UTTERING
THE
WORD

UTTERING THE WORD

The Mystical Performances of Maria Maddalena de' Pazzi, a Renaissance Visionary

ARMANDO MAGGI

State University
of New York
Press

Published by
State University of New York Press, Albany

Production by Susan Geraghty
Marketing by Anne Valentine

Printed in the United States of America

For information, address State University of New York
Press, State University Plaza, Albany, N.Y., 12246

Library of Congress Cataloging-in-Publication Data

Maggi, Armando.
    Uttering the word : the mystical performances of Maria Maddalena
de' Pazzi, a Renaissance visionary / Armando Maggi.
        p.   cm.
    Includes bibliographical references and index.
    ISBN 0-7914-3901-1 (hardcover : alk. paper). — ISBN 0-7914-3902-X
(pbk. : alk. paper)
    1. De' Pazzi, Maria Maddalena, Saint, 1566–1607. I. Title.
BX4700.D43M34 1998
282'.092—dc21
    [B]   97-38498
                                                                          CIP

10 9 8 7 6 5 4 3 2 1

This book is for my niece Marta,
who is already four years old

CONTENTS

ACKNOWLEDGMENTS

My first thanks goes to Bernard McGinn, professor of historical theology and history of Christianity at the University of Chicago. Professor McGinn has deeply influenced my interpretation of Maria Maddalena de' Pazzi. I am also grateful to Profs. Elissa Weaver and Alvises Svejkovsky. Professor Weaver, chair of the Department of Romance Languages at the University of Chicago, has been extremely helpful in clarifying the thorniest passages of de' Pazzi's texts. She has guided and enlightened my work in more than one way. During our frequent conversations at a Czech restaurant in Chicago, Alvises Svejkovsky, professor of comparative literature at the University of Chicago, offered me brilliant insights into de' Pazzi's mystical discourse.

A special thanks goes to Prof. Ann Matter, professor in the Department of Religious Studies at the University of Pennsylvania. Ann has graciously helped me correct the final version of my work.

A final thanks must be given to the sisters of the Convent of Santa Maria Maddalena de' Pazzi in Careggi, Florence. Not only did they allow me to consult the original manuscripts of de' Pazzi's visions and her private books, they also fed me with their homemade pasta and their tempting red wine.

I want to express my sincere gratitude to David Hopkins for his marvelous editing of my manuscript.

INTRODUCTION

Mystical Experience as Discourse of the Word

Isn't the Word the dearest thing to the Soul?
—Maria Maddalena de' Pazzi

The object of this study is a unique case in the history of Western spirituality. *I colloqui (The Dialogues)*, the transcriptions of the mystical monologues of St Maria Maddalena de' Pazzi (1566–1607), questions the meaning of "text" and "genre," the word's intrinsic performativity, the relationship between authorship and readership/audience, and finally the connection between gendered/sexual presence and discourse. Unlike any other mystical book, *I colloqui* is *not* the diegetic reportage of the ecstatic encounters between the divinity and a "blessed soul." Maria Maddalena did *not* intend to communicate/teach us anything; not only did she *not* care for any form of audience or readership, she did not even want this book to be written. Indeed, to approach this text correctly, two essential elements must be borne in mind: first, Maria Maddalena's oral discourses had a specific goal to attain: the expression of the Word. The mystic believed that through oral language she might be able to evoke the Word's being. *I colloqui* reports the mystic's reiterated attempt to fulfill her task. *I colloqui*, one might say, is a work in progress. Let us clarify this essential point with three brief quotations:

> [Y]our idea, your might, your goodness, everything is a language in the Word's God . . . the Word proceeding from the Word communicates us the Word and unites Him with us. (1:345)

> [T]he voice of the creatures is nothing but a little sound that one hears, and then it vanishes. But the voice of Jesus is eternal, so that Truth is God's being and His voice. (1:172–73)

> I will belch forth, I mean, I will pronounce the good word, the good Word, my Jesus, since I hold you in my heart. (1:152)[1]

Second, *I colloqui* was *not* written by Maria Maddalena de' Pazzi. Her sisters of the Carmelite convent Santa Maria degli Angeli (St Mary of the Angels) transcribed, corrected, edited, and in some cases censored her monologues. As soon as the mystic entered a rapture, the nuns took pen

1

and paper and jotted down as much as they could of her spoken words. When she whispered, screamed, cried, mumbled, Maria Maddalena was *not* speaking to her sisters. She spoke exclusively because the Word wanted her to summon His being. In the mystic's monologues the Word is the Other, that nonbeing that at once asks us to fully respond to His request for existence and dominates, gives, and subtracts sense from our own existence.[2]

Through her voice the mystic endeavored to give a body to the Other; she attempted to *embody* the Other in the physicality of her voice. As a consequence, the visionary could not help but despise her sisters' transcriptions, what were later called *I colloqui*. Left alone with one of her sisters' manuscripts, Maria Maddalena burned it, provoking the rage of her confessor.[3] The written word was of no use in her task. The Other does not reside in the written page; His being is as impalpable and transient as the oral word.

I consider it necessary to underscore that my study of de' Pazzi's texts is primarily linguistic. This book analyzes her extraordinary, albeit underestimated, mystical discourse, which formulates an unprecedented theory on the relationship between oral language and divine being. I believe that the core of de' Pazzi's mysticism lies in her "philosophy of language," which has no parallel in any other medieval and Renaissance mystic. In my view, de' Pazzi's mystical discourse is an ongoing meditation on the nature and purpose of language.

A first puzzling aspect of de' Pazzi's mysticism lies in her rejection of the manuscripts reporting her spoken words. A page from *Probatione* (*Probation*), a later transcription of her raptures, synthesizes the complex problem of the mystic's authorship:

> She happened to find those notebooks where we had written everything that had occurred during the first and most of the second year of her probation. When she realized that those notebooks concerned her, without even reading them through, she threw them into the fire and burned them. According to what she told us, she did not do that out of arrogance or conceit. Indeed, she has often told me that when she hears someone read her raptures and communications from God, . . . she feels as if she were reading someone else's spiritual book. . . . But, her superiors having forbidden her to do such a thing, from then on she has not touched anything. (1:32–33)

The sense of the above passage is apparent: when Maria Maddalena finds her sisters' transcriptions, she destroys them. The mystic both causes and annihilates the written text. We might go so far as to say that, when she speaks, Maria Maddalena erases her own text. The nuns try to explain the saint's act by saying that she did not burn those manuscripts out of conceit or arrogance, but it is not clear how the act of burning notebooks could be attributed to conceit. In any case, if the mystic did not destroy those notebooks out of arrogance, why did she do it? In fact, the nuns do not understand why Maria Maddalena had such a violent reaction to their manuscripts.

It may very well be that by burning her sisters' notebooks Maria Maddalena tells us how she interprets her own visions and the nuns' transcriptions of them. In the tradition of mystical literature, visionaries were sometimes compelled to destroy their works when they had been accused of misrepresenting Catholic doctrine. For instance, Teresa of Avila was asked to burn her commentary on *The Song of Songs*:

> She was ordered to burn this book, since it seemed to a certain confessor of hers very unorthodox and dangerous for a woman to write about *The Song of Songs*. He was moved by his pious concern that, as St. Paul says, women should be silent in God's church, which is to say: they should not preach from the pulpit, or teach at universities, or print books.[4]

There is, however, a crucial difference between Maria Maddalena's attitude toward writing and Teresa's: unlike the Italian visionary, Teresa was ordered to burn her text. Another important difference between the two mystics is that Teresa sees herself as the sole author of her work, whereas Maria Maddalena feels completely detached from her sisters' transcriptions: "she feels as if she were reading someone else's spiritual book." The Italian mystic believes that the act of writing is a betrayal. We might say that for Maria Maddalena to write means to betray or to deny the Word/Other. Whereas her monologues were pronounced once and only once, the written words become a *mirror* in which the transcribers *reflect* their own interpretations of the mystic's discourse to the Other. When they write down Maria Maddalena's discourses, the transcribers intrude upon the secrecy of her dialogues with the Word and, more importantly, appropriate her discourses to the Word through an act of interpretation. The written version reassures the nuns of the fact that Maria Maddalena's monologues are understandable, and thus belong to them. In the text/mirror they reflect their own interpretation. The written text tells them that they are not excluded from the mystic's encounters with the Word; the page makes them believe that they can participate in them, since they, the nuns, are able to grasp their meaning.

I colloqui is the biography of a performer (the mystic) who performs the biography of an absence (the Word). However, *I colloqui* is also the autobiography of the transcribers who perform their own biography simultaneously by writing down the mystic's performances and withdrawing from their own writings. Borrowing Louis Marin's words, we might say that the nuns ". . . constitute [themselves] by quoting the other and by appropriating the other."[5] As Aviad Kleinberg stresses in his study on the relationship between late medieval saints and their social environment, "those who recorded the lives of [a saint] were engaged in a dialogue, though the biographer's part is not always recorded."[6] Paradoxically, in *I colloqui* the transcribers reveal themselves by exposing the performer to her performance, as in a similar manner the performer (the mystic) *is there* when she performs the absence of the Word, who makes the mystic perceive his presence as guilt.

The Word constantly reminds Maria Maddalena of his request. We may define *I colloqui* as the narration of an excruciating obsession. Maria Maddalena is actually persecuted by the Word. As the nuns point out at the beginning of each of their transcriptions, the written word functions as the Lacanian *objet petit a*: a few lines from the Gospel read during the morning mass or the sudden memory of a passage of a psalm remind the mystic of the absence of the Other, and thus of her still unfulfilled task.[7] Although they are not the Word's being, the sacred texts contain his request to the mystic. When Maria Maddalena perceives the Other's request, so to speak, she starts to speak. Her words express her obsession with the Word. She neither speaks to the Word, nor does she speak with the Word; *she attempts to speak the Word*.[8] The Word is a *verbal body* devoid of being; he is a signifier without signified.[9] The mystic's voice both articulates her anxiety, triggered by the void of the Other, and her attempt to fill that void.[10] Maria Maddalena's voice echoes the absence of the Other.[11]

My study is an analysis of Maria Maddalena's obsession with the Word. I will analyze that obsession's various forms and various languages. In her attempt to pronounce the Other, Maria Maddalena makes use of every available language: verbal language, body language, silence, and the physicality of the world. Following St Augustine's view on linguistic expression, Maria Maddalena believes that the world itself is language. The kitchen garden, the courtyard, the chapel, the staircases, the nuns' cells, any corner of the convent is a signifier whose signified is the Word. However, her supplest language is her own body. In colloquio 48, her most complex rapture, Maria Maddalena is both the Word's corpse, his disciples, his killers, Mary Magdalen, the Virgin, numerous devils, and Satan. In this vision Maria Maddalena disappears and *becomes the biography of the Other*. She exists in order to recount the Word's death.

Maria Maddalena knows that to succeed in pronouncing the Word means to annihilate herself. When she briefly comes to articulate the divinity, she acquires a different voice. According to the transcribers, her feminine voice is replaced by a deep, authoritative, masculine one. The Father himself comes to announce his Law through the woman's voice and body. The dialogue between the Son/Word and the mystic is interrupted by the invasion of the Father. In other words, the mystic's repeated attempts conclude with the imposition of the Father's Law/denial. Mark Taylor synthesizes this fundamental point as follows:

> "God" is the name that makes the *disappearance* of the name appear. [The name "God" is] the unnameable that haunts language as a strange exteriority "within" discourse. . . . The question, then, becomes a question of thinking of the prohibition of thinking, or a thinking of the *not*, which is not precisely not thinking.[12]

For the Florentine mystic "the prohibition of thinking" is equivalent to the prohibition of "uttering" the name of the Word. If we connect Maria Maddalena's "theology of Language" with the Pseudo-Dionysius's *Mystical Theology* and *Divine Names*, we understand that the "prohibition" of uttering the Word's name essentially means the "imposition" of uttering the Word's non-name.[13] As Taylor writes, "to think God is to think the not his name names" (25). If the Second Person of the Trinity formulates a request for being, a request for incarnation, the Father *nullifies* the possibility of achieving that very incarnation, although he, the Father himself, demands that very request. The mystic *must* perform the Word's request but *cannot* fulfill it.

The first section of this introduction provides the reader with the historical background necessary to place the mystic's discourse in her time. After a biography of the saint, I investigate three major historical elements: the history and the structure of the Carmelite convent where Maria Maddalena de' Pazzi spent most of her life; the historical conditions of female spirituality in the Italian Renaissance; finally, the influence of the Counter-Reformation on de' Pazzi's mysticism.

Maria Maddalena was born on April 2, 1566, into the noble Florentine family de' Pazzi. She was baptized Caterina, but took the name of Maria Maddalena when she became a nun. Her deeply religious family raised Maria Maddalena according to the Jesuit teachings. When she was still a child, the Jesuits introduced her to their meditation techniques and to some of their basic writings. At the age of eight she had already contemplated embracing the religious life, and she joined the convent of Santa Maria degli Angeli when she was sixteen (August 1582), taking the veil the following year. She chose this convent because it was remote, rigorous, and gave her the opportunity to have communion more often than in other convents.

The Jesuits had certainly played a central role in Maria Maddalena's choice. Let us remember that through the direct intervention of Ignatius of Loyola the Jesuits had replaced the Carmelites as the spiritual guides of the Carmelite convent. For that matter, it is important to analyze briefly the origin and structure of the convent of Santa Maria degli Angeli, for its history is very similar to that of many other female institutions at the end of the Renaissance.

Although the Carmelites did accept women according to their rules and constitutions until the beginning of the fifteenth century, they still embraced old-fashioned forms of religious life that had been abandoned by most other orders.[14] The first group of Italian women affiliated with the Carmelite order formed in 1284 in Lucca.[15] However, although these women, most of them widows and young girls, had officially attained a religious status and were called *converse*, they did not leave their homes and, similar to their lay sisters, worked in male monasteries and churches.[16]

In the fifteenth century John Soreth became extremely interested in the beguines affiliated to the order, and after his election as general in 1451 he began to work for the establishment of a second order.[17] Probably influenced by Soreth, on October 7, 1452, Pope Nicholas V issued the bull *Cum nulla*, which granted the Carmelites permission to found a second order (Rohrbach, 128; Catena, AM, 23). In 1545 two houses of *converse* were founded close to each other, both depending on the same Carmelite monastery. These two female institutions later became the convents of Nunziatina and Santa Maria degli Angeli (Catena, DC, 49), where Maria Maddalena de' Pazzi spent most of her life. The fundamental ambiguity of these first female houses lies in the fact that, although the *converse* had taken solemn religious vows and thus followed the so-called first rule of the order, they still lived as "laywomen" (*terziarie*).

Santa Maria degli Angeli officially became a convent in 1480, when the general of the order granted the nuns the "scapular," the symbol of claustral life.[18] In 1520 the first eleven nuns took the veil in the new convent. A major change in the convent's structure occurred in 1521, when its jurisdiction passed from Giovanni di Antonio, its Carmelite confessor and governor, to the local episcopal power (Catena, DC, 51). This was a fundamental event in the convent's life. Indeed, it is crucial to understand that, although it formally remained a Carmelite institution, the convent of Santa Maria degli Angeli came in contact with other spiritual orders, above all the Jesuits and the Dominicans. In other words, whereas the priests influenced the convent from a jurisdictional and thus financial standpoint, the Carmelites, the Jesuits, and the Dominicans came to lead the monastery's religious life. This element is particularly important to define the complex mysticism of Maria Maddalena de' Pazzi, whose visionary discourse is molded by numerous spiritual sources.

After a second Carmelite, Clemente di Antonio, and a short time under the direction of the Jesuits, the Dominican Agostino Campi became the official confessor of the convent in 1563. Although the nuns had the right to choose their confessor, Campi remained their sole confessor for twenty-eight years, until 1591, when the convent finally lost its right to elect its confessor (Catena, AM, 52). A second crucial figure was the Florentine preacher Alessandro Capocchi, who delivered regular sermons at the convent. The library of Santa Maria degli Angeli still has the manuscripts containing the transcriptions of forty-two sermons that Capocchi delivered in more than a decade. Capocchi also gave the nuns some of the books and meditation manuals originated from his daily spiritual exercises and frequent ecstasies (Catena, AM, 30). Particularly interesting is his *Incitatione di morire spiritualmente* (*Incentive to a Spiritual Death*), which focuses on the relationship between physical and spiritual death. The originality of this text lies in its often graphic descriptions of the body's mortality and decay.[19] Capocchi's book was certainly one of Maria Maddalena's readings.[20] Moreover, thanks to Capocchi, contemplation became a fundamental and structural component of the convent's daily life.

Although in 1564 the convent's constitution had stated that Santa Maria degli Angeli could not accept more than seventy-two nuns, on August 14, 1582, when Maria Maddalena became a novice, eighty sisters lived there. As far as the structure of the convent is concerned, Vangelista del Giocondo—the severe and intransigent mother superior who exerted a crucial influence on Maria Maddalena—instituted the *novitiatus clausus* (private novitiate), which required that a novice follow the instructions of a teacher (*maestra*) and live in a separate area of the convent.[21] Although the novitiate was supposed to last one year, given the young age of many novices it could last up to ten years (Catena, AM, 34). In practice, the novitiate ended when a nun was considered mature enough to exercise her *voce* (voice), that is, when she was allowed to vote in the election for the mother superior. After the novitiate, the novice went through a three-year period of *giovanato*, during which she was instructed by another teacher.

As I have already mentioned, a fundamental rule of the convent was frequent meditation. The nuns meditated twice a day, once in the morning after the *matutino* (matins) for twenty minutes, and at night after *compieta* (compline). According to the convent's constitution, the practice of meditation was complementary to the Mass, and was meant to help the nun clarify the inner meaning of the divine office (Catena, AM, 39). Following the Carmelite rules, the constitution also increased the number of mandatory communions. Maria Maddalena de' Pazzi was drawn to this convent also because of its frequent religious offices.

The convent's daily life reflected the standardized rules introduced in the Carmelite institutions. Besides the usual recital of the breviary, one of the nuns' most important activities was manual work. The nuns worked together in the *sala di lavoro* (room of work). John Soreth himself had suggested that the nuns live as a community of sisters sharing their thoughts and concerns. Rather than a break from their meditation, working together was considered a different form of prayer.[22] In other words, the constitution of the convent wished to blend two forms of meditation, one practiced in silence and the other achieved through manual work. However, in both cases the nuns were asked to avoid any distracting behavior and focus on their inner "silence." Outer and inner silence was indeed the essential "rule" of the convent. As we shall see in chapter 1, silence is also a central constituent of Maria Maddalena's orality.[23]

The nuns were supposed to enter the room of work in a silent and respectful way and start to work reciting "Veni Sancte Spiritus" (Secondin, 60–61). Then, after spending no more than fifteen minutes to organize their work, the sisters attended to their specific duties. In the meantime, the nuns recited psalms and listened to passages from the Gospel. This practice lasted one hour. In 1579 the room of work acquired a new status. One of the older sisters was allowed to comment on the biblical passage read during the work. Often this extemporaneous exegesis resulted in a lively discussion among the nuns (Catena, AM, 46). *I colloqui* itself is the result of the discussions between the mystic and her fellow sisters on the moot passages of their transcriptions.

Very soon after entering the convent, Maria Maddalena had intense mystical experiences that led her to a mysterious and almost fatal disease.[24] In fact, this is a commonplace of hagiographic literature. Innumerable mystics experienced a similar "deadly" disease. When she recovered from this illness, Maria Maddalena started to have daily visions, during which she spoke to the Trinity, and in particular to Christ, whom she generally refers to as the Word. Despite the extraordinary intensity of her raptures, Maria Maddalena never had an influential role within her convent. Her sisters succeeded in keeping her mystical experiences secret, informing only their immediate male superiors. Moreover, when Maria Maddalena, during the last years of her life, felt urged to communicate with the external world and thus wrote letters to some bishops, priests, even to the Pope, in an attempt to express her views on the moral and religious life of her time, her letters almost never left the convent. Unlike St Catherine of Siena, Maria Maddalena's mystical message remained within the walls of her convent. She died years after her visions ended, at the age of forty-one. Maria Maddalena de' Pazzi was canonized in 1669, after a long "trial" where more than fifty nuns were asked to testify.

It is important to situate de' Pazzi's mystical discourse in the historical/spiritual context of late Renaissance Italy. Although Maria Maddalena's spirituality essentially belongs to the Counter-Reformation, it shares crucial aspects with early-sixteenth-century female religiosity. As Gabriella Zarri underscores, female saints were familiar figures in the daily life of early modern society.[25] Seen as charismatic objects of veneration, these holy women played a significant role in the political life of their time, often becoming influential counselors and guides. In their attempt to emulate St Catherine of Siena, these "living saints" apparently possessed a fundamental attribute that increased their importance: "their gift of prophecy and powers of insight" (Zarri, LS, 221).[26] For instance, the magistrates of the city often called on the "living saints" during plagues or other calamities.

A typical example of these "holy women" is Lucia Broccadelli of Narni, who bore visibly on her body the stigmata of Christ.[27] Born in 1476, Lucia married and entered the Third Order of St Dominic of Viterbo. Her stigmata attracted the attention of Duke Ercole I d'Este of Ferrara, who asked her to move to his city to lead a convent of tertiaries and to participate in his Renaissance court. The duke also publicized her "sanctity" throughout Europe (Zarri, LS, 227). When her stigmata disappeared, Lucia's holiness was questioned and this resulted in her confinement to a convent, where she died totally forgotten in 1544. Her cult was rekindled and approved in 1710.

As we have seen, Maria Maddalena de' Pazzi never became a "social operator," as Zarri defines the "living saints" of the first two decades of the sixteenth century. As I have pointed out, Maria Maddalena's "political" letters almost never reached their addressees.[28] As Vincenzo Puccini, her last confessor and first biographer, stresses in *The Life of St. Mary Magdalene of Pazzi*, at the age of twenty-three Maria Maddalena was granted the "government of the Novitiate."[29] This was the sole official role played by the mystic throughout her life. Although according to her sisters' transcriptions Maria Maddalena was immediately considered a "blessed soul," she "spent almost her whole life in instructing the youth of the Convent" (Puccini, 70). Moreover, de' Pazzi never received "external" gifts from the divinity, such as the stigmata or the power of prophecy. As we shall see in chapter 3, in her visions Maria Maddalena repeatedly asks God not to give her visible gifts, so that she can preserve the secrecy of their mutual love.

However, what de' Pazzi and the "living saints" have in common is the way they performed their holiness.[30] Like the "living saints," Maria Maddalena was rapt in ecstasy during prayer and received revelations that confirmed the Catholic faith (Zarri, LS, 238). Although Maria Maddalena was the sole visionary who performed mystical plays in which she embodied a number of different characters, the "living saints" as well were asked by their "holy Spouse" to commemorate his Passion and Death. However, rather than through actual performances, these holy women manifested their divine call primarily through physical suffering, such as sudden fevers and mysterious diseases, and simple gestures, like falling on the floor and stretching their arms as if they were being crucified.

Maria Maddalena and the holy women of the first decades of the sixteenth century also share a vehement hatred of Satan. Since visions and raptures could be caused also by "natural" illnesses and even by the devil, the Church tended to appreciate the visionary's crystal-clear rejection of the Enemy's temptations.[31] At the beginning of chapter 4 I will show how de' Pazzi and the "living saints" relate to the devil. Indeed, it is crucial to remember that two entire volumes of her sisters' transcriptions are dedicated to Maria Maddalena's mystical "probation," that is, her painful fight against the devil's subtle and disturbing enticements.

Another basic connection between de' Pazzi's mysticism and the visions of the living saints lies in the central role played by their physicality. However, the flamboyant aspects of the "living saints'" behavior are totally absent from Maria Maddalena's. In fact, the "living saints," whose social and political role had been crucial in their urban settings, "saw their fortunes fade abruptly after 1530" (Zarri, LS, 248). The advent of the Protestant Reformation forced the Catholic Church to be more cautious about the truthfulness of the women's mystical experiences. Rather than valuing stigmata and prophecy, the Catholic Counter-Reformation came to consider total humility and moral integrity the most important signs of a woman's holiness (Zarri, VS, 13). The Church prevented women "from engaging in any form of social activity and radically limit[ed] their contact with the outside world" (Zarri, LS, 253).

Maria Maddalena de' Pazzi certainly belongs to this second phase of female mysticism. The goal of the Council of Trent, described in the bull *Laetare Jerusalem* (1544), was a perfect control of every branch of the Church, both from a political and a theological standpoint.[32] A new cathechism was written in 1566 and a new edition of the Bible, the *Vulgata Clementina*, was published in 1593 (Prosperi, 39). The Church also imposed a series of strict regulations on women in religious orders, including an austere seclusion and a deferential relationship with their male confessors, who acquired an unprecedented authority vis-à-vis the religious practices of every female institution.[33] Needless to say, in some cases the confessors took advantage of their power for personal interests. Moreover, the priests themselves often found themselves unprepared to fight incorrect or even heretical assertions. Giovanna Paolin reminds us that, before the Council of Trent, priests saw their life as rather "safe" and monotonous (366), and did not expect to become paladins of the faith. The Council of Trent and Pope Pius V in particular demanded that the confessor check upon the frequency of the nuns' participation to the sacraments, particularly communion and confession. Let us remember that Maria Maddalena de' Pazzi decided to enter the convent of St. Maria degli Angeli because there, following the rules of the Council, the nuns took communion more frequently than in other convents.

However, a confessor's major task was to assess the soundness of the nuns' theological beliefs. In some instances, however, the confessor was unable to detect rather apparent "misconducts." Paolin mentions the case of the convent of St Chiara of Udine, where the nuns used to look down on their confessor and refer to him only for official occasions (370–71). For more than fifty years, this convent had been the center of an intense theological debate, which verged on a libertine rationalism. When, in 1590, the Inquisition accused this institution of heresy, Bartolomeo de' Pellegrini, who had been the nuns' confessor for more than sixteen years, was very surprised by the serious allegations. In fact, he had never doubted the nuns' orthodoxy.

To provide the confessors with the necessary and basic tools to verify the nuns' compliance, at the beginning of the seventeenth century a number of manuals were published under the supervision of Carlo Borromeo, a key figure of the Counter-Reformation and an impassioned believer in witches, demonic possessions, and thus in witch trials and capital punishment. For that matter, Borromeo inaugurated this new genre of confessional manuals with *Avvertenze ai confessori della città e diocesi sua* (Milan, 1609).[34] Thanks to Borromeo, confession became one aspect of a much larger project of surveillance. In other words, Borromeo held that the confessor had to become an actual "religious guide," that is, he had to control and influence the believer's life in a much deeper manner (Niccoli, 415).

Borromeo was a strong advocate of the Counter-Reformation Inquisition. Before analyzing the role of the Inquisition in the late Renaissance and its influence on female mysticism, it is necessary to understand that Pope Pius V and Carlo Borromeo succeeded in reforming the structure of the local dioceses by organizing periodical synods that stressed the legal power of the local bishops. In the bull *Benedictus Deus* (1566), resulting from the synod sponsored by Carlo Borromeo in Milan in 1565, Pius V underscored that the local bishops had to become severe judges of the dioceses' moral and religious habits. Borromeo himself sent the text of the Milanese synod to many dioceses in southern Italy.[35] Bishops came to embody the Church's supreme power at a local level. During periodical sydons, bishops debated a variety of matters, not only the conduct of priests and confessors, their personal lives, and the structures of the sacraments, but also the persecution of "unnatural" sexual behaviors, heresy, witchcraft, and magic (De Rosa, 321–23).

Bishops also played a key role in the Counter-Reformation Inquisition. As Jeffrey Burton Russell reminds us, initially the Inquisition "was simply a variey of the regular episcopal visitation in which the bishop sought out and prosecuted all violations of canon law."[36] It was Gregory IX (1227–41) who initiated the procedures that created the centrally directed Inquisition (Russell, *Witchcraft*, 155). In 1231 he issued a bull defining ecclesiastic legislation against heresies and entrusting the execution of this legislation to the Dominicans. In 1252 Pope Innocent IV's bull *Ad extirpanda* ordered civil authorities to apply torture in cases of heresy and to confiscate the heretics' goods. Alexander IV authorized the use of torture by the Inquisition itself (Russell, *Witchcraft*, 153). Although the Inquisition increased its power through a series of papal bulls, Pope Alexander IV made it clear that the persecution of sorcery and demonic possessions would remain under the bishops' jurisdiction (Russell, *Witchcraft*, 156).

The bloodiest period of the Roman Inquisition occurred between 1560 and 1660, due to the increasing tensions between Protestantism and Catholicism.[37] It will suffice to remember the infamous *Malleus Maleficarum* (1486) by the Dominicans Heinrich Institoris and Jakob Sprenger, which became the fundamental manual of the Roman Inquisition and a major reference for every text on demonology. Innocent VIII's bull *Summis Desiderantes Affectibus* (1484) expressed the papal support for the work of the Inquisition, and also for the ideas formulated in the *Malleus*. After 1580, "the more thorough Jesuits" replaced the Dominicans as the chief Catholic witch-hunters (Russell, *History of Witchcraft*, 83).

As far as the detection and repression of demonic activities are concerned, it is not easy to define the relationship among the religious orders (Dominicans first, Jesuits later), the bishops, and the confessors/priests. Although "it was the religious orders, rather than ordinary local clergy who tended to assume star roles as exorcists" and judges, it is a fact that bishops and confessors had a much more direct rapport with local situations, convents included.[38] In fact, only the confessors were able to detect irregularities in the believers' behaviors.

The incisive role played by local clergy is evident in the construction of Maria Maddalena de' Pazzi as the last "living saint" of the Renaissance. Although humility, social invisibility, and a silent abidance by the confessors' injunctions (the so-called "heroic virtue") were the qualities that the Council of Trent demanded from a nun, Maria Maddalena's highly theatrical raptures were not recorded as suspicious events, but rather as unquestionable manifestations of the divinity. I will analyze this aspect at the end of chapter 3. For that matter, it is crucial to bear in mind that the manuscripts containing the mystic's raptures are not the first draft of the nuns' transcriptions. The transcribers' unflinching belief in the mystic's orthodoxy derives from the fact that the mystic's confessor had previously verified and approved the nuns' notes.[39] After having received the confessor's approval, the nuns transcribed their notes in a second book, giving the mystic's raptures a narrative coherence and inserting frequent comments on the nature of Maria Maddalena's experiences. In other words, the first draft of the manuscripts reporting Maria Maddalena's visions were first and foremost textual "evidences" that the transcribers had to show the mystic's confessor, who had the last word on the truthfulness of her raptures (cf. Paolin, 376).

Maria Maddalena's visions have a distinctly oral nature. Some critics, accustomed to more traditional mystical works, regret that the saint did not write down the raptures herself: they would have rather had clear, rationally developed descriptions of her private religious experiences. Let us read, for example, what Ermanno del S. S. Sacramento, who first described the mystic's manuscripts, says about the transcriptions of Maria Maddalena's visions:

> If, instead of dictated reports of her raptures, we had a systematic book about her rich spiritual experience, without a doubt we would have a much bigger, and probably more important one than that which actually remains, given the subtlety and depth of her thought. In the present text she does not hint at the many problems she must have faced and solved in her visions.[40]

For del Sacramento a mystical experience can be only a written description of a previous experience. The fundamental element of Maria Maddalena's discourse, its orality, is seen by del Sacramento as a major flaw, which allegedly prevents the reader from following the development of a rational meditation.

For traditional students of any form of literacy, orality is what a thought is not. The mystic's sisters embrace a quite different ideology. They decided to write down her spoken words when they realized that *Maria Maddalena's orality meant something*. Over time, their method of transcription changed. They first limited themselves to composing a resumé of the saint's raptures, choosing to quote only some of her spoken words. Later, the nuns perceived that the overall meaning of her discourses could not be easily summarized, and thus developed a complex method of *live* reportage. When the mystic entered a rapture, they sat around her in a group, and each of them wrote only a short section of her discourse. In other words, the first nun transcribed the mystic's first utterances, then the second took over and wrote down the second part of her speech, and so on.

Speaking of the "historical forms imposed on orality," Michel de Certeau states:

> Because of its exclusion on the grounds of economic neatness and efficiency, the voice appears essentially in the form of *quotation*, which is homologous, in the field of the written, with the mark of the bare foot left on Robinson's island. [Orality] operates between . . . two poles defining its extreme forms: on the one hand, the *quotation-pre-text*, which serves to fabricate texts (assumed to be commentaries or analyses) on the basis of relics selected from an oral tradition functioning as an authority; on the other, the *quotation-reminiscence*, marking in language the fragmented and unexpected return . . . of oral relationships that are structuring but repressed by the written.[41]

Applying de Certeau's definition of orality as *quotation-pre-text* and *quotation-reminiscence*, we might say that the transcribers of Maria Maddalena's utterances came to perceive the necessity of overcoming the strictures of such a vision of orality. The nuns understood both the importance of giving *free* rein to the mystic's voice and the impossibility of freeing her orality from its being *a double quotation*.

The mystic took part in the editing of her sisters' transcriptions only when her confessor forced her to do so. In fact, the saint despised the nuns' work. When she happened to be alone with their manuscripts, she burned them. As I will clarify in chapter 1, according to Maria Maddalena the written version of her raptures *betrays* the deepest meaning of her mystical encounters. Indeed, Maria Maddalena believes that she is asked by the Word to articulate his being exclusively through her voice. However, the fact that the mystic articulates a human language does not mean that she does so in order to share her discourse with any possible audience. The relationship with the Other excludes the others. The relationship itself transforms language. When Maria Maddalena speaks to/with the Word in her attempt to express his being she articulates a language that "sounds like" the sixteenth-century Italian spoken in her convent. This is why Maria Maddalena thinks that her oral discourses, even when they seem to have a logical structure, become useless if they are transcribed on the page.

The saint's visions have been preserved in several manuscripts. In 1960–66 F. Nardoni, B. Visentin, C. M. Catena, and G. Agresti published her writings in seven volumes. Not a critical edition, these scholars have simply transcribed the nuns' manuscripts, without even correcting their most apparent linguistic mistakes. The titles of the volumes are the following: *I quaranta giorni* (*The Forty Days*, the mystic's visions from May 27, 1584, to July 4 of the same year; its title, not present in the manuscript itself, has been chosen because the text actually covers a period of forty days); *I colloqui* (*The Dialogues*, two volumes, it contains her raptures from Christmas of 1584 to June 4, 1585; the title refers to the fact that, after their transcriptions, the nuns asked the saint questions in order to clarify some of the unclear points of their text); *Rivelatione e intelligentie* (*Revelations and Knowledge*, the visions Maria Maddalena had interruptedly during eight days beginning on June 8, 1585); *Probatione* (*Probation*, two volumes, it reports the saint's most painful mystical experiences, from June 16, 1585, to June 10, 1590; in this text the nuns tend to summarize the content of her raptures, rather than report her actual words); *Renovatione della Chiesa* (*Renovation of the Church*, a miscellany of works of different nature [its title is a quotation from the text]: a four-day rapture [August 11–15, 1586], twelve letters written by the saint herself, and other secondary texts, such as meditations and prayers).

Although this study primarily focuses on *I colloqui*, it also examines the most significant sections of the other volumes. The present book is divided into four chapters plus a conclusion.

Chapter 1, "Orality and Time in *I colloqui*," examines the structure of the mystic's texts from a narrative and theological standpoint. I examine how, by modifying their method of transcription, her fellow sisters influenced and controlled the mystic's discourse. The transcribers turned de' Pazzi's visions into chapters of a hagiographic text, shifting, censoring, changing the order and meaning of her utterances. I prove that the transcribers, the mother superior, and the Jesuits did not limit themselves to reporting the mystic's utterances; they rather "constructed" the mystic as a holy character in order to enhance the influence of the convent where the mystic resided.

Chapter 2, "Maria Maddalena, the Word, and the Language of the Birds," analyzes both the mystic's orality and the written version of her monologues/performances. In order to fathom her mystical idiom, comparisons are drawn between Maria Maddalena's Italian and the so-called language of the birds. The birds, seen both as actual animals and as metaphors for angelic messengers, articulate a language that has striking similarities with that of the Florentine mystic. This chapter examines also the page itself seen as an "imagetext," according to John Mitchell's definition.

Chapter 3, "The Wedding, the Funeral, and the Memorial of the Word," studies two crucial visions from *I colloqui*, colloqui 39 and 48. These two raptures are examined in their theatricality, as unique forms of solo performance. In colloquio 39 Maria Maddalena performs her marriage to the Word; in colloquio 48 she participates in his funeral, enters his tomb, and waits there for his resurrection. In this vision the entire convent turns into "settings" of a miracle play, and the nuns themselves, the transcribers, are invited by the visionary to participate in the event.

Chapter 4, "The Languages of Satan," studies how the devil undermines the mystic's utterances. The devil makes the mystic doubt the reality of her experiences. To do so, the devil articulates the most subtle language, a form of speaking within the subject's mind. According to Maria Maddalena, the devil creeps into the subject's soul/heart/mind and does not allow the subject to picture the thought evoked by the devil himself. The devil thinks in the subject's mind without any apparent thought/word. The devil's thought is imageless.

In the conclusion ("Love is a Word"), I examine a powerful vision from *I quaranta giorni* (*The Forty Days*) in order to summarize the meaning of de' Pazzi's mysticism. Borrowing from Lacan's essays on the *jouissance* of the woman, I show how for Maria Maddalena "love" means nothing, or better yet, means *a nothingness*. "Love" is a word that points to the subject's desire for love and to her awareness of its "meaninglessness." "Love" is the void that follows and is concurrent with any "performance" of love.

CHAPTER 1

Orality and Time in I Colloqui

Scholars believe that the most demanding part of de Pazzi's production is *I colloqui*. In these two volumes the nuns report Maria Maddalena's most intriguing mystical experiences, such as her marriage to the Word, her visiting Hell, her speaking as God the Father, and finally her taking part in the Word's funeral and resurrection. This two-volume book is relevant also from another standpoint. In *I colloqui* the transcribers attempt to reproduce the oral tone of de Pazzi's discourses by marking down her silences, her exclamations, and her repetitions. However, as we shall see, in their editing the nuns introduce some significant corrections. For instance, they modify the order of her sentences to make her discourse "clearer," and they expand the mystic's monologues with their own interpretations.

It is necessary to explain two crucial points of de Pazzi's mysticism: the nature of her oral mystical language and the relationship between her monologues and her listeners/readers. As far as the first point is concerned, it is important to understand that Maria Maddalena is highly influenced by St Augustine's theories on language. As I have pointed out in the introduction, St Augustine's books, in particular the *Confessions*, *On Christian Doctrine*, *On the Trinity*, and *The City of God*, were fundamental readings in the convent of Santa Maria degli Angeli.

For the history of semiotics, Augustine's most influential texts are *On Dialectics* (written in 387), *On Christian Doctrine* (397), and *On the Trinity* (415). In the first book, a treatise of his youth, Augustine states that "signum est quod et se ipsum sensui et praeter se aliquid ostendit" (a sign is something that is itself sensed and that indicates to the mind something beyond the sign itself). As Hans Ruef explains, this definition describes "a double relationship. The first is between the sign itself and *sensus*. . . . The second relationship connects the sign with *aliquid* (something which is not the sign)."[1] What Augustine underscores in his first semiotic interpretation of language is "a certain nonidentity of the sign with itself, a feature arising from the fact that the sign is at once perceptible and intelligible."[2] In other words, in *On Dialectics* Augustine already stresses the communicative character of the sign, which has no essence in itself, but rather exists in the act of being pronounced for someone. Words, Augustine holds, mean things; they do not represent them. Words do not have an iconic relationship with the signified things; they point to things without embodying their "affective" content.[3] A sign is something that at once shows something to someone and exposes itself as the carrier of a given meaning (Ruef, 86). As a consequence, a sign identifies with the temporal level of its expression.[4] As we shall see later, this element plays a central influence in de' Pazzi's view of the linguistic sign.

In an important passage from his *Sermons*, which describes the phenomenology of interpersonal communication, Augustine indirectly confirms the fundamental importance of temporality in any form of verbal expression. To communicate, Augustine says, means to speak to the mind (*mens*) of others. Although the speaker does not see the others' minds, he wishes to communicate his thought (*verbum*) by means of the sound (*sonus*) of the voice (*vox*).[5] The semiotic activity of the sign is strictly connected with the social context in which the sign is manifested.[6] Moreover, investigating language's intrinsically social nature, in *Concerning the Teacher* (389) Augustine underscores that not only does the speaker sometimes fail to communicate with his listener, he also misuses his own words. Augustine goes so far as to say that the words we articulate may not correspond to the content of our thoughts. According to Augustine, our miscommunication may result from a number of factors.[7] For instance, our memory may suggest a word or expression that does not express what we mean to say. In other cases, a simple *lapsus linguae* (slip of the tongue) may occur.[8]

In *On Christian Doctrine* Augustine offers his most complete formulation of semiotic sign. In this central text of Western spirituality Augustine states that words and things share some characteristics; both things and words can be seen as signs, that is, both things and words signify something. In this work Augustine defines a sign as follows: "A sign is a thing which causes us to think of something beyond the impression the thing itself makes upon the senses. [There is no] other reason for signifying, or for giving signs, except for bringing forth and transferring to another mind the action of the mind in the person who makes the sign."[9] A sign, says Augustine, is essentially something that makes us think about something else. One crucial difference between *On Dialectics* and *On Christian Doctrine* is that in the latter Augustine's theory of the sign does not consider the "thing" as a referent. Augustine believes that "the world is divided into signs and things according to whether the perceived object has transitive value or not. Things participate in signs as signifiers, not as referents" (Todorov, 40).

Augustine further develops this concept of sign by introducing a distinction between use and enjoyment. Since things are similar to signs because both are signifiers, there are things/signs that exist in order to be used, and things/signs that can only be enjoyed:

> It is to be asked whether man is to be loved by man for his own sake or for the sake of something else. If for his own sake, we enjoy him; if for the sake of something else, we use him. But I think that man is to be loved for the sake of something else. In that which is to be loved for its own sake the blessed life resides; and if we do not have it for the present, the hope is for it to console us.[10]

It is apparent that the only "thing" that can be enjoyed is God, because everything else, both words and things, have no existence in themselves. They, rather, "refer to" something else, the divinity himself. Reality is empty, so to speak, whereas the ultimate signified is God, for Maria Maddalena the Word, the ircanate Son. Maria Maddalena's oral sign is exclusively directed to the divinity, as both an eternal and a mortal referent.

Maria Maddalena's mystical language is essentially related to Augustine's theory. If everything, both words and the world, is nothing but a sign of God, everything, language included, somehow participates in the divinity. The unique aspect of Maria Maddalena's visions is that the saint comes into contact with the divinity through language and, more important, *in* language; in her rapture she tries to convert language into the Word's *body*, the "thing" that can only be enjoyed but never used. Moreover, the "thing" itself has a double essence. God/thing embodies a mortal eternity, so to speak, for at once "he is who is," as Jesus says, and is who has entered temporality in order to die.

Another significant element is that Maria Maddalena's oral discourses are never directed to the reader of *I colloqui*. When the mystic converses with God, the transcribers can hear her voice, but not that of her interlocutor. In other words, her sisters and thus all of us, the readers of their manuscripts, "overhear" a conversation that does not concern us.[11] Paradoxically, the Other's voice can be perceived only by the speaker who articulates his, the Other's, voice. It is therefore legitimate to wonder what kind of reading/listening this text asks us to perform. When we read a literary page, we "complete" the images described by the author, assuming that we, the readers, and the writer look at reality in a similar way. In other words, by composing a text the author necessarily believes that his readers will *see* something similar to what he imagined in the act of producing his text. Conversely, the page might be seen as a mirror in which the reader reflects his understanding of the page itself; the page justifies the reader's imagining and understanding. This is not the case with *I colloqui*. Maria Maddalena's use of language is not descriptive; she does not speak in order to narrate. For the Florentine mystic language is the means through which the body of the Word *may* be evoked; the presence or absence of an audience for her discourses is absolutely irrelevant to her.

Let us remember that we do not read the mystic's words to the Word, but rather the nuns' edited texts. We might say that, by writing down the mystic's monologues and by giving them a rationally syntactic structure, the nuns translated Maria Maddalena's language into Italian. When their transcriptions still lacked coherence, the nuns felt compelled to introduce their own tentative explanations. Our contemporary debate on the topic "tradire/tradurre" (to betray/to translate) is not at stake here. We can only betray/translate an original text; *I colloqui* is the translation of a nonexistent text. Whereas the Other's discourse, the Word's words, does not exist, the mystic's utterances exist as mere attempts to articulate a foreign language. As Lacan reminds us, the Other himself does not exist and thus cannot be pronounced. However, the Other does possess a language, but he does not have a voice.[12] Maria Maddalena's ultimate task is in fact a paradox: to allow the Word to pronounce himself through her voice.

When in colloquio 48 the mystic momentarily succeeds in evoking God's discourse through her voice, two events take place. First, whereas her previous visions invoked the Son/Word, in colloquio 48 the Father takes over. The Father's Law interrupts the dialogue between the subject and the Other. Erasing both the Son as the Lacanian imaginary and the mystic as the desiring subject, the Father restates his Law. At that point Maria Maddalena disappears as a subject; she is *a body that articulates the Father's voice*. Second, the saint's voice acquires a masculine tone. Maria Maddalena turns into a hybrid; she is a female body with a male voice and identity.

How do we, readers, relate to this translation of a lost text? *I colloqui* requires a unique act of reading/listening. If we limit ourselves to processing the saint's words according to our personal perception, we betray the sense of her speaking, because her words are not for us. Whereas linguistic exchange is based on an agreement between two or more subjects who believe that they share the same linguistic field, in *I colloqui* words have a meaning that is foreign to us; we are excluded from the text itself. *We do not belong in this text.*[13] We must understand that *I colloqui* reflects our misunderstanding; no reassuring agreement exists between our comprehension and the written text. To listen to Maria Maddalena's monologues primarily means to know that we are *mis*-listening.

As a consequence, in order to perform a "respectful" listening we must bracket any interpretation we may have; we must let Maria Maddalena's words *pass through* ourselves.[14] Unlike our typical and active way of listening, *I colloqui* asks us to be "modest" or even "passive" readers and to let its words *happen within* ourselves. This is how the Italian philosopher Pier Aldo Rovatti describes this different kind of listening:

> It is this "let the words be," this act of opening up, if we are *really* able to open up to it, which prepares us for a peaceful abandonment. . . . [A]t that point language speaks, words offer themselves and come to be. It is a question of listening . . . there is a listening that overturns our obvious lending an ear to something.[15]

More than decoding the meaning of her visionary discourse according to some prepatterned interpretation based, for instance, on our knowledge of other mystical works and on our personal visual memories, we can approach *I colloqui* only if we allow its language to be listened to (Rovatti, 107).

However, although the mystic's language comes to us as a sort of echo, as a sudden message from the external world, we realize that *her words somehow concern us.* We sense that when we actually let her words occur they are not foreign to us, even though we cannot *appropriate* them.[16] It is only in this way that we can establish a basic communication with the Maria Maddalena's oral discourse in its transcribed form. Even though Maria Maddalena does not take into account any human listener, in our modest *over*hearing of her monologues we come to perceive her words *as if they were directed to us.*

Our strategy of reading must also incorporate other fundamental factors. On the one hand, in our reading we focus on Maria Maddalena's voice as it is conveyed through the nuns' transcriptions. On the other hand, the mystic's monologues are inserted into a "colloquio," that is, into a coherent chapter of a narrative structure. Each colloquio first gives introductory explanations about the forthcoming vision; then it presents the edited transcription of the actual vision; finally, it concludes with some moral remarks from the transcribers.

A second crucial problem arises when we take into account the saint's ambiguous attitude toward her own oral discourses: Maria Maddalena seems often not to remember what she said even a few minutes before. Her words seem to have flown out of her mouth, as if she had been unaware of her own speaking. As Lacan points out in "The Subversion of the Subject and the Dialectic of Desire in the Freudian Unconscious," the act of speaking is in fact a response to the Other's question: "What do you want?" ("Che vuoi?").[17] In other words, when Maria Maddalena enters a rapture and starts to speak, she attempts to respond both to the Word's request for being and to her own desire for self-expression. The articulation of the Word is equivalent to the expression of the self. We might thus say that the real author of *I colloqui* is the saint's relationship with the Word.[18] Their relating to each other, their coming in contact with each other is *the author* of this text.[19] On the one hand, Maria Maddalena is obsessed with the Word's request for being; on the other, she is tormented by her sense of guilt. The Word has been humiliated, tortured, and crucified. She wants to bring him back to life. Her sense of being inappropriate for this task devastates her. For Maria Maddalena de' Pazzi, to speak also means to give voice to her guilt. More than monologues, her utterances are often similar to tormented soliloquies.

Maria Maddalena believes that human language is not synonymous with communication, but rather with exclusion. What she says *resembles* our language, but it does not coincide with it. It is as if the language she speaks and the sixteenth-century Italian of her convent sisters, and thus the language of *I colloqui*, are different idioms, which happen to use the same phonemes. In order to render the mystic's monologues intelligible, the transcribers give them a clearly narrative character. The act of turning Maria Maddalena's words into a more or less coherent chronicle is in fact an act of translation.

In order to become a comprehensible language, the discourse between the mystic and God must adhere to the temporal categories of narration. More than transcribing the mystic's conversations with the Second Person of the Trinity, the nuns submit them to time. The words of/about the Word must become mortal in order to be understandable. We, human speakers, only perceive and exchange our mortality. In the nuns' transcriptions, the Word "becomes incarnate" in the Savior; he acquires a biography, along with sufferings, desires, and death. When we read the first chapters of *I colloqui*, in which the writers faithfully reproduce the most common topoi of every hagiography, the Other is Jesus, Maria Maddalena's anxious groom who would like his bride to respond to his love exhaustively.

Maria Maddalena is the only interlocutor of God's discourse; she is the only one who is capable of perceiving his words. However, in their transcriptions the nuns make God pronounce words that are direct quotations from the sacred texts:

My dear daughter, I want to enjoy some time with you . . . given that today is that day in which I decided to shed so much Blood for my creatures' sake, now I want to draw you, my creature, toward me [*ad me ipsum*]. You know that I said that when I was on the Cross, [that is, that] I would draw everything to me: *Omnia traham ad me ipsum*; and the other [sentence]: *Et delitie mee esse cum filijs hominum.* (1:55)

In this passage God simply comments on certain statements of his reported in the Bible: *Omnia traham ad me ipsum* (John 12:32) and *Et delitie mee esse cum filijs hominum* (Prov. 8:31). For the trascribers, the divinity can only speak the language of the Law. In fact, human language can report no actual interaction between the Word and the mystic. At times the Word's responses to Maria Maddalena might be perceived in the mystic's silences:

I do not understand anything more. In other words, you show me these things about you, but I don't understand them [*silence*] you know the strengths better than I do [*silence*] yes, last night passed very quickly [*silence*] three more nights, right? [*silence*] but last night doesn't count, right? (2:135)

The Word is present in the mystic's language as an absence. In the act of reporting Maria Maddalena's monologues the transcribers must solve a fundamental problem: If the mystic converses with the Word in silence, how is it possible to make the Word present in the text? It is simply impossible to determine how extensively the nuns have corrected and interpolated the mystic's oral discourse. As we shall see later, some passages clearly show that the authors of *I colloqui* did modify the mystic's discourse. The nuns either point it out themselves, or structure the text in a way that makes manifest a discrepancy between the oral and written level of the mystic's monologue.

In *I colloqui* the Word becomes Jesus; the page makes the Other a historical event. Similarly, the speaking subject, the mystic herself, whose identity was the words she pronounced to her divine interlocutor in a private relationship, turns into the main character of a narration. The style, content, and emotional message of each colloquio mold the identity of the visionary. Maria Maddalena, we might say, *exists* only insofar as the text makes her the main character of her own experiences. When we read a colloquio, we encounter a body that expresses itself through certain metaphors, rhetorical devices, and narrative twists. The text tells us how the mystic's body sweated, blushed, shook on the floor when the Word approached her. Moreover, in chapter 2 we shall see how the style itself of the mystic's reported discourses aims to communicate a specific emotional state. The nuns try to describe the mystic's body *through* a specific rhetoric.

Let us examine briefly the major topoi of *I colloqui*. The Son, the incarnate Word, is the unifying theme of the transcribers' text. Maria Maddalena's raptures focus on two aspects: the Son's body and his death. In *I colloqui* the Savior's body, especially his bleeding wounds, has a complex metaphorical significance. The Savior's wounds are similar to furnaces (colloquio 2, 67), to deep channels (colloquio 5, 95), to vineyards (colloquio 16, 182), and to windows (colloquio 18, 201). His body often becomes a mystical place that the mystic visits, almost always accompanied by her sisters. For example, in colloquio 4 some angels pick up the saint and her sisters by their hair and plunge them into the Son's breast: "Then she had the impression that the Holy Spirit asked the angels to pull us up by the hair . . . and so they took us into Jesus' side" (1:87).

Closely related to his suffering body, *I colloqui* speaks of the Savior's passion and death in a number of different manners (see chapters 2 and 3). According to structuralist terminology, the Son could be seen as a plot with infinite linguistic versions.[20] However, the Son pervades the mystic's narration of his existence even when he is not directly present as a character. In order to clarify this crucial point, let us compare two colloqui that revolve around the same topic, Jesus' passion, but which address it in two different ways. In colloquio 5, the transcribers state:

> She had started to accompany her beloved Bridegroom toward his passion, as she usually does all day Friday. During this period her face becomes much more pensive and grim than usual, and when she speaks and converses she almost does not seem to be herself. Nevertheless, that night we asked her to tell us everything the Lord deigned to tell her. (1:92)

According to her sisters, in this rapture the mystic holds her conversation with Jesus in her own mind, without expressing any physical reaction to the images she is seeing or the voices she is hearing. The nuns seem to understand that she is having a vision only by looking at her preoccupied expression. They state that, after recovering from her rapture, Maria Maddalena is able to talk about her experience. God, she tells them, answered her questions and showed her some powerful images concerning his incarnated Son (93–95). The mystic calmly converses with her sisters, recounting several aspects of her vision.

If we now read a passage from a later rapture (colloquio 36), we can see how here the Son makes Maria Maddalena participate in his passion by sharing with her his harrowing pains:

> Oh, what a penetrating pain! . . . *cor meum dereliquit me, et dolor passionis me assunsit me* [silence] *et peccatum omni creature* [silence] oh,

oh, now it seems as though you do not remember what you said: *Filius meus est tu* [*silence*] *et: In quo michi bene complacui, ipsum audite* [*silence*] *et non audisti eum*. Oh, oh and everything was for your creatures [*silence*] oh Word, I wonder if you mean: [*silence*] *transeat ad me penis ista*, even though it gives glory. (1:400)

In this second passage the Son is nothing but sheer despair. The transcribers report Maria Maddalena's anxiety primarily by citing well-known biblical verses: "Cor meum dereliquit me" (Ps. 39:13), "Filius meus est tu" (Ps. 2:7) and "In quo michi bene complacui" (Matt. 17:5), and by rephrasing other sacred expressions, such as "transeat ad me penis ista" (cf. Matt. 26:39: "My Father . . . if it is possible, let this cup pass from me"). All these quotations/interpretations aim to communicate and visualize the saint's disquiet, which is the real unifying theme of this discourse. The authors of *I colloqui* signify this by reproducing a fragmented syntax and citing passages from the sacred texts that allude to the mystic's sense of anxiety. On the page both the Other/Word, who conversed with the mystic in a perfect silence, and the speaking subject acquire a body through the very style of the text.

The nuns slowly learned how to mold their reportages, that is, how to edit their transcriptions. Exclamations, ellipses, biblical quotations (either uttered by the saint or chosen by the authors themselves), repetitions, and linguistic/thematic variations are the rhetorical devices that the authors use to give the mystic's discourse a narrative unity. In some passages Maria Maddalena's monologues actually take up a clear homiletic style, similar to what male preachers must have used during the morning mass in her convent. The saint's visions abound with homiletic passages:

Ubi sum ego ibi e minister meus erit [*silence*] who are these your ministers? And who can glorify your Father without glorifying you? Where you are, oh good Jesus, they are there [*silence*] you are everywhere, and they are everywhere, because they are in you who are everything, and they are everything. You are in them, who are nothing by themselves. However, since they are in you and you are in them, they are something. They are your ministers and your Christs, and (if they perform their ministery with sincerity) they acquire a name that is above every name, as is yours: *in nomine Jesu omne genu flectatur, celestium, terrestrium e infernorum*. (1:394)[21]

In this excerpt Maria Maddalena discusses the role played by male ministers within the Church. In fact, in the above quotation Maria Maddalena preaches as if she were a priest. The mystic uses some of the devices typical of a sermon: she starts her discourse by quoting a biblical passage in Latin; then she expands it, analyzing its single elements;

finally, she concludes with another Latin quotation. From a thematic standpoint, it is important to note that Maria Maddalena dares to cast doubt on the priests' sincerity. Who actually dares to express such critical doubts? The mystic? The nuns? Both the nuns and the mystic? How far was the mystic's standpoint from that of the transcribers themselves?[22]

In other passages of *I colloqui* the editors state that often Maria Maddalena's visions focus on her sisters' morality. Summarizing the alleged content of one of her monologues, the nuns tell us that in a rapture the mystic reproached some of them for being lazy and skeptical toward their faith:

> She saw that every nun had Jesus within herself. Jesus sat, slept, and took a rest under a beautiful tree, that was in the soul of each nun. Some of the nuns had a big big tree . . . some others had a small one, and others a tiny one. She understood that this tree was the charity of each nun. (1:80)[23]

In this passage, Maria Maddalena's rapture exclusively concerns her convent sisters. In other words, in this case the transcribers constructed a text about themselves. To what extent did they modify the mystic's orality? To what extent were they faithful to the mystic's discourse? These questions are particularly relevant if we remember that the mystic allegedly did not recall the content of her raptures. How can the editors create a text that is erased/forgotten by its author? What does it mean to write a forgotten text?

I colloqui is what its author *does not* know, what she *does not* remember. Whereas writing is usually conceived of as an act of memory, in *I colloqui* writing is equivalent to forgetfulness. What we read, what the transcribers wrote down is the mystic's oblivion. As we have seen in the excerpt from *Probation*, although the nuns report that Maria Maddalena does not recall the content of her visions she is forced to abide by her confessor's order: Maria Maddalena must become editor of her own raptures. After having spoken, the saint sits down with her sisters and takes part in the editing of her own words:

> She spoke for a long while and said many beautiful things. By the grace of God, we wrote them all and we shall transcribe them in their right place, after having checked them with her, although she remembered very little. (1:264–65)

The mystic supposedly said "many beautiful things," which the editors respectfully wrote down, along with her subsequent remarks and clarifications. Her "beautiful things" are legitimized, we might infer, when the transcribers involve her in their editing. What her words *must* obtain in their passage from the oral level to the written one is a logical, narrative sense.

The written text attempts to reinstate the connection between voice and hand, which is split in the mystic's orality. In *I colloqui* what the hand composes is not what the voice expresses. The voice speaks, and the hand interprets. Whereas the mystic's voice is primarily the attempt to articulate the Word's being, the hand tries to capture the voice's logical message. As we shall see in chapter 2, although the mystic's monologues cannot help but use Italian and Latin as their main languages of expression, they mean something radically or partially different from what they seem to say.

Prior to any specific content, that is, prior to any given signified, the saint's voice *speaks* her effort to utter the Word. Asked to help her sisters to edit her monologues, Maria Maddalena has difficulty in pinning down a single moment in the development of her past emotions, since written words cannot reconstruct her internal conditions. She directly refers to this problem in colloquio 27, when she states that she retains only what she has perceived rationally, whereas she forgets all her feelings (1:288).

By taking part in their interpretation of her discourses, Maria Maddalena validates her sisters' work. Sometimes it is not clear who has actually explained an obscure passage, Maria Maddalena or her sisters; the nuns use expressions such as "we understood that," "it became clear to us that," without specifying the source of a particular insight. To conclude, we may say that in *I colloqui* Maria Maddalena plays two distinct roles: she is not only considered by her convent sisters the actual author of their transcriptions, she is also one of their editors. In her second role she authenticates her sisters' edition of her raptures.

Maria Maddalena's convent sisters are directly present in the text when they insert their comments on some obscure passages of the saint's monologues. The nuns claim that their interpretative work is primarily based on their conversations with Maria Maddalena; however, on some occasions the sisters directly introduce their own interpretation. For instance, in "colloquio 9 the transcribers say that it was so difficult to obtain any explanation from the saint that they felt forced to guess at the meaning of her words (1:129). In some of the most complex passages, Maria Maddalena's words, other saints' alleged statements, and the nuns' comments, become interwoven. The nuns transcribed what Maria Maddalena said, but Maria Maddalena actually repeated what another saint had just told her. As a result, it becomes nearly impossible to understand who says what. An example of this can be found in colloquio 7, wherein Maria Maddalena reports her dialogue with St Agnes:

First, St Agnes said (she told us), from the mouth of my groom I have received milk, that is charity . . . although it is sweet, honey is quite raw; this means that love for our neighbor makes us suffer, especially holy persons like Saint Agnes . . . since God gave her this charity, not only toward God Himself, but primarily toward her neighbor [St Agnes] could feel this rawness when she endured so many insults. (1:110)

In this passage the editors write that Maria Maddalena reported to them what St Agnes had told her about her experience with God. All of a sudden, the text shifts to the third person. Who then is the narrator? Maria Maddalena or the transcribers? Who is speaking about Agnes' charity?

In some other passages the nuns censor the mystic's words. They believe that Maria Maddalena's remarks about specific persons or situations may not be included in their final edition, as in the case of colloquio 31: the nuns explicitly say that the saint's comments on a certain Florentine convent are unbecoming, and thus they will not write them down:

[S]he said many more things about a certain convent here in Florence; Jesus would like to warn them, but we shall not say more, and shall not report the words she spoke in this rapture, because it is not appropriate. (1:315)

In several other pages, Maria Maddalena speaks about those of her convent sisters who seem to have difficulty in their faith. In these cases, the names of the nuns are not written down.[24]

The nuns' primary effort is to turn their own transcriptions into chapters of a narrative text. It is important to remember that I colloqui is not a series of unrelated raptures, but rather a cohesive narration. It encompasses a specific period of time, from December 1584 to June 1585, and describes a specific place, the convent of Santa Maria degli Angeli in Florence. To compose a coherent literary product, the editors manipulated the notions of time and space, modifying the temporal and spatial categories of the first draft of their transcriptions, shifting passages, inserting various remarks, eliminating excerpts that would disturb the coherent structure of their text.

In I colloqui time and space are synonymous with structure. However, to organize the mystic's monologues with the Word, that is, to insert them into time and space, essentially means to silence the voice of/to the Other. As the final section of I colloqui clearly shows, language in time and space can only be the language of the Father. In colloquio 48, when God finally articulated his Law through Maria Maddalena's mouth, neither the mystic's voice nor the Word's responses were reported. In *I colloqui* the Word does not come to express his will, because the Father takes over in that moment when, after the first half of the text, Maria Maddalena has completed an excruciating mystical purification. When the actual encounter with the Word seems close to its realization, the Father invades the mystic's body and starts to express his Law through her mouth. Time and space, seen as narrative constructions, mold a text that reveals the Law of the Father.

Let us examine first the temporal composition of the text. To begin, we must distinguish between two different temporal categories: time within each colloquio and time as a result of the relationship among all the colloqui. As far as the first category is concerned, we can easily notice that the writers marked not only when each vision took place, but also which saint was celebrated that day and how long the rapture lasted. Also, since in each rapture the mystic was reported to interpret a particular episode of the Gospel, the transcribers constructed each colloquio on two interrelated levels: (1) the historical time of the vision itself, and (2) the mystic's interpretation of the biblical time. According to the writers, when she acted out a moment of the Savior's life, Maria Maddalena never followed consequential time, but she rather went back and forth from the biblical past to her present moment. The nuns believed that the mystic's interpretation of the sacred texts was influenced by her psychological condition. We might say that an essential part of the editors' literary construction is based on a sort of "emotional time," that is, the constantly changing of the mystic's psychological responses to her divine interlocutor. When, after the first half of the book, the nuns modified their rhetoric they started to reproduce on the page the oral cadence of the mystic's discourse, that is, her silences, exclamations, repetitions. They felt compelled to construct a narration of the mystic's emotions. Maria Maddalena's feelings became chapters of a private story, her love relationship with the Word.

In order to better understand this point, let us study briefly the temporal structure of colloquio 36, one of the most interesting chapters of the book. The editors state that in this rapture Maria Maddalena celebrated Good Friday and reexperienced the Word's pains. From a temporal standpoint, we may distinguish at least three different narrative levels. The first level is the present of the nuns' and of the saint's comments on this vision. On the one hand, the transcribers describe her gestures and her movements, and try to explain her words. On the other, Maria Maddalena converses with the Word and the Virgin Mary about the sense of his past sufferings. For instance, at a certain point Maria Maddalena reminds the Word of his mother's anguish over his forthcoming death: "This narration of your action made Mary suffer a lot [*silence*] *elegi eam apud te* [*silence*] *et confirmasti eam de manu tua*; because she was going to give birth to you, I believe that too" (1:384). On the second temporal level the mystic merges her commentaries with the account of Jesus' sufferings, as if they took place at that very moment:

> So wonderful are the vision that you wanted to give us and the glory that you wanted us . . . I would not say to participate in, but rather to taste and enjoy, that if it were not more intense than the suffering I would not speak any longer [*silence*] vision [*silence*] vision. Only vision of truth and of the Word [*silence*] but today it is a day of Passion and not of vision, yes, but. (1:385)

In the first part of this passage, the mystic comments on a past event, the Savior's passion, whereas at the end she seems to say that the two temporal levels, the time of her commentary and that of the commented event, coincide.[25] The text states that through her own suffering the mystic is capable of connecting the two distinct times of her rapture. On the third level, Maria Maddalena totally identifies with the Word's experiences. The present time is the time of the biblical event. For example, toward the end of this colloquio Maria Maddalena addresses the mob that saves Barabas and condemns Jesus:

> You say that Caesar is your king, but in reality you do not deserve my Spouse to be your king; He will be your judge [*silence*] *ecce Rex vester* [*silence*] what are you doing, ungrateful people? What did you say before? *Benedictus qui venit in nomine Domini*, but now you say: *Crucifige, crucifige eum*. (1:414)

Maria Maddalena participates in the Word's passion as his spouse; she reenacts the last moments of the Savior's life and yells at the crowd that rejects his message. However, unlike other mystics, Maria Maddalena does not make frequent use of this third temporal level. In most cases, the time of her rapture and that of the Gospel intermingle, that is, the saint both recounts a past event and actively participates in it.

We have seen so far that in the nuns' transcriptions time is multi-faceted; the present of their commentary interacts with other temporal levels. The writers also gave their edited text a temporal structure by interrelating the visions among themselves. The nuns attempted to show that Maria Maddalena's discourse had an intrinsic coherence that went beyond the basic unit of a single vision.

The writers constantly refer to previous or future raptures, highlighting similarities, repetitions, passages, or images that clarify, say, ambiguous past utterances or the roles of certain persons who witnessed one vision and are reported deceased in a later one. In *I collo-*

qui time goes by not only within each single rapture, from its beginning to its end, but first and foremost in the lives of the saint and of her biographers.

The most evident time sign is at the beginning of each colloquio, when the writers mention the date of that vision. This is how colloqui 1 and 4 begin: "Tuesday January 1st . . . we got together with the blessed soul" (1:51); "Sunday night, January 13th . . . we decided to have our usual dialogue with her" (1:82). In most cases the transcribers also mention how long that vision lasted. We know that the vision reported in colloquio 48 is extremely long; it lasted exactly forty hours. Moreover, at the beginning of some colloqui the nuns summarize previous visions that they were unable to write down. The writers condense in one chapter what has actually occurred in more than one day: "Sunday evening, January 6th, 1584 . . . we began our second conversation . . . we asked our blessed soul what the Lord had communicated to her the past Friday" (1:62); "On Saturday, April 27th 1585, we conversed again with the blessed soul . . . but first we will recount what she experienced last Monday, the second day of Holy Week" (1:428).

The nuns also use flashbacks at the beginning of a colloquio and throughout their transcription of a particular vision. In order to make the mystic's discourse clearer, sometimes the nuns modify the structure of her reported monologues. Sometimes the nuns believe that by reversing the order of her sentences, the sense of the mystic's words becomes more apparent. For instance, in colloquio 32, after having reported a passage of her discourse ("Oh my ingratitude, oh my ingratitude! [*silence*] my ingratitude causes every evil," 1:320), the nuns add: "We believe that here she referred to the Church, because right before she had said: "Your bride cries [*silence*] oh Catherine, if you were here, you would force God." The transcribers have reversed two passages of the saint's speech in order to connect one idea (the solitude of the Church) to Maria Maddalena's following exclamation "oh my ingratitude!"

Let us now move on to analyze how Maria Maddalena's single visions, the so-called colloqui, are related to each other. Two basic kinds of events hold the text together: first, mystical occurrences that testify to a change in the mystic's relation to God; second, historical facts that span more than one colloquio. As far as the first element is concerned, the transcribers never fail to notice that each of the saint's visions corresponds to a different facet of her relation to God. Maria Maddalena experiences all the traditional signs of divine love. In colloquio 42 the nuns state that the she is ready to receive the Savior's crown of thorns, because a week before, like Catherine of Siena, she had married the Word (2:72).

If we look at the second element that unifies the mystic's raptures, we see that historical events play a central role in connecting the individual chapters with each other. A historical occurrence is mentioned in a vision, then developed in the following one, and finally summarized in a third. For instance, in colloquio 15 the nuns state that Lady Camilla da Bagnesi, who had been one of the convent's most influential "friends," is very ill: "While she was praying for the Father Confessor and for Lady Camilla da Bagnesi, who was sick, she was told that . . . Lady Camilla was suffering so much in this latest disease of hers because of her love for her son" (1:177). In the next colloquio the nuns speak of Maria Maddalena's meditation on Jesus' blood offered to God during the morning mass. The nuns specify that the day before, February 20th, the morning mass had been dedicated to Camilla da Bagnesi, who had just passed away:

> Wednesday, February 20th, 1584, we met with the blessed soul in the name of God and conversed with her. She told us that yesterday morning many masses had been celebrated for the deceased Lady Camilla da Bagnesi. (1:179)

In a much later colloquio the nuns write that during her vision Maria Maddalena mentioned Camilla da Bagnesi. The saint had seen her in heaven praying for her son, who had given her so much pain: "I saw Lady Camilla in heaven. She wanted to pray to God for her son Niccolò" (1:284).

The concept of time expressed in this text derives from the interaction between two complex temporal notions. On the one hand, the mystic's utterances, which correspond to the nonsequential, "mystical" temporality,[26] are the actual *signifiers* of the text; what each chapter "says" lies in the mystic's reconstructed orality. On the other, the temporal, historical time of the literary construction is the text's *signified*. It is apparent that *I colloqui is a text that is signified by an absent signifier*. When the mystic's oral words became instrumental to a coherent, narrative temporality, her language had already been converted into a signified. The act of appropriating the visionary's utterances *marks* the disappearance of her voice.[27]

Similar to the notion of time, space is the result of the interaction between the nuns' transcriptions and their own editing. First of all, her sisters understood that Maria Maddalena spoke not only through her voice but also through her body. The transcribers perceived that the description of the saint's body was an important factor in their editing; her body completed, or rather, enriched the sense of their reportage. Before and/or after each part of the saint's reported discourse, the nuns introduced a description of her physical conditions:

> As soon as she knelt down she entered a rapture, and for three hours she did not come out of it, although through gestures and words she showed that she was suffering a lot; large drops of sweat ran down her face and tears ran from her eyes, and she also had such a rheum and breathlessness that we really worried for her. She drooled . . . as when one is dying. (1:312)

This form of narration of a visionary's suffering is common to many hagiographic texts. In the above passage the nuns compare her with the Savior, since during this vision Maria Maddalena reexperienced his pains on the cross. What distinguishes *I colloqui* from previous hagiographies is the fact that similar physical descriptions accompany almost every utterance of the saint. As I have already pointed out, the mystic's emotional states help the editors construct a logical text. The nuns did not limit themselves to introducing brief excerpts from the saint's inspired discourses with an account of her gestures or movements, they also connected almost every section of Maria Maddalena's often long speeches with her inconstant physical positions. Her body and her words are very closely related to each other:

> She joined her hands and stood still, looking toward the sky . . . she said the following words: "God prays to God. . . ." She showed that she was in great pain: "Oh, what excruciating pain!" And one could see that she was participating in it, since her face was slowly taking a sorrowful expression . . . then she gave a painful howl, which apparently came from inside her, and then she said: "In her bosom you desired to suffer, and now? . . ." And after these words she fell down . . . with her hands joined and her arms down like an exhausted person, and she kept her eyes fixed on the floor . . . and then she said: "You suffered all of this for your chosen ones." (1:399–400)

In the above passage each utterance pronounced by the mystic is accompanied by a description of her sorrowful body. In one sense, each word of *I colloqui* contains a specific gesture; each word *is* a gesture.[28] The mystic's body "speaks" a language that interacts with that of her voice. By carefully noting Maria Maddalena's physical reactions, the nuns endeavor to give her spoken language a sort of visual perspective.[29] In *I colloqui* words speak the visionary's body. If to exist means to be engaged in the effort to articulate the Word, since both our words and our gestures cannot help but be a response to his request for being, *I col-*

loqui itself expresses a desire for existence. This text, we may infer, is a body that longs for incarnation.

According to the editors, the mystic's gestures accompany her words as she acts out a particular episode of the Gospel. Being language, the human body *must* have a meaning; its gestures *must say* something. However, in some cases the nuns' transcriptions of the mystic's physical expressions fail to convey a clear meaning. When this happens, the editors add an interpretative key by referring her gestures to the overall sense of the saint's vision. In colloquio 30, for example, the nuns begin their transcription by reporting a brief, fragmented sentence: "Not insertion, no, but through infusion." Maria Maddalena accompanied these words with an *unclear* movement of her hands, as if she were receiving, welcoming something or someone. The writers relate both her words and her gesture to the fact that this rapture occurred on Easter Monday, and therefore conclude that on that day Maria Maddalena must have received spiritual, though invisible, stigmata. The mystic reminded her sisters of Catherine of Siena:

> When the blessed soul was in the garden with the novices . . . she leaned against a pole, with her eyes fixed on the sky. Soon a sister noticed it and took her to the dormitory of the novices . . . she held her hands open, staring at a figure of Jesus that she had on top of her bedstead; she looked like St Catherine of Siena. So, we thought that at that point Jesus gave her his holy stigmata. (1:331)

The nuns insert Maria Maddalena's silent movements into the general frame of their mystical narrative, composing their text as if they were both authors and readers, that is, both as addressers and addressees of their literary discourse. They know how things actually went: how the saint behaved and spoke, how her words resounded in their convent, how painful or cheerful the tone of her voice was.

However, the nuns are aware of the fact that the mystic's words do not suffice to "give body" to her linguistic expression. The editors understand that the mystic's body and her words are two facets of the same signifier. This double-sided signifier both multiplies and weakens its ultimate expression. If, on the one hand, the connection "body-orality" enriches the sign, its potentiality, on the other it jeopardizes the sign itself. In fact, in the written text the mystic's body is both signifier and signified, the sign that says and the sign that is said; her body is both part of that "world" the authors want to initiate the reader into, and the means through which they perform that initiation. As a consequence, if on the one hand we can appropriate the mystic's body as a signified through a phantasmatic association, because by the act of writing the authors allowed us to do so, on the other hand we fail to perceive it as a signifier because of its strict relation to that orality, which is irremediably lost. The sign's capability of working as a signifier is thus in doubt; the body of the text, we may say, is signified on the page, *it is said*, that is, it is constantly compelled to say something, to mean something, even though we, and the editors, cannot be sure of what it is saying. As the mystic strives to summon the Word's being, *I colloqui* tries to perform it in its own language.

CHAPTER 2

Maria Maddalena, the Word, and the Language of the Birds

And Solomon was David's heir; and said, "O ye folk! you have been taught the speech of birds, and we have been given everything; verily, this is an obvious grace.

—The Koran

Oh Angels, come and bury my beloved Son . . . every bird will praise Him and sing with delight.

—I colloqui

For centuries scholars have attempted to define and categorize mystical language. It is apparent that no rhetorical transition is conceivable between the "language of unsaying," as Michael Sells defines mystical language, and our metadiscourse on that very language.[1] In Lacan's words, our "discourse of the University" endeavors to tame the *objet petit a*, which is the erotic/rhetorical element present in every text and which is irreducible to any form of interpretation, in order to turn the text into a subject of discourse.[2] Mystical language never becomes subject of/to its own saying and strongly resists what Barthes calls "the libido dominandi" of critical discourse.[3] Mystical texts have never been particularly popular among scholars primarily because of their alleged lack of "clarity," that is, of a clear and distinct sense.[4]

This superficial dismissal of mystical literature derives from the fact that the academic "fascism," as Barthes says (Barthes, *Leçon*, 14), perceives that mystical literature defies every expression of "knowledge." Indeed, a fundamental premise of every critical metadiscourse is that language cannot express a "void"; language, and in particular literary language, must say something, must *mean* something, so that that "meaning" may be appropriated by the rhetoric of knowledge (Barthes, *Critique et vérité*, 70).[7]

The fundamental problem of any act of interpretation is indeed a matter of rhetoric. As I pointed out in the introduction, our rhetoric becomes even more problematic if we attempt to appropriate the monologues of Maria Maddalena de' Pazzi. If rhetoric, our "discourse of the

University," is supposed to transform and "absorb" a mystical expression, the manuscripts of Maria Maddalena's visions trouble this process of appropriation. First, Maria Maddalena does not speak for us; second, Maria Maddalena does not write anything down; third, Maria Maddalena opposes the very act of writing. In other words, the seven volumes of the mystic's visions distance themselves from any rhetoric, and thus reject any "translation."

I colloqui manifests the radical impossibility of speaking about Maria Maddalena's discourses. Instead of saying what her monologues "actually say," that is, instead of "translating" her words, *I colloqui* paradoxically suggests that we summon the physicality of the mystic's words, so that her discourses might be present here and now as signifiers, rather than signifieds. Signifieds can be appropriated; signifiers can only be listened to. Signifiers are phonetic events, whereas signifieds are written objects, and thus can be turned into subjects of knowledge. The Lacanian *objet petit a* is nothing but the remnant of the original signifier that makes the act of appropriation questionable, or better yet, a question.

We must read the signifiers of Maria Maddalena's monologues as linguistic occurrences preceding any signified discourse. More than *what* the mystic says, we must investigate *how* she says what she says. The actual message of her utterances resides at the performative level of her discourse. As a consequence, we must constantly move from the content of her discourse to the missing performance of that very content, that is, the mystic's body, her voice, her gestures, her audience, the place(s) where her saying took place, the light of the day or night of that performance. What she said once and for all lies in the perceived physicality of her saying. To summarize this crucial point, we may say that the mystic's divided identity, that is, her being both speaker and "spoken" by the nuns' transcriptions, her being absent as speaker and present as narrated event, cannot help but be reflected in our analysis of her saying, itself split between a no-more-existent orality and *I colloqui*, the reconstruction of the mystic's orality through a variety of rhetorical procedures.[6]

In this section I focus on the mystic's missing orality. In order to clarify this essential aspect, we may refer Maria Maddalena's saying to the angelic language, often defined as "the language of the birds." In *The Bestiary of Christ* Charbonneau-Lassay points out that medieval iconology frequently uses the image of a bird, whose body is reduced to a head with two wings, in order to depict the image of an angel.[7] Speaking of the angelic presences at the beginning of *Purgatorio*, Dante writes:

"Then he—that bird divine—as he drew closer/ and closer to us, seemed to gain in brightness,/ so that my eyes could not endure his nearness" (*Purgatorio*, 2:37–39).[8] The Gospel reminds us of "the birds of the air" in the parable of the mustard seed:

> He also said, "What can we say the kingdom of God is like? What parable can we find for it? It is like a mustard seed that at the time of its sowing in the soil is the smallest of all the seeds on earth; yet once it is sown it grows into the biggest shrub of them all and puts out big branches so that the birds of the air can shelter in its shade." (Mark 4:30–32; Matt. 13:31–32; Luke 13:18–19; GT 65)

Another example of the relationship between birds and angels can be found in Gregory the Great. In the tenth *Homiliarum in Ezechielem* Gregory compares the music performed by the angelic spheres to the birds' singing. According to Gregory, the melody of the birds/angels is similar to the harmony within the Church.[9] Finally, as the quotation at the beginning of this chapter shows, Maria Maddalena herself uses a similar image. The angel's words, "the language of the birds," and Maria Maddalena's utterances share some crucial aspects. As linguistics speaks of "families" of languages, we may say that Maria Maddalena, the birds, and the angels speak three cognate, albeit distinct, idioms.

The angels' speech, the birds' language, and the mystic's utterances are all similar yet distinct entities. Moreover, the term "birds" signifies both the animal and a linguistic metaphor. The "birds" are themselves and the momentarily identity/image of the angelic being. In other words, angels are birds and are like birds; Maria Maddalena's language is the language of the "birds" and is *like* the language of the birds. The inner duplicity of this double comparison is of central importance. The three languages are distinct but similar idioms.

Before examining the three idioms, we must realize that the three speakers in question have no name. The birds, the angels, and the mystic do not possess a subjectivity as speakers. Honorius reminds us that "angels do not need names. . . . Michael, Gabriel, Raphael are not names, they are rather *agnomina*, given to them by the human beings. Angels have no names in heaven."[10] "Maria Maddalena" herself is not mentioned in *I colloqui*. The transcribers call her "the blessed soul," "our beloved soul," or just "this soul." The fact that the three speakers are devoid of any name reflects the intrinsic nature of their speech, a language that transcends/annihilates its own speaker.

Let us analyze now the speakers of the three similar but distinct languages, starting with the birds. We often happen to be drawn to the "language of the birds." We cannot help but wonder whether the birds are frantically trying to say something or actually saying something, and whether that "something" somehow concerns us, is directed to/comments on us and on our being unable to perceive what they are saying. As René Guénon reminds us, "there is often mention, in different traditions, of a mysterious language called the language of the birds."[11] Before the sounds of the birds' speech make us aware of the space/distance filled by that very speech, before our mind/rhetoric takes over and sets the parameters of time and space, our body *echoes/is traversed by* the "language" of the birds. As Lacan stresses, the act of thinking initiates our perception of the void that creates language itself.[12] The act of thinking occurs exclusively in the past tense. The hearer cannot make sense of the sounds uttered by the birds. As a consequence, the birds' speech produces *no* memory of itself. It leaves *no* trace of itself. The birds say something as if they were unaware of their own discourse. Their language exists as appearance.

Appearance is also the central element of the angels' speech.[13] Debating the nature of angelic bodies (*Summa*, Ia 51: 3), Thomas Aquinas writes:

> Certain vital functions have something in common with other activities: speech, considered simply as sound, is like the sounds pronounced by inanimate things. . . . To the extent, then, that vital functions resemble other activities they can be performed by angels through the bodies they assume. . . . An angel does not really speak through its assumed body; he only imitates speech, forming sounds in the air corresponding to human words.[14]

Angels "do not really speak." Like birds, they articulate sounds "in the air." Angels are not even totally aware of what they are saying. If their major power is their being "hermeneut[s] of the divine silence,"[15] they do not perfectly master this faculty "proceeding from the ordering wisdom of God, for this surpasses their comprehension."[16] Thus, the angels communicate a communication that transcends their understanding. As de Certeau says, an angel "crosses, short-circuits the hierarchies of beings and mediations" (AN, 199). Like the birds, angels have *no* memory of their discourse.[17] Like the birds, they forget their message in the very act of articulating it. Angels do not even possess a discursive reasoning, which necessarily implies the categories of past, present, and future; they rather speak the appearances of the present (Cacciari, 56; De Certeau, AN, 203). They exist as communication, although their language is not a language but "sounds in the air."

As Thomas Aquinas stresses, since they constantly contemplate God's face, the angels receive from the divinity a degree of knowledge corresponding to their level within the angelic hierarchy. However, even the highest angels cannot formulate a thought *directed to* the future, since their contemplation is an eternal present. They can only speak in the present tense: "the angelic mind, and every created mind, falls short of the divine eternity. Therefore by no created mind can the future be known" (Thomas Aquinas, qa 57:3, 133). Along with the knowledge of the future, the angels lack perfection. Their utterance/being might err. In the words of Thomas Aquinas, "[I]ncidentally an angel may fall into error [because he does not possess] the *supernatural* factor of God's governing will" (58: 5, 159). Indeed, as Origen writes, the angels constantly long for the Word; they feed on the bread of heaven, *panem intellegi- bilem.*[18] Their contemplation is, in fact, an immutable desire.[19]

The angels are their request for the Word; their being nameless and bodyless reflects the absence of the Word and communicates the absence/Word to the human kind. Thomas defines the manifestation of the Word in the world "the word of the Word."[20] However, the angels pronounce a word that risks being mis-pronounced, mis-uttered, as a result of their mis-interpretation of divine silence. For that matter, Hieronimus goes so far as to say that both mankind and the angels will be judged on Doomsday according to their "virtues."[21]

In her visions Maria Maddalena directly compares the angels' language to that of the birds. In a long passage from *Revelation and Knowl- edge* she draws up a list of birds/angels, each of them having a specific message to convey to the soul:

> And there are various birds that fly over the human being in order to serve him [*silence*] these are the three theological virtues of the soul: faith, hope, and mercy; and the four cardinal virtues: justice, fortitude, temperance, and prudence. They are innumerable because great is the variety of the birds [*silence*] faith is communicated by the familiar and well-known pigeons, which live in their dwellings and feed on what the dwellers give them . . . the song of the pigeon is a mourning. In fact, it mourns and sings, and mourns singing. Similarly, the soul mourns see- ing the creatures' lack of faith and sings knowing God's greatness and goodness . . . there are also various, enchanting, and useful little birds, such as the goldfinches and others. And in the soul these are the virtue of hope . . . there is also the rare and fast eagle, and in the soul this is the virtue of mercy. (234–36)

Maria Maddalena goes on to describe other birds, such as the turtle, the pelican, the falcon, and the partridge (237–39). In the mystic's discourse the birds are creatures that speak to the soul and, more important, *serve* the soul, exactly like guardian angels. Indeed, by speaking to the soul, or better yet, by letting their speaking be perceived by the soul, the birds/angels mold the language of the soul itself. If the soul's ultimate goal is the expression of the Word, the soul can accomplish its task by internalizing the theological and cardinal virtues/languages of each bird/angel. The birds speak *within* the soul, teaching it how to articulate the divine idiom. Let us remember that, according to Origen's third homily on Luke, when we pray to God our guardian angel recites our own words without being heard by us.[22]

In her monologues Maria Maddalena expresses a language similar to that of the birds. Although she is fluent in Italian, she attempts to learn another language, the "language of the birds." The analogy between Maria Maddalena's utterances and the "mysterious" language of the birds is more than a mere metaphor. As we have seen, birds have been often seen as synonyms for angelic messengers, for those almost-divine beings who, more than saying something, say that something is going to be said.

Like the birds/angels, Maria Maddalena announces that the Son is going to be spoken. The crucial similarity between the mystic's language and the birds' lies in the fact that the actual message does not coincide with its signifiers. The language of the birds announce a forthcoming language, the transparent, perfect dialogue between the Word and the human subject. The birds hint at the fact that the Word needs both to speak and to be spoken. This is also the never fulfilled task of Maria Maddalena's monologues.

Let us move now to the mystic's written orality. First of all, we must bear in mind that the nuns who composed *I colloqui* saw orality as an essential element of Maria Maddalena's visions. According to Peter Dinzelbacher, three categories of mystical visions can be distinguished:

1. Visions in which the spoken word is almost irrelevant. These primarily consisting of descriptions of divine images and encounters.
2. Visions that intermittently contain brief dialogues between the mystic and the divinity, but all in all still rely on descriptive narrations.
3. Visions that depend exclusively on the spoken word. Dinzelbacher calls this third kind of vision *Wortoffenbarungen* (word revelations).[23]

However, in the medieval tradition these visions are almost exclusively sermons reproducing a formal conversation between God and the mystic. For instance, the blessed Brigitta of Sweden dictated some of her mystical revelations, often characterized by a dialogic form, at the same time she experienced them. A comparison between a passage from Brigitta's work and one from *I colloqui* will clarify the unique character of the Italian text. In *The Fifth Book of Revelations* or the *Book of*

Questions, Brigitta begins every vision by describing a religious man standing "on a high rung of a ladder which was fixed in the earth and whose summit touched the sky."[24] In the "eleventh interrogation" Brigitta hears that religious man ask God the following questions:

> *First question.* O Judge, I ask you: Since you are both God and man, why did you not show your divinity as well as your humanity? Then all would have believed in you. . . .
>
> *Response to the first question.* The Judge answered: "O Friend, it is you that I answer—and yet, not you. On the one hand, I answer you in order that the malice of your thought may be noted by others. On the other hand, it is not you that I answer, for these things are shown . . . as a benefit and as a warning for others. (124–25)

Other mystical texts limit themselves to echoing the oral word, such as the monologues of the Blessed Angela of Foligno (ca. 1248–1309). Since she was illiterate, Angela dictated her visions to Arnaldo, a friar, who translated her words into Latin. The main difference between Angela and Maria Maddalena de' Pazzi is that Angela was aware of the fact that someone, a male transcriber, was constructing her discourse, that is, was performing a double translation, from Angela's dialect of central Italy into Latin and from the rhetoric of an oral discourse into a literary text. Moreover, as Aviad Kleinberg reminds us, the male transcriber "later translate[d] his own text back into Italian for Angela and translate[d] her corrections into Latin again."[25] Her mystical message does not reside in her orality as such, but rather in her dialogue with Arnaldo, her male scribe. Let us read a short passage from Angela's *Memorial*:

> Afterward she added: It seems that whatever I say about it is a blasphemy. And when you asked me if this darkness drew me more than everything I had ever experienced, what I answered seems to me to be blasphemy. That is why I fell very sick when you asked me those questions and I answered them the way I did.[26]

As this passage shows, Arnaldo actively contributed to the construction of Angela's *Memorial* through questions and requests for clarification. Angela's mystical message is also the result of a conversation.

Let us examine now a short excerpt from *I colloqui*. In colloquio 48 we read:

> Oh my Jesus, it's clear to me, yes [*silence*] *si ascendero in celum tu illic es, si descendero in infernum ades* [*silence*] oh good Jesus! [*silence*] you are only love, but you are absolutely pure [*silence*] oh Word, when are you coming? [*silence*] oh good Jesus! My Jesus, you want to, yes, yes [*silence*] good Jesus, good Jesus [*silence*] I understand neither you nor myself. If I am in you, you know it, you come out of yourself [*silence*] if I'm on earth I am not sure, if I'm in heaven you know it.[27]

The authors of *I colloqui* structured their text as a reportage of the mystic's monologues. In this passage, for instance, by breaking the mystic's discourse into fragmentary segments the authors aimed to convey the dialogic nature of Maria Maddalena's monologue. Even the first section ("Oh my Jesus, it's clear to me, yes, yes") hints at the fact that the mystic was in fact responding to an unheard question uttered by the Son, who presumably asked her whether she had understood a previous statement of his. Moreover, strictly speaking, the constantly repeated "oh good Jesus," "oh Jesus," "oh my Jesus" are superfluous expressions; they do not convey any specific narrative content. The reader perceives an implicit difference between the above three exclamations, without being able to rationalize it. Like the birds' language, Maria Maddalena's utterances at times say without saying or allude to unheard discourses. Like the birds/angels, the mystic utters an idiom of mere signifiers.

According to the nuns, Maria Maddalena's discourse is a response to the Son. Maria Maddalena enters a rapture after having remembered or listened to a passage of the sacred texts. In some cases, she has a vision after having attended morning mass. For instance, at the very beginning of colloquio 4 the nuns state: "she told us that she felt drawn by the Lord during the meditation of the last part of the Gospel that had been read at mass" (1:82); in colloquio 14 the editors directly report the Saint's explanation on when she entered a new rapture: "when the priest began the mass that was, as you know, about the Holy Trinity, as soon as I heard those words *Benedicta sit Sancta Trinitas atque indivisa Unitas, confitebimur ei quia fecit nobiscum misericordiam suam* I was drawn out of myself" (1:163). In other cases, the mystic is compelled to speak by simply bringing to mind a specific passage of the Gospel. For instance, in colloquio 6 the nuns write: "it crossed her mind the last word Jesus said on the cross: *Consummatum est*, and when she started to consider it she was drawn by the Lord as usual" (1:99).

A fragment, a brief verse, a sudden memory of a excerpt from the Gospel arouses the mystic's obsession for the Word. If Lacan's *objet petit a* is that bodily, physical element that enacts every desire, the sacred texts are reminders of God's absent body. Maria Maddalena perceives fragments from the biblical books as repeated requests for being. From the written page the Other asks the mystic to articulate his essence, his body, his being. The Other, we might say, exists as long as the subject perceives his request.

In order to clarify this point, let us refer to Searle's well-known concept of "illocutionary acts," those linguistic performances through which a speaker expresses his/her personal intention to a hearer.[28] Searle distinguishes among five categories of "illocutionary acts":

assertives, when we tell our hearers . . . how things are; *directives*, where we try to get them to do something; *commissives*, where we commit ourselves to doing things; *declarations*, where we bring about changes in the world with our utterances; and *expressives*, where we express our feelings and attitudes.[29]

The Word articulates *directive acts*; he asks the mystic to do something. His statements, as they are reported in the sacred texts, contain a request.[30] However, it is crucial to understand what kind of rapport the Word entertains with the subject. When I say that *from* the written texts the Son articulates a request, I do not mean that the Word speaks some sort of language. By stressing that the Word does not possess the physicality of human language, or of any language for that matter, I intend to put aside the intricate discussion concerning what Nicholas Wolterstorff defines as "manifestational revelations" and "nonmanifestational revelations," the former meaning revelations communicated through "a natural sign of the actuality revealed," the latter referring to revelations "in which the means is not a natural sign of the actuality revealed."[31] The Word's request to the mystic is neither a *transitive* nor an *intransitive* revelation, that is, it is neither intended nor unintended, neither *manifesting* nor *nonmanifesting* (Wolterstorff, 30–31). In fact, Maria Maddalena's physical pain performs both the Other's demand and her, the mystic's, attempt to respond to his demand.

Maria Maddalena, as every other mystic, embraces and develops the Augustinian concept of language's intrinsic physicality. God is first and foremost the biography of his Word. In sermon 53 of his German works Meister Eckhart emphasizes that

> God is a word that speaks itself. Wherever God is, he speaks this Word; wherever he is not, he does not speak. God is spoken and unspoken. The Father is a speaking work, and the Son is a speech working . . . all creatures want to utter God in all their works; they all come as close as they can in uttering him, and yet they cannot utter him. . . . God is above names and above nature.[32]

God, says Meister Eckhart, is a word "that speaks itself" through his Son, the Word. As Bernard McGinn underscores, following a Johannine terminology Meister Eckhart gives a central role to the Son in the act of creation.[33] According to Meister Eckhart, the Second Person of the Trinity is "the Image, Logos, Idea, and Ideal Reason of all things" (ES, 39). Indeed, in his *Commentaries on Genesis* Eckhart states: "the principle in which 'God created heaven and earth' is the ideal reason. This is what the first chapter in John says, 'In the principle was the Word' (the Greek has 'Logos,' that is, 'reason'), and, later, 'All things were made through him, and without him nothing was made'" (ES, 83). According to Eckhart, for God to create is equivalent to speaking: "He speaks in begetting the Son because the Son is the Word; he speaks in creating creatures (Ps. 32:9)" (ES, 85).

If we examine the relationship between the Father, the Son, and the creature ("the Father is a speaking work, and the Son is a speech working"), we understand that for Eckhart the creature is asked to be an "ad-verb to the Word," to complete the Word's linguistic expression. In the German sermon 9, "Quasi stella matutina," Eckhart compares the creature with the planet Venus. Like Venus, the creature should accompany the Word, following and completing his self-expression:

> God called himself a word. St. John said: "In the beginning was the Word" (John 1:1). He means that one should be an ad-verb to the Word. The planet Venus . . . has many names. When it precedes and rises before the sun, it is called the morning star; when it so follows that the sun sets first, it is called an evening star. . . . In contrast to all the other stars it is always equally near the sun. [One] should be like the morning star: always present to God. . . . One should be an ad-verb to the Word.[34]

As I have already stressed, Maria Maddalena knew the German mystics through some anthologies in Italian. Eckhart's linguistic interpretation of the divinity is present in a number of passages of her visions. In colloquio 12, after having remembered the biblical expression "Eructavit cor meum verbum bonum, dico ego opera mea Regi," the mystic clearly states that she aims to "belch forth" the Word:

> Oh my Jesus, now that you are in me I can really say David's words: *Eructavit cor meum verbum bonum, dico ego opera mea Regi.* I will express, that is, I will articulate the good word that you are, my Jesus, and that I keep deep in my heart. (1:152)

The expression "ercutavit verbum bonum" has a totally different meaning in St Bernand's *On the Song of Songs.* In the sermon 67, Bernard actually interprets the verb "eructare" as "to belch forth." He holds that, when the soul is full with God's grace, it "belches forth" the Word:

> [T]he Bride, aflame with holy love, doubtless seeking to quench a little the fire of the love she endures, gives no thought to her words or the manner of her speech, but impelled by love she does not speak clearly, but bursts out with whatever comes into her mouth. . . . The bride thinks it no robbery to take to herself the words of the Prophet: "My heart has belched a goodly theme," since she is filled with the same spirit.[35]

St Bernard maintains that the spouse/soul overcomes language when she is replenished with love. "She does not speak clearly, she bursts out" (*non enuntiat, sed eructat*). The difference between Maria Maddalena's interpretation and St Bernard's is apparent: whereas in St Bernard the act of belching out the Word signifies the soul's contentment with his grace, in Maria Maddalena "eructare" primarily means "give linguistic expression" to the Word. "Eructare" is synonymous with "to speak." Maria Maddalena perceives the sacred texts, either read or listened to during the mass, as God's request for being.

Indeed, the most frequent term used by the mystic to address the divinity is "Verbo" (Word). In the first colloquio the initial words pronounced by Maria Maddalena are "Verbum caro factum est" and "in principium erat Verbum et Verbum erat apud Deum," as if the nuns/editors wanted the reader to perceive the Word as the leitmotif of the entire text. As we have already mentioned, "Word" is and is not a first name. In our analysis of the mystic's performances (chapter 3) we shall see that "Word" functions as a Peircean index, a sign signifying the memory of a sign, like a hole in a wall might remind us of a lost bullet.

We should also remember that the first colloquio opens with a fundamental religious feast: the Holy Name of Jesus (il Santissimo nome di Gesù), celebrated on January 1st. Still, in colloquio 1, the nuns go back to some of Maria Maddalena's previous raptures, starting with that one she had had at Christmas, which commemorated the incarnation of the Word into the world. These are the central premises of all of *I colloqui*: the name of the Son and his birth among and within us:

> on Tuesday, January 1st, 1584, the feast of the Holy Name of Jesus, we gathered, in the name of Jesus, with the beloved soul [Maria Maddalena] . . . we started by asking her what the Lord had wanted to communicate to her on Christmas night [and she] started with the words of Saint John: "Et Verbum caro factum est" and also "In principio erat Verbum et Verbum erat apud Deum." (1:51)

In the passage that immediately follows, Maria Maddalena underscores a second crucial theme of *I colloqui*, the difficulty she faces in expressing the divine Word. Indeed, Maria Maddalena tells her sisters that St John had previously scolded her because she had not recited her morning prayer with the necessary intensity (1:52). The entire first colloquio is actually dominated by the relationship between St John and the Son. By resting on the Word's chest, Maria Maddalena says, St John had been able to experience his infinite love and wisdom, and thus to write his Gospel, that is, to utter the Word for all of humanity:

> While Saint John was resting on his chest, Jesus poured in him. This is how he [Saint John] acquired so much wisdom . . . that *he belched forth that divine conceived Word*, as he later wrote in his holy Gospel. (1:54, emphasis mine)

St John also tells her that three virtues are necessary in order to utter the Word: "humility, purity, and love" (1:52). In particular, humility is crucial for the soul who wants to receive the Word's holy love, so that she totally loses herself in the divinity and becomes like him:

> And he who has this perfect humility also has very easily the third virtue which is his holy love. his love comes to the soul without being requested, because it depends on holy humility. If we have this perfect love we can perfectly unite with God and thus we can become something similar to him. (1:53)

In order to receive the Word, the soul must become completely humble and passive toward the divine will. In this respect, it is clear that the first colloquio is meant to set the tone for the entire book.

The term "Word" appears throughout the two volumes of *I colloqui*. "Word" is a reminder, an *index*, of the mystic's unfulfilled task. According to the authors, in some passages the mystic discusses the meaning of "Word," as if she aimed to clarify some of its unique aspects. For instance, in colloquio 38 Maria Maddalena distinguishes between the word, human linguistic expression, and the Word, divine language. She reminds us that God's glory lies in the Word's voice:

> [Y]our idea, your might, your goodness, everything is a language in Verbo Domini. In Verbo Domini I hoped, rested, and abandoned my soul. . . . The Word, proceeding from the Word, communicates us the Word and unites him to us. She meant that the word of God, which is pronounced by the mouth of the incarnate Jesus, communicates to us and unites us to its source, Jesus himself, while he utters it and we listen to it. (1:435)

In another passage from colloquio 15 the saint goes on to distinguish the human voice, which can only convey an ephemeral word, from God's voice, which is his eternal being:

> The eternal Father has placed . . . his right to his right, primarily for the three virtues that he practiced throughout his life, but particularly during his holy passion. . . . Truth is his holy voice, because it lives forever. *The voice of the creatures is nothing but a little sound that one hears and then it disappears, whereas the voice of Jesus stays forever. Truth is God's being, and also his voice.* (1:172–73, emphasis mine)

Finally, in colloquio 33 Maria Maddalena is reported to describe the Word's mouth. As she says, "the Word's mouth speaks":

> But there is that sweet mouth . . . are so many the virtues of that mouth . . . as from there breath comes out, they will draw the Spirit out of you so that they can infuse in the others [*silence*] then *that mouth speaks*. Oh, how necessary this is! (1:335, emphasis mine)

Whereas the divine word coincides with his being, the mystic's language is only a repeated attempt to evoke the divine presence.[36] In the mystic's language the signifier, coinciding with the physicality of the Word, is never fully expressed, or better yet, the speaker, the mystic herself, constantly doubts that the ultimate signifier, the Son, can be expressed through her words. Indeed, repetition is one of the most frequent rhetorical devices of the saint's narrative style.

Let us examine briefly the central role played by repetition in the construction of the mystic's narrative. In fact, Maria Maddalena's frequent use of repetition contradicts a fundamental assumption of mystical studies. Students of mysticism usually believe that a "blessed soul" progressively moves toward a higher level of enlightenment, even though this "upward" path may be characterized by sudden regressions and impasses. Certain signs manifest the mystic's achievements, such as, for instance, St Francis's stigmata or St Catherine's mystical marriage to God. These events are *unique* occurrences that take place once and only once, because they signify that the mystic has attained a closer contact with God.

If we read the entire seven volumes containing the visions of Maria Maddalena de' Pazzi, we realize that her mystical apprenticeship, so to speak, does not follow a similar pattern. In Maria Maddalena's mystical experience, no event has a stable, once-and-for-all meaning. For Maria Maddalena, every mystical event embodies a certain performativity. More than the event itself, such as the gift of receiving the Word's wedding ring (colloquio 39) or that of being allowed to participate in the Word's burial (colloquio 48), Maria Maddalena focuses on the performance that enacts a given event. Indeed, her mysticism questions the nature of any form of expression. Since every act, every word, every thought, is directed to the Word and aims to embody the Word, every act, every word, every thought is nothing but a rehearsal of itself. Whereas, at least according to their hagiographies, St Catherine of Siena or St Catherine of Genoa perceived their mystical marriage as a "grounding" experience, as Deleuze would say, Maria Maddalena repeats this act at least twice. For Maria Maddalena, "to ground is always to ground representation," that is, she experiences a given mystical event as the remembrance of a forthcoming occurrence.[37]

Maria Maddalena interprets the world as a set of innumerable signifiers that are merely simulacra of themselves, since their signified, their "ground," still awaits to be performed. We might define Maria Maddalena de' Pazzi as "the mystic of the Word." No other mystic of the Western tradition comes to such a radical conclusion about the world's "ungroundedness." If negative theology is based on the premise that nothing can be said about the Word, Maria Maddalena pushes this assumption even further. For her, not only linguistic expression, but also the world itself is unable to say anything about the Word.

Every act, every word, every thought, are performances that attempt to "ground" the Word in the world. However, Maria Maddalena knows that this act of "foundation" cannot be achieved unless the Son himself grants it to the world as a grace. Every performance (words, deeds, thoughts) is thus an invocation to the Word; each performance reminds the Word of his request for incarnation in the world. Only the Word can fulfill his own request.

As a consequence, Maria Maddalena cannot help but perceive her mystical experiences as "rehearsals" of a forthcoming "première," when the Word will actually marry her, when he will actually take her to the places of his passion and death, when he will actually grant her his infinite love. George Bataille conceives of a mystical experience in a rather similar way. As he writes in *L'experiénce intérieure*, "I'm convinced that I can hit the bottom only in a constant repetition, in what I am not sure I have attained, and never will be sure to attain."[38]

However, Maria Maddalena never questions the validity of a given narrative/performance, such as her mystical marriage or her being in the Son's tomb. Although her rehearsals essentially perform a similar performance, they introduce significant variations and unique details. The performance of/for the Word can never be exactly the same. As Deleuze writes,

> repetition occurs when things are distinguished *in numero*, in space and time, while their concept remains the same. In the same movement, therefore, the identity of the concept in representation includes difference and is extended to repetition. A third aspect follows from this: it is apparent that repetition can no longer receive only a negative explanation. In effect, it is a matter of explaining the possibility of differences without concept. (Deleuze, 270)

Deleuze offers a clear definition of repetition. Repetition occurs when a series of performative acts share the same concept, what Lévi-Strauss calls mythème. However, repetition does not always have a "negative explanation." Maria Maddalena de' Pazzi makes clear that repetition and the human condition are closely connected with each other. Repetition founds a dialogue, a request to/from the Word to/from the world. Repetition is the creature's and the Word's calling to each other.

Repetition's intrinsic "negativity" is in fact the essence of our being in the world. As Maria Maddalena underscores in her raptures, our life unfolds as a constant repetition and variation of memories. To be human and mortal means to rehearse, to vary, to meditate on one's own "ungroundedness." Indeed, Maria Maddalena does not cling to any aspect or event of her life. Not even the gifts sent by the Son are "grounded." What the Father defines as "perfect purity" in colloquio 48, which is the fundamental requisite in order to meet with the divinity, is in fact the soul's rejection of any "personal effects," including its own memories. Memories do not belong to the soul; they do not constitute the soul, since the soul is a project, a work in progress. The soul is the forthcoming Word. Thus, memories are "things that happen to the soul" but do not grant it a stability, a "ground," an identity.

The seven volumes of Maria Maddalena's raptures are "scripts" with a number of possible variations. In the next chapter I will analyze two major events in the mystic's life, her marriage to the Word and her participation in his funeral. In fact, these very experiences occur to her more than once. However, each time they "say" something slightly or significantly different. Each time these performances focus on different "zones," "chapters" of their script.

Let us start with the topos of mystical marriage. In colloquio 39 Maria Maddalena stages an actual wedding, inviting St Catherine of Siena and St Augustine to accompany her to the altar. Moreover, she describes in detail the ring that she receives from the Word. In a quite long monologue she also recounts what she is going to see reflected in her wedding ring. She makes the gesture of actually receiving a ring, and looks at her hand as if she wore a ring.

In *The Forty Days*, which contains visions that occurred before those of *I colloqui*, Maria Maddalena has a very similar experience. On June 16, 1584, she enters a vision by meditating on "Eructavit cor meum verbum bunum, dico ergo opera mea regi" (Ps. 64:2). This biblical verse concludes colloquio 39 (2:152), the vision in which the mystic performs her mystical marriage. A first difference thus comes to the fore. Whereas in *The Forty Days* the mystic's marriage to God is introduced by the above quotation, in colloquio 39 the same "line" ends the performance of an identical event.

Colloquio 39 sees the act of "belching forth" the Word as the mystic's overwhelming joy for the gift she has just received. In *The Forty Days* she marries the Word at the end of a long description of different forms of divine contemplation. After having meditated on Psalm 44:2, Maria Maddalena states that first the Father "belches forth" a Word, which is his creature (180). Then, the Virgin recites the same verse twice, the first time in order to give birth to the incarnate Word, and the second one to convince the Father to sprinkle the world with his infinite graces (181). Finally, the Son himself pronounces this verse and, by so doing, he recreates the creatures, freeing them of their sins.

In other words, in *The Forty Days* Maria Maddalena *does not* pronounce "Eructavit cor meum verbum bonum"; the divinity and the Virgin belch forth this biblical expression. After reciting this verse, the Son gives the mystic a ring:

> Then it seemed to me that Jesus gave me a ring and married me to himself, in a union of love. The ring was out of gold for love and mercy, and the stone was white for purity, and its enamel was all purple for humbleness, because I must ascribe nothing to myself, but everything to God's goodness. And when Jesus put that ring on the ring-finger of my right hand, he told me: "Every time you feel the urge to honor and love me, and also to love every creature in me and for me, keep in mind that I have given you this ring. Also, remember that you are not mistaken . . . I want neither you nor the others to be able to see it externally." And this pleased me a lot, because with the eyes of the mind I always have the impression that I see it. (*The Forty Days*, 181–82)

The mystic's marriage is here the account of a visualization. Maria Maddalena does not enact her actual wedding. No saints or angels are invited to participate in it. It is a totally private event, that the mystic discloses after it took place.

Paradoxically, Maria Maddalena marries the Word twice. She seems to have erased from her memory her first marriage and her first ring, as if *that* marriage needed to be repeated, varied, performed in a more "convincing" way. Even though the mystic claimed that Jesus told her "and remember that you are not mistaken," that is, you must believe that I actually married you, years later the same event takes place one more time. What has changed is its "genre." In *The Forty Days* the wedding is a narration, a sort of autohagiography in which the "blessed soul" herself unveils her being chosen by God; in *I colloqui* the same wedding is a solo performance, half narration, half mime. Her wedding is not a secret anymore. The Son asks her to manifest the event to the world, even though his gift remains invisible. Maria Maddalena walks toward an invisible altar; she addresses her guests, St Catherine and St Augustine, and explains aloud the form and the divine qualities of her ring. In other words, the same event is a concept (mystical marriage) that can be reproduced and varied because it is embodied in different forms of performativity. Performativity and mysticism coexist in Maria Maddalena's raptures.

As far as the second experience is concerned, the mystic's participation in the Word's burial, the nuns themselves underscore that it took place at least twice. Indeed, in *Probation* the transcribers relate that on March 26, 1592, their sister Maria Maddalena was granted by Jesus the gift of participating in his passion.[39] The nuns point out that he had already done this seven years ago, that is, in 1585, as one can see in the book of *I colloqui*, where it is written everything she did and said during that rapture of the passion. And when she understood this, at once the blessed soul of the Lord besought him not to give her his gift in a way that it would be apparent to us like that other time, when she physically moved from one place to another, gestured, and acted as Jesus had been forced to do in his passion. (*Probation*, 2:48)

The rapture in *Probation* is thus introduced by the nuns as a mere repetition of a previous "gift." However, *strictu sensu* the mystic was granted his privilege several times. Each of her visions is in a sense a reenactment of the Savior's sacrifice. Maria Maddalena speaks exclusively about the passion and death of the incarnate Word. However, what the nuns mean is that seven years later her sister performs her vision of the Word's passion using a very similar performativity, that is, involving the whole convent, its rooms, the kitchen garden, the staircases, and so forth, in her solo mystical play. The transcribers stress this point one more time when the vision actually starts:

[S]he left the oratory and went to the scriptorium of the procuratrix, which for her was the Virgin's house; and during this passion she went to the same rooms and places where the other time the Lord communicated to her, as one can see in the book of *I colloqui* that reports everything she did and said in that rapture of the passion. (2:49)

However, what the nuns state is not correct. The vision recounted in *Probation* deeply differs from colloquio 48. From a narrative standpoint, the two raptures have simply nothing in common. In fact, whereas colloquio 48 narrates the moments after the Word's death, *Probation* deals with the actual "stations" of the Word's passion, such as his dialogue with Pilate, his being exposed to the crowd, his being whipped at the column, and so on. In colloquio 48 the Savior is already dead, and Maria Maddalena's rapture takes place in his tomb. What the two visions do share are the "backgrounds," the places where the two raptures were staged. Reading pages 47–86 from *Probation* we cannot help but recall that in colloquio 48 Maria Maddalena had already used the kitchen garden, the dormitory for the novices, the chapel, and so forth, to enact her vision.

It is important to note the basic difference between the two visions on the mystical marriage and the two on the passion of the Word. The former share an identical subject, but they are performed through two different "genres" (an "I" narration and a solo play); the latter share a similar performativity, but they recount a totally different subject. In other words, the structure of the two pairs of visions is perfectly opposed. The two visions on the mystical marriage have an identical theme but a different style; the visions on the passion of the Word have a similar style but a quite different theme.

The transcribers fail to stress the radical difference between colloquio 48 and the vision from *Probation* because they underscore their similar performativity. They have already "seen" this play because they have already seen how Maria Maddalena turned their everyday places into "settings" for her memorial of the Word's passion and death. Without offering a detailed description of the second vision on the Savior's death, we will limit ourselves to enumerating its major scenes. The vision opens in the dormitory, where Maria Maddalena sees the Virgin and the Son converse for the last time. When they kneel down because they are overwhelmed by disquiet, the mystic shares their anguish and kneels down like them (2:54). Then she rushes to "a large room, upstairs" (2:56), where she recounts the Last Supper:

> While you were eating the lamb you stood [*silence*] I think I see you eating: end, end, this law must end, and another one must begin. Word, you'll be the lamb, well-roasted, and soon you'll be taken and dead on the Cross [*silence*] one must eat all of you . . .

While Jesus washes his disciples' feet, she addresses each of them:

> She said something to almost every apostle, so that we could know who she was washing. After St Peter, she went to St Andrew, and said: "Blessed Andrew, you won't dare to say anything."
>
> St John
> "Oh pure John, you are the beloved [*silence*] I wouldn't like to have to find that Judas!"
>
> St Thomas
> She didn't say anything to Saint Thomas, but she gazed at him with a joyful and delighted face.
>
> St James
> "You are one of those who wanted to participate in the reign [*silence*] and still you tolerate that God, your Master, washes your feet. But you heard what he said to Peter: you do not want to miss that part, as if one tried to stay at his right and the other at his left."[40]
>
> St Philip
> "You are my Philip. I believe that you loved my God with sincerity and purity of heart."
>
> When she got to Judas, she became distraught and started to cry and to shake, saying: "And you will be the one who betrays my Christ." (2:58–59)

This "scene" reminds us of that passage from colloquio 48 when, after the burial of Jesus, the mystic (as the Virgin) meets with her son's disciples, and says something to each of them. Again, from a performative standpoint colloquio 48 and *Probation* have significant points of contact, even though the content of their performance is absolutely dissimilar.

After the Last Supper, Maria Maddalena moves to another room, which is supposed to be next to the garden of Gethsemane (2:62). Here the mystic holds a rather long monologue that touches upon themes present in the Father's sermon from colloquio 48. Indeed, Maria Maddalena meditates again on the relationship between the Father and the Son before the Word's incarnation. In particular, like colloquio 48, *Probation* describes the different "clarifications" (*clarificationi*) that the Father's and the Son's mutual contemplation generate in each other (2:63–67). In this specific passage, the two visions' performativities coincide. Indeed, like the Father, Maria Maddalena simply enumerates the different kinds of "clarifications."

The major difference between the two visions is the fact that in *Probation* Maria Maddalena finally plays the role of the Savior himself:

> We saw that she was taken and tied up with her hands behind her shoulders, because she made a gesture to signify that; and then with great violence and fury she was led to Anna's. In other words, she left that place and went to another room that was much more distant. Along the way she suffered a lot, because we saw that once in a while she was wrenched with the ropes behind her back. Hence, she suffered very much. (2:73)

The final section of this vision is sparse of words. The mystic's body suffices to signify the stations of the cross. After having confronted Pilate and the crowd (2:75–78), Maria Maddalena mimes the act of being drawn to the column. She leaves the second floor and walks down to a room on the first floor:

> She stood against a column with her hands behind her back and her eyes downcast. She stayed here an hour, hardly saying a word. She continued to keep silent also during the other mysteries of the passion, that is, Jesus's coronation of thorns, his carrying the cross, and his crucifixion. (2:79)

The referential narrative allows the mystic to keep silent throughout the last part of her performance because, it does not need to be "acted out" by means of words. The act of miming the crucifixion is indeed a common trait of female mysticism. For instance, when she relives Jesus' last moments, Vanna da Orvieto (1264–1306) lies down on the floor, stretches out her arms, and puts one foot on the other, in this way "depicting" the Savior's passion.[41]

As this brief excursus on two crucial visions has shown, repetition expresses Maria Maddalena's awareness of the failed "embodiment" of her word. Mystical language indeed expresses the "insane" tenacity to give the Son a second body.[42]

As I have already pointed out, toward the end of *I colloqui* the nuns note that the mystic has acquired a twofold voice. The Father has erupted in her voice in order to restore his power, coinciding with the prohibition of uttering his being. In colloquio 46, for instance, her convent sisters are amazed by her capacity to change radically the tone of her voice. When she talks as the Father, they say, the mystic has a powerful, masculine voice, whereas when she speaks as herself her voice becomes very humble:

> Throughout this rapture she spoke with the eternal Father, and the Father spoke with her, responding to her questions, like a form of dialogue . . . it was amazing to hear her, because she spoke those things with such a dignity and might. And when she spoke as herself she had a submissive and humble voice, almost whispering her words. (2:195)

Before accomplishing the so-called *unio mistica*, the amorous encounter between the Son/Word and the mystic, the Father reinstates his Law. The divinity expresses an apparently contradictory request: on the one hand, he asks the mystic to incarnate his being/Word, on the other he prevents the mystic from achieving this task. The mystic is aware of the fact that the Word is in fact the negation of the Word. Maria Maddalena knows that she has difficulty in uttering the Other. However, although she senses that her repeated attempts are doomed to fail, the saint never rejects God's request. She knows that she must respond to him; she cannot help but speak.[43] Prior to any specific content, her language expresses a necessity; the actual theme of her discourses is temporally secondary to her urge toward language, what de Certeau calls "l'impétuosité d'une énonciation [mystique]" (FM, 202).

Maria Maddalena's monologues arise from her being aware that the Word cannot be uttered. The actual source of her utterances is her disquiet, her uneasiness that pervades all her visions. Her speaking, one might thus say, is an act of awareness. Indeed, in colloquio 6 Maria Maddalena says that language always springs from "a copiousness of the heart" (*un'abbondanza del cuore*, 1:101). In other words, speaking springs from a *jouissance*, a "more-than-feeling" that annihilates rationality. Speaking, we may infer, *occurs* when the subject *does not know* what he/she is saying.

Do the mystic's words have an addressee? In fact, Maria Maddalena's words have no specific, stable audience. No actual interlocutor takes part in her monologues; her words rather engage *partial* interlocutors, characters who limit themselves to justifying, expanding, sustaining the mystic's rhetoric. The apparent addressees of her monologues are rhetorical devices she uses in order to give rein to her monologues. Both her speech and her addressee is her utterance itself.

In all her visions Maria Maddalena "converses" with angels, devils, several saints, among them St Augustine and St Catherine of Siena, as well as the Father and the Son, and the Virgin. However, the mystic frequently exchanges only brief statements with her interlocutors; she moves from one holy figure to the next without any apparent logic. For instance, in colloquio 48, Maria Maddalena simply hints at her numerous interlocutors, such as the Magdalen, the Virgin, many of Savior's disciples, his murderers. More importantly, we must remember that in several cases Maria Maddalena does not have an interlocutor at all; she rather talks to herself.[44] For example, let us read a short passage from colloquio 30:

> Yes, to the crown of thorns [*silence*] nine and [*silence*] oh the angels and [*silence*] the Holy Trinity [*silence*] oh, I don't understand [*silence*] oh, so much ignorance [*silence*] and and there's something that doesn't let me understand [*silence*] oh, and then to honor you. (1:308)

Who is the addressee of these words? In other passages the saint seems to be talking to someone, but she is actually speaking to herself. For instance, in colloquio 32 Maria Maddalena apparently addresses St Catherine, but in reality she uses a conversational style to discuss with herself her private emotional states: "Oh Catherine, if you were on earth you would force God [*silence*] why am I not able to convince him myself? [*silence*] oh my intellect, why are you not able to make others able to do it? I would be more than willing to give it away" (1:320). As this excerpt shows, the mystic seems to move brusquely from one addressee to another: first St Catherine, then her own intellect. The above passage proves that her interlocutors are in fact *rhetorical figures*, closer to metaphors than to actual beings.

The mystic's performances sometimes engage the nuns who are transcribing her words. Indeed, during her visions the mystic is sometimes aware of her sisters' presence.[45] For instance, in colloquio 48 she invites them to follow her toward Jesus' tomb and to mourn with her over his body. In another vision, contained in the second volume of *Probation*, Maria Maddalena goes around in the convent asking her sisters if they possess love and if they know where love is. We will analyze this powerful vision when we speak of Maria Maddalena's concept of "love." However, Maria Maddalena never speaks *with* her sisters, she speaks *to* them. St Catherine, the devils, or Christ's murderers, and the mystic's convent sisters are *connectors, figurative devices* present in, but not essential to, the development of the mystic's discourse. In her performances the nuns take up momentary roles. In one occasion they are the crowd that shows up at the Savior's martyrdom, in other raptures they are undefined sinners the mystic yells at.

In fact, Maria Maddalena directs her words to no one. As de Certeau reminds us, "[the mystical words are] 'adressées,' sans qu'on puisse savoir finalement . . . à qui" (FM, 195). The mystic neither converses, nor does she ask for advice or help. Maria Maddalena lets her language occur. Like that of the birds/angels, her speaking forth is *necessary*, without being dialogic. In other words, whereas the Word's request for being is an illocutionary act *expressed but not said*, Maria Maddalena's utterance speaks without expressing. Like the language of the birds, her monologues *seem to announce something*. As the birds announce the day, as the angels will descend to announce Judgment Day, Maria Maddalena announces the forthcoming, but never actually occurring, embodiment of the Word through her utterance (de Certeau, PA, 207).

The Word *might manifest itself* in the actual body of the mystic's language. However, it is crucial to underscore one more time that for Maria Maddalena language, the physicality of its signifiers, the signifieds they seem to refer to, the mystic's body, the day or night when she entered a rapture, are one and only one entity. Language occurs like breathing, like pointing to something, like walking, like reciting the Savior's death and ressurection, like running down the stairs of a convent in total despair, like ringing the bells in the kitchen garden and asking whether we know love and why we disregard love. As we shall see in a close analysis of colloqui 39 and 48, the transcribers realized that the actual message, if such a thing exists in the mystic's utterance, occurred in the materiality of the voice, that is to say, in the mystic's mouth, her body language, and all the physical details that composed the mystic's act of speech. This is why the nuns understand that the mere content of the mystic's words does not suffice to convey the "message" of her monologues. Thus, they break down her utterance with pauses, silences, exclamations, repetitions. The editors endeavor to recreate the *happening* of her speech. Let us take one of the many examples, a passage from colloquio 32 in which the nuns explain that they mark the saint's silences and exclamations in order to stress the rhythm of her discourse:

> [A]s one can see and understand in the words she said, which we transcribed as carefully as we could, and will write them here leaving the space between one word and the other in order to show when she kept silent and when she spoke. (1:319)

What does it mean "to leave the space between one word and the other"? What role do the mystic's exclamations play within the structure of her overall monologue?

Let us explain this central aspect. The nuns/eye-witnesses perceive the mystic's performances as manifestations of the Lacanian *real*.[46] For the Florentine nuns, the *real* is manifested through the mystic's performance, which gives voice to the Word's request for being. Although they perceive the mystic's performances as evocations of the unspeakable *real*, the editors understand that the *real* is missing from their writing. By inserting exclamations and pauses within their written discourse, the writers aim both to allude to the *real* and to tame it. Silences and exclamations work as allusions to an unrepresentable, albeit fundamental, core, the *real* evoked by the mystic.

The hypothetical readers of the nuns' reportage are asked to perceive the presence of the *real*, without processing it into language, because this process is impossible. Similar to the allusive language of the birds, Maria Maddalena's utterance questions the basic relationship between image and word.[47] The ultimate challenge of the mystic's discourse is its overwhelming, and thus obscure, allusiveness.

It is important to underscore the twofold character of Maria Maddalena's utterances. On the one hand, as a response to the Word's request for being, the mystic's utterances function as response to an *objet petit a*, since they attempt to quench the mystic's desire and its related sense of guilt. The mystic's words try to transform the *real* into language; they aim to give a linguistic form to the absent Divinity. On the other hand, in their written version her words endeavor to hint at what they cannot materialize. We might summarize this decisive point by saying that Maria Maddalena's words *occur* as a response to an *objet petit a*, and are later turned into a tame allusion to the *real*, which is conjured up by the mystic's performance itself. *I colloqui* is thus the mystic's performance turned into a tame allusion to that very performance.[48]

In the nuns' edition the text acquires a *visual connotation*, that transcends/integrates the meaning conveyed by the rhetoric of the mystic's transcribed orality. In other words, the page itself performs a phantasmatic connotation. As Jack Goody reminds us, "writing . . . provides auditory information with a visual, and hence spatial frame. In fact it changes the channel of communicated language from an auditory to a visual one."[49] The transcribers of Maria Maddalena's monologues wished to "picture" her performances in the page itself. In *I colloqui* tha page becomes a field where the nuns themselves perform their interpretation of the mystic's orality. Syntax is the body of the nuns' performance; the transcribers' body is the "gestures" of their syntax. For an illustration, let us read a crucial page from colloquio 39:

When the twentieth hour rang, after a deep sigh she cried out: "Oh good Jesus, as much as you want." Then, after a short silence, she said: "Oh, I don't know [silence] et relaxabo me in liberalitate tua [silence] oh good Jesus, oh, oh, oh [silence] oh Word, oh good Jesus! [silence] oh bonitas immensa [silence] vir linguosus non dirigetur in terra [silence] oh, aren't they like curses! [silence] oh good veritas, you give strength, even though both the Soul and the body consider it impossible. Oh Word, let me die a living death, so that I can carry out your project. Omnes declinaverunt, non est qui faciat bonum, non est usque ad unum [silence] oh, let blindness see, whose seeing gives it pain, whose pain gives it glory, this glory is its beatitude, and its eternity is incomprehensible, inscrutable, and it can only be understood by you, for you and in you [silence] but no novelty is novelty to me! [silence] omnes declinaverunt a te, and non cognoverunt te, et nolunt intelligere ut bene agerent [silence] they don't know you, and they don't want to know you. But in any case they will know you. Et mors depascet eos [silence] oh Word, even though always, you always show them in the same way [silence] you showed us your wounds, your hands, your chest, so that we are not incredulous anymore, but rather faithful [silence] oh great is the ingratitude of your creatures!"

The nuns's syntactic performance makes use of a number of devices: First of all, brief direct discourses (Erlebte Rede), sometimes characterized by an ambiguous, truncated rhythm, such as "Oh, I don't know." These short sentences are not related to each other as clauses of a written syntax, but rather as references to the mystic's oral rhetoric, as sequences of exclamations expressing suprise, insight, and so forth ("Oh good Jesus, oh, oh, oh;" "oh Word, oh good Jesus!"). The syllable signifying exclamations (oh) is itself a mark constructing the rhythm of this visual performance (oh, oh, oh). Brief expressions are, however, followed by well-constructed gestures/sentences ("Oh good veritas, you give strength, even though both the Soul and the body consider it impossible. Oh Word, let me die a living death, so that I can carry out your project"). The contrast between the two syntaxes is itself a mark of performativity.

The "hole" in the page, that is, the pauses marked as "——" and that I render as "[silence]," are the most striking device. They are marks of interruption, of doubt, of unaccomplished linguistic gestures. "[silence]" depicts a reiterated, syncopated gap, a rhythmical lack of meaning.

The rhythm of the nuns' gestures is given also by the constant shift between two idioms, Latin and the vernacular: "Oh Word, let me die a living death, so that I can carry out your project. Omnes declinaverunt, non est qui faciat bonum, non est usque ad unum."

In his study of Chicano poetry, Lauro Flores examines the meaning of "code-switching," which can be either (1) "situational," "associated with the manner in which the poet manipulates his or her relationship with the public," (2) "metaphorical," occurring "when a poet feels compelled to change language because a given concept is better expressed in one language than in the other," or (3) "phonetic," which enhances the musical quality of the text.[50] In the page from *I colloqui*, the passage from Latin to Italian and vice versa can signify a more intimate or more respectful way of addressing the Other (situational code-switch), a device to raise the tone of her monologue (metaphorical code-switch), or a combination of the above two aspects, with an enhancement of the melodic sound of her saying (phonetic code-switch). Given their phonetic similitudes, the mystic's Latin and Italian almost merge. Finally, often expressions or words in Latin echo in an following Italian translation, usually after a pause: "*Omnes declinaverunt a te, and non cognoverunt te, et nolunt intelligere ut bene agerent* [*silence*] they don't know you, and they don't want to know you. But in any case they will know you."[51] The rhetoric of the page performs the nuns' perception of the *real* through a procedure of "iconization." Western poetry has often made use of writing to visualize a specific connotation, from the inventive strategies of the Baroque, like the compositions of Giovanbattista Marino, which sometimes have a quite obscene configuration, to Marinetti's "words-in-freedom,"[52] Mallarmé's "Un coup de dés,"[53] the avant-garde,[54] and Cummings's floating syllables.

The writers of *I colloqui* draw the reader's attention toward the visual emptiness of the page recording the mystic's performance. Maria Maddalena's silences and sudden exclamations depict a constructed chaos. In fact, in *I colloqui* the page *shows* a double absence, both at the denotative level (the absent Word, his death, his request for being) and at the connotative one (the mystic's pauses, the holes in the page itself). Moreover, a third form of lack arises from the page, the mystic's voice itself. Indeed, the nuns' attempt to reproduce the oral level of Maria Maddalena's discourse depicts her voice as a productive absence, as "a speaking nothingness." The transcribed silences and exclamations, along with the mystic's truncated expressions and repetitions, formulate an *image* of the radical nothingness (the Word) that constitutes the text itself.

As Giorgio Agamben reminds us, any linguistic expression arises from a lack; language *comes after* an implicit sense of absence. Language reports, we might say, what is already missing.[55] Rather than actually communicating facts and feelings, language springs from our perception (what Maria Maddalena calls "the copiousness of the heart") that our being "here and now" is based on a fundamental absence. Maria Maddalena knew that her sisters' reportage would not modify the inner sense of her orality; the mystic knew that spoken language exists only at the moment it is expressed. As Agamben says, spoken language plays the same role of a moan.

Let us analyze in detail how the nuns shape Maria Maddalena's exclamations and silences. As far as her exclamations are concerned, it is important to notice that the nuns vary the way they report them. The most frequent sign used to mark her exclamations is "oh": "Oh, oh, oh, [*silence*] oh *bonitas* . . . Oh death that gives life [*silence*] I die alive [*silence*] oh, oh, oh [*silence*] *appone iniquitatem super iniquitatem* [*silence*] ah, almost nobody understands her. Wisdom seems folly, and folly seems wisdom [*silence*] oh iniquity! . . . oh, oh, oh, good Jesus" (2:15). We cannot say, for instance, if capital "Oh" has a slightly different meaning from "oh." Moreover, we cannot know how the mystic actually pronounced the three "oh"s in a row. Were they uttered in the same way all the three times? In the above passage we also have another, albeit less frequent, exclamation: "ah." Is this "ah" (in Italian "uh") similar to that present in the expression from colloquio 46: "Ah, you are really what you are"? (2:246) A third kind of expression used to mark the saint's exclamations is "ah" (in Italian "eh"): "Ah, my little one, your small feet are so nice, ah, ah [*silence*] Ah, ah, poor one [*silence*] Ah my Spouse, I would like to kiss you . . . ah, ah, ah, he has given himself those small ears in order to listen to us" (2:182). Some of the most striking passages of the entire book are almost entirely based on exclamations. In colloquio 48 the mystic repeats "Oh good Jesus!" several times:

> Oh good Jesus! [*silence*] oh my Jesus, it is clear to me, yes [*silence*] *si ascendero in celum tu illic es, si descendero in infernum ades* [*silence*] oh good Jesus! [*silence*] oh good Jesus, you are all love, but you are all pure [*silence*] oh Word, when are you coming? [*silence*] oh good Jesus! [*silence*] my Jesus, your will, yes, yes. (2:312)

It is, of course, impossible to ascertain if the above exclamations were uttered all in the same way. Nor is it possible to determine the temporal gap between two similar exclamations. By transcribing her exclamations, the nuns allude to the saint's orality without being able to transcribe it on the page. The writers *picture* the mystic's feelings more than describing them. However, although we cannot come in contact with Maria Maddalena's performativity, we sense that this excerpt aims to communicate a private sorrow. To clarify this important point concerning the impossible communication of a private feeling by means of language, let us read a passage from Wittgenstein's *Philosophical Investigation*:

> Suppose everyone had a box with something in it: we call it a 'beetle.' No one can look into anyone else's box, and everyone says that he knows what a beetle is only by looking at his beetle.—Here it would

be quite possible for everyone to have something quite different in his box. One might even imagine such a thing constantly changing.—But suppose the word 'beetle' had a use in these people's language?—If so it would not be used as the name of a thing.[56]

In this passage Wittgenstein denies that a so-called private object can ever exist. In fact, Wittgenstein claims, if we hypothesize that we can only know from our own case "what a beetle is," we can never be sure that our "beetle" coincides with someone else's "beetle." The term "beetle" points to something, but we cannot determine what this something is or whether it really exists. Beyond the metaphor, Wittgenstein believes that we cannot know something only out of our private experience; reality can only be shared through a common use of language. What cannot be shared through language cannot be said necessarily to exist. Therefore, given that, according to Wittgenstein, we cannot communicate private pain or joy, we might say that these sensations are indefinable. One's interpretation of the word "pain," as one connects it to one's personal experiences, can never totally correspond to someone else's "pain."[57] However, as I have already pointed out, the nuns' primary goal is to summon the Lacanian capital phi, the passage from the real, perceived as overwhelming and incomprehensible, to its imaginary level, where the subject can *look at the real* without being *blinded* by it. The nuns' "imagetext," according to John Mitchell's definition, both hints at and hides the impossibility of the expression of the real.[58]

The second essential aspect of the mystic's reported utterances are her frequent pauses.[59] The "wholeness" of Maria Maddalena's discourse thus depends on the reader's capacity/willingness to read between the lines, "to perceive" silences when the editors ask her to do so. As Deborah Tannen points out, in every linguistic interaction silence "is the extreme manifestation of indirectness; [silence] can be a matter of saying nothing and meaning something."[60] Silence's indirectness, however, "contributes to a sense of involvement through mutual participation in sensemaking."[61] If we apply Tannen's remarks to *I colloqui*, we could say that the saint's silences ask us, the readers, to "make sense" of her utterances. The act of "making sense" is shared among the speaker, Maria Maddalena, her listeners, her sisters, and the readers.

In *I colloqui* silence is multifaceted:

1. It can refer to the unheard words of one of the mystic's interlocutors, in particular the Word.[62]
2. It can represent a pause in her meditations, as if she were developing some unexpressed thoughts.
3. It can mark a sudden and overwhelming sense of despair, which often follows an exclamation.

Let us examine these three kinds of silence. As the following excerpts will clearly show, the different types of silence very often merge in the saint's discourse. However, we can find passages in which one of them dominates over the others.

Let us start with the first kind. In some passages of the text Maria Maddalena clearly responds to a unheard interlocutor. She keeps silent because someone is talking to her. We read her silences, we could say, as if they implicitly contained the other's voice. We might say that her silences are thus implicitly expressive. We could even imagine single words or full sentences that her interlocutors might be saying to her. Let us read, for instance, a passage from colloquio 39. While she is describing her wedding ring, she enters a brief conversation with the divinity: "[*silence*] add the third to the first and the second [*silence*] and what will it be? [*silence*] but, my Jesus, I do not want to give you orders [*silence*] oh, the purity!" (2:18). In this passage the reader perceives the absent presence, so to speak, of the mystic's interlocutor. Indeed, when the nuns insert a silence in the mystic's discourse, sometimes they allude to the Word's unheard expression. Through the mystic's silence the divinity manifests its absence, according to the well-known concept formulated by the "negative theology."

In a passage from colloquio 44 Maria Maddalena talks with the Trinity about her imminent fight with the devils. Her battle against them will last for three days, the same length of time as the Savior's passion:

> Oh, Father; oh, Word, oh, Holy Spirit [*silence*] I do not understand anything else. In other words, you show these things about yourself, and I do not understand them [*silence*] you know my strength better than I do [*silence*] yes, this night has passed very quickly [*silence*] three more nights, right? [*silence*] or this one doesn't count, right? (2:135)

The reader overhears, one could say, the above dialogue without perceiving the voice of one of the speakers. In other passages Maria Maddalena asks her interlocutors to raise their voices, because she cannot hear them well. For example, colloquio 46: "Raise your voice [*silence*] I do not understand [*silence*] I don't know [*silence*] oh yes, yes, but I hear this voice, and then I do not understand what you say" (2:235). In other points (colloquio 43) Maria Maddalena hears the devils scream at her: "you can yell and scream as much as you want, but you only intensify your pains [*silence*] even here you will not take me. I know that I was created out of earth and that I will become food for worms" (2:106). Finally, in some extraordinary passages her silences summon her physical interaction with her interlocutors. For example, in colloquio 43 Maria Maddalena asks Jesus to defend her against the devils who come back to attack her:

\Oh, Word, help me. They are coming back [*silence*] verbum caro factum est [*silence*] oh, Word, send them away [*silence*] *sursum corda*
[*silence*] why are you doing that? [*silence*] oh you, stupid and ignorant,
what do you think you can accomplish? You harm yourself! [*silence*]
oh, do you not see that the others have left? And you are so shameless
that you come up to me. Do you not see that my Word defends me?
[*silence*] go, go! (2:100)

In this passage the mystic's silences not only allude to the devil's
responses, they also picture the mystic fighting with her enemy. The
mystic's linguistic performativity becomes a crucial element of her discourse. In this sense, if we postulated the above passage as the description of an image (a sculpture, a picture) of the mystic against the
demons, we might see it as an example of *ecphrasis*, "the description in
detail, usually of an art object."[63]

More often the mystic's silences do not allude to a unheard speaker;
they are pauses in her private chain of thoughts. In colloquio 32, for
instance, Maria Maddalena speaks about her being a nun. In particular,
she states that "they," probably referring both to her sisters and to herself, are ungrateful to Christ, because they do not remember all the pains
he suffered for them and the constant help he gave to their souls:

[M]y narrow-mindedness does not understand that she is blessed, sorrowful, arduous, laborious and glorious [*silence*] oh, we really behave
like those people [*silence*] oh, we really pay off what he does for us, but
we do not pay ourselves [*silence*] *ego sum* a worm *et non homo*. He
suffers in an impenetrable way; he actually tolerates so much ingratitude [*silence*] he helps everybody cooperate [*silence*] oh, who will be,
who will be, who will be able to cooperate in the way you do with the
soul, with the Father and the Holy Spirit? [*silence*] I don't understand.
(1:319–20)

In this page the saint's words actually spring from her pauses.[64] She
develops her thought in a complete silence; her utterances are the debris
of her internal thinking. If we try to grasp their overall meaning, we
could say that in this excerpt Maria Maddalena slowly becomes aware
of insensitivity toward the Word's generosity and his desire to collabo-
rate with the soul. Indeed, her silences refer to an increasing sense of
guilt: "My narrow-mindedness does not understand that it is blessed,
sorrowful, wearisome, and glorious [*silence*] oh, we really do like those
ones [*silence*]." As, it seems, her anguish increases, the mystic directly
addresses the Word, even though one cannot tell whether she actually
talks to him: "Oh, who is going to be, who is going to be capable of such
cooperation that you do with the soul, with the Father, and with the
Holy Spirit? [*silence*] I don't understand it [*silence*]."

Let us now examine another passage containing Maria Maddalena's silences. In this second example (colloquio 39) the nuns do not report the mystic's chain of thoughts. Her short sentences are mere exclamations:

> Oh, good Jesus, how much you want [*silence*] oh, I do not know it [*silence*] *et relaxabo me in liberalitate tua* [*silence*] oh good Jesus [*silence*] oh, oh, oh [*silence*] oh Word, oh good Jesus [*silence*] oh immense goodness. (2:14)

In this last case, exclamations overwhelm and destroy the syntax of the mystic's discourse. The nuns make use of a number of different rhetorical devices in order to vary the mystic's discourse. The interaction between pauses and exclamations can be differentiated in an almost infinite manner, resulting in an extremely nuanced expressivity. The written page is a "map," a pictorial performance of the text's variations and repetitions.

I would like to conclude by reporting a short vision entirely dominated by the saint's silence. In *Revelation and Knowledge*, a transcription of her later raptures, Maria Maddalena's sisters state that one day the saint kept silent throughout her vision:

> [T]he blessed soul entered a new rapture as usual around eleven o'clock. In this rapture she did not speak at all, although it was clear that she was suffering, because she looked sad and rapt, except at the moment when she usually received the Holy Spirit. At that point she was happy and through her gestures she made us understand that she was receiving him. After a long while she became sad and suffered again, until 11 in the evening. (175)

The mystic's silence dominates the entire vision. What the nuns can notice are only her physical expressions: her face is tense; she seems to be suffering. Later, she looks relieved. Her silences are all we have. Her sisters believe that her sudden joy is due to her usual encounter with the Holy Spirit. Whereas in other raptures her recurrent pauses may help one apprehend the meaning of her words, in this vision her complete silence denies our participation in the text. In the above passage silence has invaded the page. No semiotic sign signifies the mystic's absent saying. Since the text has constructed a specific relation to "[*silence*]" as a graphic mark that both empties and builds the icon-page, in the vision from *Revelation and Knowledge* silence is articulated by language itself, since language in its totality comes to connote silence.

Before concluding, it is necessary to give a closer look at the ideology that lies behind the writing of *I colloqui*. Indeed, we must remember that, in the sisters' opinion, the written texts of Maria Maddalena's speeches could be considered as a sort of hagiography, although their work was denied as hagiography the very existence of its main character. Hagiography narrates a death. The "blessed soul" must be already dead. *I colloqui*, and for that matter the entire corpus of Maria Maddalena de' Pazzi's visions, is an oxymoron. As de Certeau says, "the rhetoric of this [the hagiographic text] 'monument' is saturated with meaning, but with *identical* meaning. It is a tautological tomb."[65] The tautological meaning of any hagiography lies in its being a "discourse of virtues" (de Certeau, WH, 277), of a variety of seemingly different narrations that in fact have the same meaning, the perfect adherence of a given saint to God's will. Hagiography is a tomb of signs.

However, as Aviad Kleinberg clarifies, it would be erroneous to think that this literary genre does not offer some ideological variations. "The biographer of a new saint," Kleinberg writes, "had to produce just enough hagiographical commonplaces to convince the reader of his subject's sanctity. . . . In the *Lives* of accepted holy men and women of the distant past . . . events are often written in a 'generic' form, even when they are based on real occurrences."[66]

Typically, a hagiographic book reported not only the extraordinary events of a saint's life, but also debris of his or her inspired words. For instance, the author of the fourteenth-century *Vita di Santa Chiara della Croce*, Berengarius of Saint Affrique, not only reports some words uttered by the saint in question, but he also describes the way she speaks and moves in her raptures:

> And after having been in this way for a long while, she spoke and said: "Let me go, let me go." And then she said: "Take me with you." Then she raised her arms, she stood up and sat down. Her sisters were astonished because for a long while she had kept still, being incapable of any movement. And she said: "Everything is burning, everything is burning, and you, what are you doing?" Then she began to sing sweetly.[67]

The style of the above passage is very similar to that of *I colloqui* in that, by inserting the visionary's alleged words, the author aims not only to render a more vivid portrait of the visionary, but also to preserve some of her words. In the tradition of hagiographic texts the reported words acquired the same sacred value of a saint's relics, that is, they were seen as "remnants" of a saint's human experience.[68] Unlike the manuscripts of Maria Maddalena's visions, the medieval and Renaissance hagiographies insert debris of "holy" sentences into a diegetic, discursive structure. In fact, those "holy" fragments, similar to the physical relics of any given blessed soul (her vestments, her rosary, her shoes, her hair, her nails, etc.) derive their "holiness" from their alluding to the Word. Even a brief reported speech thus works as an *objet petit a*, a reminder of the lack of the *real*. However, the Lacanian *a*, the site of desire, is in fact the result of the subject's projection. We decide that a relic is a relic. In other words, the writer of a hagiographic text turns the debris of orality into "holy" remembrances/souvenirs, into stones of the speaker's tomb.

But, what message, what request were a blessed soul's reported words supposed to convey to the reader? Edith Wyschogrod gives us a clear answer: "I define hagiography as a narrative linguistic practice that recounts the lives of saints so that the reader . . . can experience their imperative power."[69] A hagiography communicates, as Wyschogrod says, an imperative, moral request. The reader is supposed to compare his sinful life to that of the saint in question, so that he feels compelled to repent and change his life. Indeed, it is the author of the hagiography, not the saint, who formulates the request directed to the reader. A saint is usually depicted according to some commonplaces, which devoid him/her of his/her personal identity. As de Certeau stresses, hagiography is interested more in characters than in identities: "The same features and the same are passed along from one proper name to another" (WH, 276). Every hagiographic text, we may conclude, formulates the same request. Indeed, the authors of *I colloqui* began to write their text as a hagiography. In fact, the first chapters do not reproduce the saint's whole speeches, but, according to this religious genre, only "remnants" of them. Given that they could not hear what the saint's interlocutors said to her, in the first colloqui the nuns felt free to invent, for instance, plausible dialogues between God and Maria Maddalena. A clear example of a reconstructed conversation between the saint and the divinity is at the end of colloquio 4, where the nuns write:

> And in our opinion she answered him . . . and he must have spoken to her. And then, as usual, she was drawn by the Lord, and he said to her: "You honor me." And, in our opinion, she must have answered: "I would like to honor you" And Jesus must have said to her: "I like you very much, because you follow the path of respect and faith." (1:90)

In most of the first colloqui, however, the writers do not signal the passages that they have clearly reconstructed. Let us read, for example, colloquio 2, where the writers imagine a conversation between the saint and God concerning the damned souls. According to the nuns, God seems almost to apologize to Maria Maddalena for sending the damned souls to hell: "And, my dear daughter, what could I do for this creature? What could this creature ask me for?" (1:66).

Hagiographic texts formulate a standardized request to the reader: compare your life to that of a saint, recognize your faults, and repent. As far as *I colloqui* is concerned, even though at the beginning the transcribers had in mind a hagiographic work, they slowly transformed their work into something different. Rather than a sequence of clichéd descriptions, the nuns' manuscript turned into a two-volume monologue performed by the saint herself. The nuns perceived that the mystic's discourse had two fundamental facets: on the one hand, the actual content of her words; on the other, the unique traits of her performances.

The nuns understand that, like the angels/birds, Maria Maddalena announces that something is going to be announced. She speaks *of* a language that is going to be articulated. *The Word is going to be spoken.* This is why the mystic's utterances have an unmistakably figurative element. The mystic's utterance makes use of images/words similar to Lévi-Strauss's *mythèmes*, the smallest units of a mythic narration. *Mythèmes* are thus the necessary, unavoidable fragments of the "phonetic meaning" that allows the mystic to *allude to the Word's forthcoming language/discourse*: "They [*mythèmes*] share with the 'constitutive units' of discourse the property that they are phrases, yet they are distinct from specifically literary texts in that they do not exhibit any style."[70] A myth, in its distinct units or *mythèmes*, designates a prerational and thus prelinguistic narration, which needs language to express itself, even though it is prior to language.[71]

Mythèmes are thus the essential element of language; they allow the speaker to articulate her utterance, even beyond the literal meaning conveyed by the words/*mythèmes* themselves. Language expresses itself as a chain of syntactically united *mythèmes*. More than signifying something, *mythèmes* give a form to language. *Mythèmes* are the imageless body of language. The birds, the angels, and Maria Maddalena necessarily draw their language from specific *mythèmic areas*. *Mythèmes* offer any discourse the illusion of meaning.

But which are Maria Maddalena's most frequent *mythèmes*? They revolve around the incarnate Word (Secondin, 237). Their sources are both the Gospels and some medieval devotional manuals recounting the Savior's life and death, so that the reader would remember all the pains Jesus had endured for her, and thus she would repent of her sins. The saint's convent still has two copies of Maria Maddalena's very first reading: *Instrutione et avertimenti per meditare la passione di Cristo nostro redentore, con alcune meditationi intorno ad esse* (Instructions and Suggestions in order to meditate on the Passion of Christ, our Redeemer, With Some meditations about them, Rome 1571), an Italian devotional text written by the Spanish Jesuit Gaspar Loarte.

The mystic's *mythèmes* repeat and vary the event of the Savior's sufferings and death. Yet, in some parts of her visions, we cannot clearly perceive any religious narrations, but only disturbed feelings, anguished states of mind. The Word's biography is present in Maria Maddalena's raptures as linguistic fragments or brief allusions, more than complete descriptions. The most frequent "mythic units" revolve around word-images such as "sangue" (blood), "costato" (chest), "cinque piaghe" (five wounds), "fonte" (source), "croce" (cross), "corona di spine" (crown of thorns), "cuore aperto" (open heart). Maria Maddalena's monologues address the Word's sufferings, more than the Word himself (Secondin, 292–94). We might say that Maria Maddalena's numerous visions, contained in several volumes, vary on one basic mythic image: the Savior suffering on the cross for all of humanity.

The Word, the mystic explains in colloquio 4, wants us to "practice" more pain than love because, although love is sweeter, it is through pain that the believer becomes closer to him and she is able to share his sufferings:

> Jesus wants us to practice more suffering than love, because suffering is a sort of going toward martyrdom, and in this way we recognize and honor his sufferings for all of us. And with our suffering we can share his pains, and cry and lament his passion. (1:88)[72]

The primary source of communication, Maria Maddalena holds, is the Word's sufferings. The *mythèmes* of her discourse announce that Christ has suffered and is suffering in the exact moment of the articulation of language. The mystic's *remembrance* of the Word's pain is twofold: on the one hand, it is founded on her incapacity to express the Word's word and thus springs from her sense of guilt; on the other, it represents her urge to give a body to the Word's sufferings themselves. In the same colloquio 4 Maria Maddalena stresses the importance of bathing in the Word's blood, which comes out of his wounded chest. By bathing in his blood, the soul purifies and transforms itself into him ("his Blood adorns and afterward [the soul] turns into God, becoming like him" 1:86).[73]

Maria Maddalena's *mythèmes* are not merely repeated throughout *I colloqui*. The mystic's convent sisters reelaborate and vary the mystic's "mythic units." Indeed, the nuns' variations and interpretations of Maria Maddalena's performances take a different form in each colloquio. According to the nuns' transcriptions, Maria Maddalena's discourse makes use of at least three basic forms: first, in some cases her speeches, often characterized by complex allegories and a dense syntax, have a clear sermonic tone, even when they are not structured as actual sermons.[74] Second, her words are presented as a mere *reportage* of a visionary discourse. In this second case, the syntax and the coherence of her speeches is loose without being illogical. Third, her speech can also turn into a solo mystical play, in which the mystic identifies with several characters who witnessed the Savior's sufferings. Let us see now how in the manuscripts one theme is varied in the above three different ways. In several visions, Maria Maddalena is reported to talk about the Word's blood. In colloquio 5 she describes in detail the Savior's five bleeding wounds, and her soul's progress through contemplation of those wounds, in a well-structured and powerful discourse:

> I say that . . . first in his left foot his blood annihilated and the soul came to know herself. In his right foot his blood purified and the soul became stronger. In his left hand his blood enlightened and the soul came to know God. In his right hand his blood embellished and the soul learned charity. His chest nourished and the soul transformed itself into his blood, so that she perceived only his blood; she saw only his blood; she tasted only his blood; she perceived only his blood; she thought only of his blood. (1:97)

In colloquio 33 the mystic allegedly reelaborated the above theme, indirectly referring to St Catherine's well-known insistence on Christ's blood.[75] The main difference from the above excerpt lies in the style of Maria Maddalena's discourse. Here she expresses herself through broken sentences and brief exclamations:

> You will add to *Verbum caro factum est* Sanguis unionis [*silence*] and who did the first has to do also the second [*silence*] the blood is there [*silence*] the ink-pot is open, Augustine, do not be late [*silence*] Oh, Catherine, you were enraptured in this blood! [*silence*] oh, John made the world know it, you make me know it. (1:343)[76]

We have seen so far that Maria Maddalena's discourse is presented as a response to God's request for the expression of his Word. The mystic perceives that to evoke God's Word means to reexperience his sufferings, passion, and death on the cross. Nevertheless, she senses that her goal, the expression of divine Word, is impossible to attain. In her visions, repeated attempts to conjure up God's Word, the saint varies themes related to her own linguistic and religious history. *I colloqui* is thus the reiterated announcement of a forthcoming linguistic event. Similar to the language of the birds/angels, Maria Maddalena's discourse fails as self-expressing message; it rather suggests that something, the Word himself, might be articulated soon and thus announced to the world. Like a biblical messenger, the Florentine mystic does not refrain from repeating one basic *mythème*: the humanate Word has suffered for all of humanity and his language is imminent.

CHAPTER 3

The Wedding, the Funeral, the Memorial of the Word

This chapter analyzes de' Pazzi's two most compelling visions, colloqui 39 and 48. As a premise, I would like to underscore a fundamental aspect of the mystic's performances. The actants present in *I colloqui*, the transcribers/audience, the performer, her female body, Christ, the Father, the secondary "presences" summoned by the performer (devils, angels, Mary Magdalen, St John, the Virgin, etc.), and the text itself act out their own erasure.

As Louis Marin reminds us, every text, by this term meaning a literary "field" caracterized by a given performativity, possesses both a body and a space, the space of the text being that of its, the text's, body as it is dismembered/articulated in its existence, in its being performed. The text, Marin writes, is "the most powerful revenant of its own body."[1] Colloqui 39 and 48 as a body/text are not only "dismembered," as Herbert Blau defines postmodern physicality; they are denied/annihilated in their actualization.[2] Moreover, these two monologues question any form of structure, including narrativity, time, and space, but they also question the denial of any structure. These mystical performances *occur* as a linguistic flux that both accepts and denies any structuring. Some sections of these visions are decontextualized, nondiegetic, and thus make the transcribers feel compelled to insert their exegesis, which itself decontextualizes the flux of the mystic's decontextualized orality.[3]

A second crucial element of Maria Maddalena's raptures is that both the mystic's orality and the nuns' transcriptions make the message dependent upon both the performer's body/voice and the audience, the transcribers themselves. For the moment it will suffice to say that *I colloqui* is the performance not only of the mystic, but also of the nuns who "are there" when the "thing" happens and who "make the thing happen" by writing down the "happening of the thing." Colloqui 39 and 48 thus result from a double performance, a perfomance within and after a performance.

In vision 39 the mystic goes through a severe process of internal purification, which concludes with her mystical marriage to the Word.

According to her sisters' manuscript, in vision 39 the mystic mimes the act of receiving a nuptial ring from the Word. The nuns connect the mystic's silent gestures to a topos of medieval hagiography, the narration of St Catherine's spiritual marriage to the Son. The mystic's gestures trigger the transcribers' association. No gesture, the nuns seem to infer, is devoid of meaning. The fact that the mystic stretches her hand necessarily *means* something. Each "act," as the nuns define the mystic's movements, is an *index*, a sign that asks the viewer to *recall* its meaning. Thus, colloquio 39 speaks of Maria Maddalena's wedding even though she never pronounces this term.

Since her marriage to the Word signifies the completion of her purification, in vision 48 Maria Maddalena is allowed to participate in the Word's funeral. This is the second crucial moment in Maria Maddalena's mystical experience. The vision starts on May 17, 1585, a Friday evening, and lasts forty hours, until Sunday morning. It is the longest vision/text of the entire book. Christ himself warns Maria Maddalena of the arduous task she is going to face. The Word asks her to follow him into his sepulcher. The first words of the mystic's longest monologue are indeed a response to the Word's (unheard) request:

> Oh eternal Word, so long? [*silence*] as long as you were underground, forty hours I mean, in the sepulcher, and during that time you were in limbo in the Father's bosom, and underground? And I'll follow you with admiration. (2:285)

The entire vision thus "takes place" in the Word's tomb, and is a meditation on the Word's corpse and on the act of dying. The tomb is in fact the Father's bosom, as if the Father were pregnant of the dead Word. As we shall see later, the mystic's performances repeatedly blur the limits of sexual subjectivity.

The above passage is the leitmotif of vision 48, which takes up seventy pages of the entire book. As we shall see, the words themselves are repeated and varied throughout both portions of the text, the excerpts from the mystic's monologues and the nuns' exegesis of those very excerpts. After inserting their *a posteriori* interpretations of the dynamics of the forthcoming/past vision, the nuns transcribe a second introductory excerpt from the mystic's words:

> And it will be fulfilled the time of forty hours [*silence*] so that at the dawn of your happy day of Sunday I'll be there, yes [*silence*] one can really call it the day of the Lord. (2:286)

The nuns stress that these words are in fact a dialogue between the mystic and the Savior, even though they, the audience, cannot hear him. A third passage concludes this sort of proem:

> Oh yes, you were not in the sepulcher at this time. Yes, I'll get there myself later, yes, sure! [*silence*] Oh yes, during this time the mystery of the Trinity will be fulfilled, 'cause it'll be two nights and one day. (2:286)

As the passage clearly shows, Maria Maddalena is going to perform a solo mystery play, reenacting the death of the Word by means of a constant shift of the temporal categories. She reminds the Word of the fact that *now* he *was* not in the sepulcher yet.

The actual vision though starts with an act of identification. The mystic is at the same time the Virgin and herself who acts the role of the Virgin. Her gestures express despair, the nuns point out; she seems to be cleaning the Word's corpse of his clogged blood and of the spit of the Roman soldiers. While she kisses the floor as if, the nuns write, she were kissing that corpse, Maria Maddalena articulates her sorrow by referring to the Word both as "my Son and my Groom" (2:287).

This is a central aspect of the performances of the Florentine visionary. We must keep in mind that the meaning of her gestures is the result of an interpretation. The nuns are adamant about this. They state that the mystic's movements remind (them) of some *Pietà*, the traditional image of the Word's removal from the cross, with his mother and the other pious women bent over his body ("she seemed as if she had before her one of those images of Jesus when he is removed from the cross, as one sees in some *Pietà*," 2:287). The mystic's performative identity is *given* to her by the anonymous writers who see her vision as a form of "translation" of a pictorial image into a body performance. Colloqui 39 and 48 are thus two texts performed in complete anonymity. The transcribers refer both to herself and to themselves either as "one," or "we," or "I," although we have no clue who this "I" is. Moreover, the mystic herself has *no* name; at the most she is "the blessed soul." The mystic takes up several (fictional) identities, starting from the Virgin whose name "Mary" is clearly stated in both colloqui, later the "Magdalen," and finally the "Father." Otherwise, Maria Maddalena does *not* exist within the performance; she is erased *in* the act of performing. She *acts herself exclusively as a body in pain*:

> Oh Word, no more offences [*silence*] no more offences [*silence*] where are you, good Jesus? [*silence*] Oh Word, so much pain [*silence*] Oh good Jesus.[4] (2:310)

In colloquio 48, by becoming and/or identifying with the role of the Virgin, the mystic enters a diegetic performance. However, later she discards her identification with the Mother; she is a physicality that allows the performance to perform itself at random. Expressing her despair before that dead body, she first talks in the person of the Mother

("Come, Angels, take and bury my Son and your Creator . . . please, come take it," 2:290), then she is a virgin, the Spouse of the Word: "I prided myself on having an immortal Groom and now I see them bury you."[5]

This constant transformation of performed identities is a basic trait of Maria Maddalena's two visions. The main performer of the vision acts "in-between identities; in this sense, performing is a paradigm of liminality."[6] This essential anonymity/liminality of the text primarily involves the Second Person of the Trinity. The entire *I colloqui*, we must remember, is the remembrance of an occurred absence; the Word is a non-Word, is a nonexistant presence.

That the Word is a non-Word is particularly evident in vision 48, which revolves around a corpse. Only invisible presences are allowed to be called by their names (Magdalen, Peter, John, etc). The text is grounded on an absence; its diegesis acts out the Word's death. "The dead, rotten body," Jean-Luc Nancy says, "is this thing that no longer has any name in any language . . . and the unnamed God has vanished together with this unnameable thing."[7]

It is crucial at this point to discuss the absence of the name of the third performer, the Word himself. If, as Louis Marin underscores, every first name is a Peircean *index*, that is, it is a sign that refers to an object in a dynamic way since it refers both to the object itself and to the *memory* of that object, we may infer that a first name is similar to a gesture that at the same time signifies and shows its object, even if this object is absent (Marin, SP, 24). Therefore, a first name says *nothing* and *everything* of its object (Marin, SP, 25). This a crucial element of Maria Maddalena's performances. "The Word" is an *index* that points to a void and that obliges the erased main performer, the mystic, to hold a diegetic discourse on his nonbeing.

That the deceased Word in vision 48 possesses no given identity is evident in the way the mystic uses his two first names, "the Word" and "Jesus." Whereas during the diegetic sections of the vision, that is, the mystery play concerning the burial of the Son of God, the mystic addresses the second person of the Trinity as "the Word," thus summoning his nonpresence, when she embodies her self in her expressions of sheer pain she pronounces the term "Jesus." However, "Jesus" is not an *index*; "Jesus" is the annihilation of any diegetic performance. "Jesus," or "my Jesus" or "good Jesus" signify a despair that imposes itself as an absolute, all-erasing saying. "Jesus" and "the Word" thus indicate two different "objects." "The Word" exists as an absent actor of a mystery play. "Jesus" is *not* a first name of someone whose first name is "Jesus." "Jesus" is the name of someone else's disquiet.

Colloqui 39 and 48 are the biography of a void, or better yet, these texts are the biography of a performer (the mystic) who performs the biography of a void (the Word). A void marries a Florentine nun; "it" dies and is mourned by "its" spouse. However, these two texts are also the *auto*-biography of the transcribers who *perform* their own biography by withdrawing from the performer's performance. As Marin states, "the subject, the 'I' constitutes itself by quoting the other and by appropriating the other."[8] The transcribers reveal themselves by exposing the performer to her performance, as in a similar manner the performer (the mystic) *is there* when she performs the absence of the Word, who makes the mystic perceive his presence as guilt. In other words, the mystic, the Word, and the nuns are both performers and performed, both presences and silenced bodies.

A central theme of colloquio 48 is Maria Maddalena's encounter with the devil. After having met with her Groom's disciples she lowers the tone of her voice to a barely audible mumbling (2:299). All of a sudden, the mystic stands up and opens the window exclaming: "Yes, confused before but now in everything [*silence*] and he placed them in hell [*silence*] Who has ever seen such a speed?" According to the nuns, the visionary is being attacked by a horde of devils. She defends herself by throwing the "bad angels" out of the window down into the courtyard (2:300). Her fight with the devils introduces the most dramatic passage of colloquio 48. The devils have instilled in the mystic's mind the awareness of the Word's irrevocable death. The mystic is "enlightened" by the devils. The devils expose the mystic to "the vortices in which the body that lets loose its hold on the levels of the world . . . gets drawn."[9] By recognizing the Word's nonexistence, the mystic's body "becomes the double of the other," putting itself "wholly in the place of the death that gapes open for the other" (Lingis, 181). Maria Maddalena's body starts shaking and wriggling, "as if she were dismembering herself inside." Her body becomes the articulation of the devil's idiom.

Vision 48 recounts a second, even more powerful "invasion" of the mystic's body. All of a sudden Maria Maddalena has acquired a male voice. She is no longer the Mother/Spouse; she speaks as the Father (2:314). The Father is entitled to specify the modalities of the soul's purification. Whereas so far the vision has focused on the Word's corpse, now it relates the word of the Father. The mystic "lends" her female body, her mouth, her tongue, to the Father who states his Law. From now on, the text is essentially, but not exclusively, the Father's sermon. The mystic plays the role of a male preacher who delivers a well-articulated speech on two major themes, the procedures necessary to attain an interior purity and the "acts" that the dead Word "operated"/"operates" in his, the Father's, bosom during the three days of his, the Word's, death.

However, the Father's sermon is intersected by two different kinds of aside discourses: (1) the mystic's (female) voice who often asks herself/the (male) preacher to repeat and to clarify his sentences because they are too "hard" for her, and (2) the mystic's (female) expressions directed to the Word's corpse. In fact, in the final section of her vision, the mystic performs two double performances at the same time. First, she is herself as a female disciple/daughter who listens to the Father who imposes his discourse of the Word, the deceased Groom of the (female) Father's (female) audience. Second, the mystic also is/performs the (female) soul who at moments feels lost because of "her Word's" absence, and thus cannot help but interrupt her (male) monologue with expressions of despair.

It is crucial to remember that the Father's violation of the female body has occurred when the mystic suffered from intense physical pains and then came into contact (through Communion) with the divinity's flesh. The Father thus enters her body in order to impose his discourse about physicality, gender, and the Word's relation to the (female) soul.[10] The discourse about the body (body as corpse; body as resurrection of/*from* the body; body who "operates" in the male bosom during its own death) *belongs to the Father*. A female voice cannot pronounce *the* sermon of the body. As Hélène Cixous reminds us, theater has always asked the woman to perform her own annihilation:

> [The woman] is always the Father's daughter, his sacrificial object, guardian of the phallus . . . it is always necessary for a woman to die in order for the play to begin. Only when she has disappeared can the curtain go up; she is relegated to repression, to the grave, the asylum, oblivion, and silence.[11]

We will subsequently examine the preacher's discourse in detail. Here it will suffice to say that the first theme of the Father's sermon revolves around the acquisition of a perfect purity. The mystic/preacher stresses that, to obtain a flawless purity, "the soul must guard its frailty" (2:316). Without embracing its fragility, the soul cannot earn the Father's purity, which is his being itself. As a consequence, without its frailty the soul has no being. Interestingly enough, the mystic is addressed by herself/the male preacher as "the soul"; her identity becomes even more impalpable. In a similar way, the Word is not the incarnate Word, a dissected corpse any longer. In his Father's speech, the Word is the Word's soul, dead and "active" in his Father's bosom.

The second topic of the Father's speech is the "operations" of the (dead) Word's soul in the Father's bosom. The preacher says that the soul of the dead Word "performed his operations" by contemplating him, the Father, and by being contemplated by the Father. *The Father's gaze performs the Word as a manifestation of the Law.* Let us summarize this pivotal point. An erased/female body performs the male Law that performs a corpse's performance, in which *no disruptive improvisation is allowed.* We may say that the Father erases both female and male physicality, insofar as he first annihilates the woman by violating her "voice," and then denies the Word his diegetic status of (dead) body." The only form of unexpected improvisation within the text/sermon are thus the sudden, female expressions of disquiet for the Word's death. The mystic's panic breaks the discourse of the Father and thus the performance of his Law.

Colloquio 48 ends with a final, unexpected change. The male voice disappears; the mystic herself carries on the male discourse. The conclusion of the sermon is performed by a female voice that develops the themes initiated by the Father. In other words, the Father has molded the mystic's discourse. Even though the transcribers fail to mark the gender of the speaker, the structure/ideology of the speech itself is male-gendered.

Once she has embodied the Father's discourse, the mystic is allowed to go back to her diegetic performance. The Father has conceived of his speech as a sermon. The style of the mystic's monologue thus becomes eloquent and solemn. It is also important to note that in the final part of the transcription the mystic's gestures have disappeared from the text. The nuns do not report her movements anymore. The text has become "opaque." As I have pointed out, the male discourse rejects any form of improvisation, because improvisation disturbs the structure of the male sermon. The absence of improvisation (for instance, the mystic's sudden exclamations, her bodily performances, her moving from one room to another, her miming the battle with the devils) negates the creation within the text of "a symbolic interpretive space."[12] The negated body of the performer is in fact the negated spatiality of the text itself.[13]

The vision concludes with the resurrection of the Saviour. However, as the mystic herself states, the Word/Jesus does not express his resurrection *in* the mystic; he "narrates" it to his Mother: "Oh, you narrated your operations, and now you narrate your operations to Mary, yes, they will generate admiration and love in us" (2:368).

The mystic does say that she is seeing the resurrected Jesus ("Oh my Word and Spouse, how beautiful you are!"), but she also stresses that the Word "is visiting" his Mother and that the "soul" (whose soul?) must follow the Father's instructions if it wants to be visited by the Word (2:369). Vision 48 thus ends as the Father's sermon was supposed to end, by reminding the audience of the procedures necessary to attain a perfect internal purity, which equals a perfect internal "fragility." The mystic is both the soul who has already married the Word and the soul who wishes to be allowed to marry the Word. One more time, the text is the instability of the performer's identity.

Colloqui 39 and 48 perform the ungrounded foundations of any performance. Maria Maddalena de' Pazzi is and is not herself. Her being as spatiality is made of remnants, debris, memories, images of previous performances, performers, and narrations. The mystic attempts to "utter" the Word by summoning identities, physicalities, "spaces" that have the consistency of pure emptiness.

COLLOQUIO 39: THE WEDDING
AND THE MEMORY OF THE WEDDING

The transcribers introduce the theme of this colloquio by writing that on Sunday, April 28, 1585, a young girl took the veil (2:11). It was during the celebration of that mass that Maria Maddalena entered a rapture. It is apparent that the nuns compare the girl with the mystic. As the girl marries Jesus Christ by entering the convent, so does Maria Maddalena experience her mystical wedding with the Savior. The girl's wedding is a sign of the forthcoming mystical wedding between the mystic and the Word.

Considering the nuns' reportage as a textual performance of the mystic's performance, we may say that the authors structure their writing according to a standard form of hagiographic narration, which leads the reader through three major phases/acts: the soul recognizes its sins and suffers for them; the Word forgives her and marries her; having experienced an amorous encounter with God, the soul thanks him and extols his goodness. The nuns follow this three-step pattern: first, Maria Maddalena feels that she cannot marry the Word because of her sinful nature; second, after having suffered because of her infinite distance from God, she is allowed to marry him; finally, the mystic ends her rapture by praising the Word's generosity.

The introductory part of Maria Maddalena's vision discusses the relationship between orality and writing. "Ancilla Christi sum" (I am the servant of Christ) is the first quotation from the songs performed during that morning Mass, when that girl took the veil.[14] The authors state that while the novice pronounced that verse Maria Maddalena saw in a corner of the church an angel writing down everything the girl was saying. At the same time, the angel marked down the past of the novice, that is, her past thoughts, actions, desires, and finally her wish to marry the Word. The angel makes it sure that the words pronounced by the novice *now* (her confession, her promise to be a faithful spouse, etc.) match with the novice's *past* words or thoughts.

A divine voice tells Maria Maddalena that God always sends an angel when a girl marries him (2:12). At the girl's death, her reported words will be used in her favor or against her. At its very beginning, this colloquio thus emphasizes the importance of the act of writing as an expression of temporality. We may say that this vision is founded on an intrinsic parallelism: as the angel writes down what the novice says during her marriage to God, so will the nuns transcribe what Maria Maddalena says during her mystical marriage to the Word.[15] The spoken discourse—the words pronounced by the novice and the ecstatic utterances of the mystic—are *relics* of the two brides' body/corpus of utterance/being. The two brides also signify two distinct temporalities. On the one hand, the novice is *like* Maria Maddalena when she joined the convent years before. The girl that takes the veil is the actualization of the mystic's memory. The words pronounced by the novice are the words that the mystic herself uttered when she took the veil. Their gestures are the same gestures. If in the nuns' text both the girl's words/gestures and the mystic's are, as de Certeau says, *quotations-pre-text* and *quotation-reminiscence*, events that turn into relics in the moment of their occurrence, the girl's words/physicality are *already* relics of relics, quotations of quotations, commentaries on an already performed performance. It is crucial to keep in mind that, according to the nuns, the mystic was rapt when she heard the words uttered by the novice. Moreover, the transcribers underscore the division that occurred in the mystic's identity. Her body looks at the event of the novice's wedding, which is a past event of the mystic's body, whereas her soul becomes engaged in its own present encounter with God. Although the theme of the division soul versus body is a topos of mystical literature, it is almost never present in *I colloqui*. As we shall see, colloquio 39 is indeed a meditation on the disruptive power of memory.

Maria Maddalena's vision actually begins with the mystic's disappearance. All of a sudden Maria Maddalena is missing (2:13). The mother superior sends some sisters to look for her. They find her in the dormitory for the novices (*la soffitta per le novizie*), where she is lying on the floor. The nuns notice that she is talking to herself in a very anguished way. This new section of the colloquio begins with another imperfect biblical quotation: "Circundederunt me dolores inferni," a reference to Psalm 114, "Circundederunt me dolores mortis et pericula inferni invenerunt me."[16] The first quotation ("Ancilla Christi sum") signifies the optimistic projection of a young spouse who sees her future as resulting from her good (present) intentions; the second quotation reverses the sense of the first one. Lying on the floor and mumbling to herself, Maria Maddalena feels the pangs of her sinful nature. Her wedding has not realized its expectations. The fulfillment of her marriage entails the realization of its failure. In order to perform her marriage to the Word, the mystic must come to terms with her nonwedding to the Word himself. The girl taking the veil *shows* the mystic the nonbeing of her own past marriage. The mystic has *mis*-interpreted, *mis*-performed her marriage. Instead, she has shared the iniquities of all human beings. This is the sense of the second reported sentence: "Comedit me dolores inferni pro multitudine iniquitatum nostrarum."[17]

After having stated the topic of this section, the authors report three excerpts of her spoken discourse. They connect the three parts by inserting explanatory commentaries at the end of each section. In these three passages the mystic slowly intensifies the emotional content of her discourse, as is particularly clear in the last excerpt of the three, which is almost entirely dominated by her fragmented exclamations. However, some key terms and expressions connect the three parts. Indeed, the two sentences cited above not only state the topic of this section of her vision, a meditation on human sin, they also mention some key words and expressions that will be present throughout the mystic's discourse and the nuns' exegesis. Let us read the first excerpt of Maria Maddalena's words:

> Oh Word, I can't anymore, *iniquities*, oh no, no more, no more, if they don't want to remove their sins and their *iniquities*, please remove these *iniquities* from my view, because I can't anymore.

Then, after a while, she said:

> *Respiciunt* vanitatem, and *cadunt* in *iniquitate*; respiciunt elevationem, and *cadunt* in profundum abissi. . . .[18] Non habitavit in domum tuam qui blasfemant nominis tui. . . . *Comedi ego iniquitates* eorum, *dolores inferni circundedit me.* Discedit ad me anima eius, and accedit a te.[19] (2:13, emphasis mine)

We could say that in this passage Maria Maddalena's discourse varies and expands the two biblical verses reported at the beginning of this section: "circundederunt me dolores inferni" and "comedit me dolores inferni pro multitudine iniquitatum nostrarum." The key words are "iniquity," "respiciunt," "cadunt," and "dolores inferni." These terms in fact refer both to "them" (humankind) and to herself as subject of her own past. "I have eaten their iniquities," Maria Maddalena says. When she saw the girl taking the veil, she saw (as "they see," *respiciunt*) her own iniquity. The mystic fell (she fell on the floor; she fell as sinner) as the humankind falls. "The pains of hell" are the natural result of her/their falling.

The two sections of her reported words express the same content. If in the first part the mystic has a personal, intimate style ("Oh Word, I can't anymore"), in the second, by expressing herself in Latin, the mystic restates the same theme in a formal, albeit grammatically imperfect, manner. Formality versus informality, a stylistic division that runs throughout the mystic's monologues, entail a constant shift of *audience*. In the first reported words she speaks *to* the Word, in the second she speaks *of* the Word, or better yet, of his absence from the humankind, and its consequential "iniquity." She addresses both Christ and herself as audience of her own words. She delivers a sermon to herself, knowing that a third interlocutor, the absent Word, *listens to* the words directed to humankind, that is, to the speaker herself. In other words, Maria Maddalena engages her betrayed, and thus unexpressed, Word in a painful dialogue and manifests this very dialogue to herself in the person of a nun who has been unfaithful to her divine groom.

In some points Maria Maddalena's discourse might be seen as a *confessio laudis*, as St Augustine developed it his *Confessions*. In several passages of his book, St Augustine praises God's generosity by recounting his beneficent interventions in his life. At the same time he also accuses himself of being incapable of responding to God's goodness. However, in accusing himself St Augustine also reprimands all of humanity for the same insensitivity toward the Lord. Therefore, a *confessio laudis* style has two interlocutors: God and all of humanity. However, the human kind as audience is absent from Maria Maddalena's text. She is the audience of herself. Whereas St Augustine is aware of the fact that his speaking is both a private communication and a teaching imparted through his seemingly private speaking, Maria Maddalena exclusively engages herself into her private debate.[20]

The transcribers interrupt their reportage by describing the mystic's physical dejection. She sighs, cries, shakes on the floor. The nuns mark the exact hour (8 p.m.) of the mystic's tormented acting. In order to enact their textual performance of the mystic's performance, the nuns put her physicality "under scrutiny." The mystic's body is "controlled by the gaze and read as a text for its symptomatic acts, its unwitting self-revelations."[21] Her body is asked to speak what her words do not reveal. However, the language of the body enacts a double rhetoric. On the one hand, the body is what is *seen*; the body gives a body to the mystic's performance. The body says that the mystic is suffering because it *shows the signs of suffering* (tears, "unbecoming" gestures, such as shaking on the floor). On the other, although it shows the *signs* of pain, the body *does not* tell the pain itself. The body is a language of signs that *may* be signs: "Pain is invisible. We infer the presence of pain in someone else indirectly, from observation (e.g., a broken leg) or through communication from the sufferer-pain behavior" (Jackson, 139).[22] Pain's visibility in the body is pain's *in*-visibility in the language of the body.[23]

> Oh Word, let me die of a living death, so that I can realize your project. *Omnes declinaverunt, non est qui faciat bonum, non est usque ad unum*[24] [*silence*] Oh, let blindness see. Seeing gives it pain, its pain gives it glory, its glory is beatitude, and its eternity is incomprehensible, inscrutable, and it can only be understood by you, through you and in you [*silence*] but nothing is new to me! [*silence*] *omnes declinaverunt a te, and non cognoverunt te, et nolunt intelligere ut bene agerent*[25] [*silence*] they do not know you, and they do not want to know you. But in any case they will know you. *Et mors depascet eos* [*silence*] Oh Word, even though always, you always show them in the same way [*silence*] you showed us your wounds, your hands, your chest, so that we are not incredulous anymore, but rather faithful [*silence*] Oh great is the ingratitude of your creatures! (2:14)

This long passage partially reproduces the rhetoric(s) of the previous excerpts. Maria Maddalena does and does not have an interlocutor. She invokes the Word ("Oh Word, oh good Jesus!"; "Oh Word, let me die of a living death"; "Oh, let blindness see"); she seems to be responding to him ("Oh, I don't know"); she also treats the Word as a topic of a sermonic saying. She discusses the *theme* "Word" addressing a second/third subject who listens to her speaking about the Word. Like a sermon, her sentences shift from Italian to Latin quotations, sometimes without any "[*silence*]." She translates her lack of the Word into words. The language of the lack of the Word is her body; her voice is a text translating the speaking of the body. Her narrative of the Word's benefits translate "a message from one language into another. She [is] a psychodramatist."[26] Maria Maddalena translates from the language of the body into the language of the voice exclusively for herself. She is speaker and interlocutor, performer and audience of her performance. *She listens to her self.* The absence of the Word, the *failure* of the mystic's marriage to the divinity, is the means through which she becomes aware of her being another. *She sees and speaks through the absent Word:*

> Oh, let blindness see. Seeing gives it pain, its pain gives it glory, its glory is beatitude, and its eternity is incomprehensible, inscrutable, and it can only be understood by you, through you, and in you. (emphasis mine)

Her complex, even chaotic rhetoric is the most accurate translation of her painful awareness. Indeed, her long monologue clearly revolves around the faulty and wicked nature of human language. Man's words, Maria Maddalena says, are similar to curses: "*Vir linguosus non dirige-*

tur in terra" (A man of wicked tongue shall not abide in the land); "Oh, they almost curse!" Man's language only expresses his propensity toward sin.[27] Since both her body and her soul must be born to new life, Maria Maddalena asks the Word to let her die a "living death." Like her utterance, which is split between the utterance of the body and the opaque utterance of the voice, her dying is both annihilation and self-revelation. Her voice articulates her death as a linguistic process toward the formulation of death. The self that delivers a fragmented sermon, and the self that is the addressee of her sermon reflect each other in the Word. The mystic's self/selves display its/their "sinful" rhetoric.

Let us examine the main aspects of the rhetoric of the mystic's discourse.[28] A first important element is a frequent use of *iteratio*: "Oh good Jesus . . . oh good Jesus"; "Oh Word . . . oh Word." *Oxymoron*, a rhetorical figure present in every mystical text, plays here a crucial role: "let me die of a living death." This expression also contains a thematically complex *polyptoton*: "dying/death." Furthermore, the long sentence "Seeing gives it pain, its pain gives it glory, its glory is beatitude, and its eternity is incomprehensible" is a complex *gradatio* or "repetition in contact." Finally, from a sentence in Latin ("and non cognoverunt te") Maria Maddalena develops a long *polyptoton*: "and non *cognoverunt* te . . . they *do not know* you, and they *do not want to know* you. But in any case they *will know* you." The above passage ends with a renewed invocation to the Word. Maria Maddalena remembers that he has clearly shown us his hands and his bleeding side, so that we would repent and believe in him. The very last exclamation, following a pause in her discourse, marks the mystic's resentment of man's insensitivity to the Word: "Oh great is the ingratitude of your creatures!"

The third and final monologue of the first section (the soul's awareness of its sinfulness) marks the mystic's utmost despair. Her discourse falls apart and turns into mere exclamations. "Oh, oh, oh [*silence*] oh *bonitas*," a simple invocation to the Word's goodness, is the first reported expression. The nuns tell us that Maria Maddalena looks desperate; she sighs and cries shaking on the floor. The mystic cannot articulate her discourse any longer; she limits herself to moaning. Her soul, we may say, lies in the language of the body. What remains are the debris of her physicality, as it is *performed* in the nuns' textuality:

> Oh, death that gives life [*silence*] I die alive [*silence*] Oh, oh, oh [*silence*] *appone iniquitatem super iniquitatem* [*silence*] oh, it is so little understood. Wisdom seems folly and folly wisdom [*silence*] Oh iniquity! [*silence*] they exercitate them, even though they are not aware of that, oh yes [*silence*] Oh, oh, oh good Jesus. (2:15)

This short passage develops the mystic's previous words in an extremely complex way. In particular, while before Maria Maddalena had asked the Word for a "living death," now, in this second excerpt, the mystic says that she is already "dying alive." This modified oxymoron might refer to a second step in her purification. A second crucial difference between the two passages is the intensification of the mystic's suffering. The second passage opens with an interesting *complexio* (combination of repetition at the beginning and at the end of two groups of words) that combines two oxymorons: "Oh, death that gives life [*silence*] I die alive." The above *complexio* is connected through a *polyptoton* to the preceding descriptions of the transcribers through "dead": "she fell on the ground as she were dead" (2:15). By repeating the concept of "death" in various form, this excerpt recounts the final moment of the mystic's preparation to her *real* wedding, the mystical one.

The second half of this excerpt then focuses on the word "iniquity." However, at the core of the entire passage are her three brief exclamations "Oh, oh, oh" that are reported in the middle of the text. The two key terms "death" and "iniquity" are in fact synonyms. Iniquity has finally taken over both selves of the mystic. Her words are not directed from one performer of a *confessio laudis* to a listener. The two selves tend to be reunited in their mutual annihilation. The rhythm of the transcribers's text is rendered by mere exclamations. As Pozzi says in his anthology of *I colloqui*, the nuns' transcriptions are similar to musical scores of an unknown composition. A sense of fundamental lack continues to dominate our reading (Pozzi 1984, 41).

Between the first and the second "acts" of their hagiographic narration, the authors of *I colloqui* insert a page focusing on Maria Maddalena's physical conditions. She cries as if she were dying; she howls and writhes in such pain that her sisters do not feel like staying next to her (2:16). The only reported word is "good Jesus," preceded and followed by disturbing screams. Since her rhetoric has been shattered by the iniquitous nature of her selves, the mystic has no protection against the attack of the devil. Her language to the Word, that sort of monologue articulated in the night of the soul, as St John of the Cross writes, is no longer a defensive veneer. Devils have total control over her body abandoned to its silenced physicality. The Lord, the nuns write, lets the devils curse in the mystic's ear in order to achieve her complete purification. The devil thus participates in the mystical marriage of the soul. The devil screams and swears so that the mystic might be "purged" (2:16).

We may summarize the first, and most important, section of vision 39 by saying that the mystic's performance deals with her "breaking through" the language of both the body and the voice. The body of her rhetoric is shattered. However, the conclusive moment of this purification is the evocation of the devil's language, an idiom of disarticulated and offensive sounds. When the devil speaks his words, the mystic has concluded her clarification.

Whereas the first part of this colloquio recounts the painful purification of her soul and of her language, the second section narrates the actual event of the mystical wedding between Maria Maddalena and the Savior. The mystic, whose identity was an identity on its way toward annihilation (the tears, the sufferings, the shaking on the ground), becomes the main character of the nuns' narration. As de Certeau says, hagiography is more interested in characters than in identities. Her reported words turn into the lines of a hagiographic story. The nuns's exegesis becomes a central feature of the text. The mystic's utterances finally *make sense*; they are not ambigous signs any longer. They narrate a joyful wedding.

The writers introduce Maria Maddalena's mystical marriage to the Word by reminding us that on that day the convent commemorated St Catherine's mystical marriage ("celestial wedding," 2:16). Given her deep devotion for St Catherine, Maria Maddalena will have the same experience that very day. At the very beginning of colloquio 39 I have stressed the essential similarity between the novice's wedding and the mystic's forthcoming wedding. If the novice is the mystic as she was years before, St Catherine was what the mystic will be. In other words, the novice embodies the failure of the past, the misarticulation of the Word, whereas St Catherine assures the successful announcement of the Word.

The two brides, the novice and Catherine, are each other's negative. The novice signifies that the *future has been* nothing but aphasia. Catherine's image says that the *future has been* eloquent love. The nuns' writing goes back to the central topic of remembrance. Maria Maddalena *is going to rewrite her past by adopting St Catherine's own past.* As the novice's gestures were Maria Maddalena's misperforming gestures, the hagiographic memory of St Catherine's well-spoken gestures are incorporated in the mystic's solo play.

The first reported words, which are also the point sentence of the entire subsequent passage, underscore a dramatic change in the mystic's feeling. She exclaims: "Oh immense liberality" (2:17). The nuns tell us that she pronounces these words because she already sees the gift she is about to receive: the Word's wedding ring. We are asked to see the whole passage as the mystic's response to God's gift. His ring becomes the unifying theme of the whole excerpt:

Oh immense generosity [*silence*] when she saw the gift that Jesus wanted to give her, she rejoiced . . . Oh Word, you too [*silence*] she meant: you too married St Catherine [*silence*] oh Word [*silence*] oh, your holy hands are so beautifully adorned and full of so many wedding rings for your spouses. (2:17)

The nuns attempt to merge the mystic's words with their commentaries. It is apparent, however, that in one case their explanation does not really match up with her words. The writers complete the fragmented expression "Oh Word, you too" by adding "she meant 'you too married Saint Catherine'" (2:17). What the nuns meant to say was "Oh Word, you married St Catherine too," but the passage does not lend itself to such an interpretation. Indeed, we cannot clearly define what Maria Maddalena words actually meant. The mystic's last sentence thematically links the above passage to the next one, in which she states that she wants St Catherine and St Augustine to be present at her wedding: "I will have her as priest, even though she is a bride [*silence*] and I will have Augustine [*silence*] Oh, both of them!"

After having welcomed her two major guests, Maria Maddalena directly discusses with the Word some details of the forthcoming ceremony. Whereas she would like to have a private ceremony, keeping the audience (which audience?) unaware of their engagement, her Groom has other plans in mind:

Oh my Jesus, your will [*silence*] but you promised me that as you hid, I would hide too [*silence*] who will understand the value and the beauty of this ring? I don't care about its importance and its beauty, only about who gives it [*silence*] when they receive their groom, the spouses ask. I too, I will ask. However, since your creatures give me pain, I will ask for your spouses, although I will not forget all the other creatures. But now I will pray for your spouses, so that you will help them become more pious and keep the promises they made to you. I will also ask that you give them a Christ according to your heart [*silence*] I will also ask for those you force me to ask for [*silence*] *Cantabo Domino canticum novum*[29] [*silence*] *Omnes gentes plaudite manibus*[30] in honor of the marriage of pure souls [*silence*] on the enamel of the ring you will write what is already written in the heart: *Verbum caro factum est, and Sanguis unionis* [*silence*] to the first and to the second you add the third [*silence*] and what will it be? [*silence*] but my Jesus, I do not want to give you orders. (2:18)

Maria Maddalena's first words stress once again her complete abandon to the Word's will. However, she dares to remind him that he had promised her to keep their marriage secret. In other visions Maria Maddalena asks the Word to keep secret their encounters.[31] In fact, she would prefer that her visions were not apparent to her sisters (*Probation* 2:48).

An interesting element in the above passage is the mystic's use of the future tense. Her whole account of mystical marriage oscillates between the present and the future. After having reminded the Word of his promise of keeping their marriage secret, Maria Maddalena poses a question: Who will understand the beauty of her ring? In the following statement ("I don't care about its importance and its beauty, only about who gives it"), she quickly corrects herself: one should not care about the ring's beauty, but only about its giver. Then she reminds the Word that, when she meets her groom, every bride is allowed to ask for something. The mystic connects the above passage to the first phase of this vision, her painful perception of man's sinful nature: "since your creatures give me pain, I will ask for your spouses." Does/did the novice that took the veil that day signify a spouse that gives suffering to the mystic? Did the mystic see the novice's wedding as the announcement of her forthcoming suffering?

Later, at the end of her requests to her Groom, Maria Maddalena describes her wedding ring. She talks about her future ring as if she did not see it right there. Her frequent use of the future tense is perhaps intended to suggest that Maria Maddalena is at the same time experiencing her mystical encounter with God and narrating what she is going to experience in the future. Once again, Maria Maddalena's performance is in fact a rehearsal of her future wedding. However, as a rehearsal her performance is the enactment of that future, *real* performance. Any performance announces its instability, its non-quite-being-there. As Schechner writes,

> the stage is first a physical space waiting to be filled. But when the stage is full, it is filled with propositional emptiness. . . . [T]he performer acts in-between identities. (295)

Is not this "in-betweenness" the cipher of one's desire? Is not desire the site of nonexistence? Examining how St Augustine uses the future tense in his *Confessions*, Louis Marin speaks of the mystic's "future of desire" (*future du désir*).[32] We might thus infer that the mystic both sees her wedding ring and desires it. When she comes to describe it, Maria Maddalena says: "on the enamel of the ring you *will* write what is already written in the heart: *Verbum caro factum est*, and *Sanguis unionis*." Moreover, rehearsing the ceremony of their wedding, the mystic says: "I *will* also ask that you give them a Christ according to your heart."

The Virgin and St Augustine, along with St Catherine, will participate in the mystic's wedding. Mary will offer the mystic her nourishing milk and St Augustine will put away everything the Word will grant to his bride.[33] As the nuns remind us, Maria Maddalena often associates St Augustine with the act of writing. Indeed, in a previous vision (colloquio

33, 1:343), she had asked Augustine to write "Verbum caro factum est" in her heart.[34] The nuns interpret her words ("Augustine, please put everything aside. This will please his liberality") as a new request for writing. The act of writing, the nuns say, guards what otherwise would disappear.

As we have seen at the very beginning of this colloquio, one of the first images evoked by the mystic is an angel who writes down the novice's words. At the moment of her death, the novice's entire life will be interpreted according to the angel's transcriptions. It is apparent that colloquio 39 is constructed on the basis of a series of correspondances and oppositions. First, the novice and St Catherine are opposite aspects of the same image, the bride of the Word. Second, the vision opens with an angel writing what the novice is saying and what she has said in the past, and it concludes with St Augustine who will participate in the mystic's wedding and will write down the details of the event. Third, the mystic articulates a double idiom, that of the body—in itself double because it signifies but it does not say—and that of the voice.

After having described her future wedding ring, the mystic mimes the act of receiving it. While she raises her right hand toward her divine groom, Maria Maddalena mentions St Catherine and St Augustine again. They *will* hold her hand, she says, but only the Word *will* actually put his ring in her finger (2:20). In fact, throughout the final part of this vision the future tense indicates that Maria Maddalena's mystical wedding is both an actual event and the expression of her desire.

After having invoked St Catherine, who has had the same experience, Maria Maddalena asks herself how she could preserve her mystical marriage. She will use her marriage to the Word as a mirror in which she will see reflected different aspects of Jesus' love.[35] At this point her discourse has lost its previous dramatic tone; no exclamations or pauses are reported. Maria Maddalena expresses herself in long, well-articulated sentences that share the same incipit:

> Oh Catherine, you preserved this wedding so well! How will I preserve it? [*silence*] I will use it as an extremely clear mirror, in which, by constantly contemplating it, *I will see* how the generosity, goodness, and gentleness of my Word has married the Holy Trinity, in the same way He has married my soul. . . . Later, in this mirror *I will see* my Word rest in Mary's womb like in a valley of purity. . . . *I will also see* Catherine's loving kindness and Augustine's santity. (2:20–22)

In this monologue the usual traits of her spoken discourse, that is, her pauses and her exclamations have disappeared. In a quite formal style,

Maria Maddalena describes the images that she will see reflected in her mystical mirror. As in some previous passages, the mystic's use of the future tense expresses the complex nature of her mystical performance. On the one hand, the writers want us to understand that the Word has actually given her his mystical ring; their marriage has actually taken place. Even the radical change in her spoken style, from a fragmented discourse to a formalized sermon, underscores this highly formalized moment of her vision: after having received her ring, the mystic thanks the Word by praising his generosity. The page "acts" a different plot. On the other hand, however, the mystic expresses herself as if she were still going to receive her wedding ring, or, more precisely, as if her mystical ring corresponded to an internal state that she would experience in the future. The mystic's discourse does not exclude one or the other of these aspects, but rather merges them.

We could summarize the content of her discourse in the following manner: first, Maria Maddalena will see the Word on the cross in her wedding ring, which becomes like a bright mirror. He will be crucified in her, the mystic, and she will appear crucified in him. The Word will also express the passionate desire of redeeming all of humanity to his Father. Second, in her ring the mystic will see the Word rest in his mother's womb. Coming out of her womb, the Word will benevolently intervene in his creatures' lives. By contemplating his divine acts, Maria Maddalena will understand that she is incapable of fully imitating him. She will thus learn to be humble and submissive toward God. Third, her ring will show her the Word's infinite love. The mystic will thank him for having given his believers the holy sacraments, so that they can remember him forever. Fourth, she will see in her ring how the Word's love has prepared the glory of his creatures. As the stars embellish the sky, the mystic says, so do the souls enhance the Word's majestic glory. Each of the blessed souls adorns a different part of the Word's body: some of them are in his chest, others are in his mouth, some others are in his hands or feet.

Concluding her monologue, Maria Maddalena reiterates the primary topics of her vision. To this end, she reminds us of some key expressions of the previous sections of this rapture: talking about Mary's purity, which united the Virgin to the Word, Maria Maddalena says: "Puritas coniunsit Verbum ad Maria, and Sponsum ad Sponsam." Furthermore, the mystic *will also see* Saint Catherine's gentleness and Augustine's sanctity. Her ring-mirror *will become unclouded*, Maria Maddalena concludes, because the Word's blood, like a strong wind that cleans up the sky of every cloud, will always keep her mirror clear and bright.

The conclusive quotation from the mystic's orality equals the future/present ring to the act of "belching forth" the Word:

> *Eructavit cor meum verbum bonum,* I mean, the wedding of the Word
> and my soul [*silence*] *Non cor meum, sed costatum tuum; non verbum,*
> *non* word, but a bond of a ring, of union, of love, of preciousness
> [*silence*] *ortus conclusus* [*silence*] *conserva me domine, quoniam inno-*
> *centia mea regeneravit me Sanguinis sui* (2:25)

The first sentence of this long passage is particularly significant. It is
moot whether the mystic means that she herself "belched forth" the
Word, or whether she limits herself to using a biblical passage to express
her joy for her forthcoming wedding. Maria Maddalena had already
tackled this topic in colloquio 12, in which she had expressed the desire
of belching forth "the good word":

> Oh my Jesus, now that you are in me I can really say those words of
> David: *Eructavit cor meum verbum bonum, dico ego opera mea Regi.*
> *I will belch forth,* that is, *I will express the good word,* the good word
> that you are, my Jesus, now that I keep you locked in my heart. . . . I
> mean that *I want to express it* through words (1:152)

This passage might shed some light on the ambiguity of the mystic's
wedding. In colloquio 12 the mystic has received Jesus in herself. To
express her sense of "fullness," she quotes the biblical verse on the act
of "belching out the Word." However, Maria Maddalena also specifies
that the fact that she has received the Word does not mean that she is
able to utter him. The act fo receiving the Word has stirred in herself the
desire to utter the Divinity.[36]

The passage from *I colloqui* confirms this interpretation. Maria
Maddalena clearly states that her bond with the Word is not based on
linguistic expression. The bond/wedding is bound to a future ring that
will ratify the occurred event. In other words, the signifier "ring" relates
to a doubled signified, as if the signified "ring," like any other element
of the mystic's performativity, had both a present/past and a future
materiality. The mystic *might* have received the ring, but the significance
of that "ring" will be evident at a later moment. As a consequence, the
mystic's task, the articulation of the divinity through language, is still
unfulfilled.

As I have pointed out at the beginning of this chapter, according to
the topoi of hagiographic literature the three-step experience of Maria
Maddalena's wedding must end with her praising the divinity's generosity. Indeed, the last words of the mystic confirm this structure:

> Oh Word, who will be ever able to thank you for the present you gave
> me? [*silence*] only your blood will be able to do this; and all the drops
> you shed will be voices thanking you. But in order to thank you for
> having married me, I want to offer you every drop of the blood that
> you shed for me with such a burning love. (2:26–27)

In the final sentence the mystic states that the wedding did take place. Thus, she did receive the wedding ring. However, the wedding itself is not complete yet. The mystic believes that the Word's blood *will thank* him. She limits herself to offering the language that will articulate a homage to the Word. This language is the Word himself. The Word *will utter* the Word through his blood. Only the Word can pronounce his name.

Through a series of identifications/distinctions (the novice versus the mystic, the mystic versus St Catherine, St Catherine versus St Augustine, the present tense versus the future tense, the writing angel versus St Augustine, orality versus writing, the mystic's language of the body versus her verbal language, the nuns' textual performance versus the mystic's performance) the text leads us to a better understanding of the mystic's "philosophy of language." Whereas the human condition exists as a dialogue of oppositions, the Word is his own blood. The Word is himself. His own body, through his blood, articulates his being. Whereas the mystic's dialogue with her split self is a sign of division resulting from the sudden awareness of being as iniquity, the Word's dialogue with his blood, the "words" that the blood directs to his body, are *signs* of the perfect and harmonious unity of Being. Thus, the human subject utters the Word *insofar as* she activates the unity of the Word. The blood is the voice that thanks the Word for his existence.

COLLOQUIO 48: THE WORD'S FUNERAL AND THE FATHER'S MEMORIAL

After marrying him in colloquio 39, in colloquio 48 Maria Maddalena approaches the very essence of her bridegroom, both in his divine and in his human nature. In her mystical progress toward a perfect fusion with God, the mystic first is allowed to marry him and then, after celebrating their (forthcoming) mystical wedding, she comes to "share" his past. Whereas in previous visions the mystic had always experienced the Word's past, that is, his passion and death, as a reminder of her "baseness," in colloquio 48 she actually reenacts the moments following his death. Unlike other raptures, colloquio 48 does not focus on the well-known details of the Word's trial, humiliations, crucifixion, and death. Colloquio 48 begins when everything has already occurred. In terms of memory and remembrance, the mystic *enters* the Word's past, so to speak, when his past has already turned into memory, when the incarnate Word has already withdrawn from the world. In colloquio 48 the Word is a corpse.

We may say that from a narrative standpoint this vision is nothing but a memorial. Maria Maddalena commemorates her Spouse. Colloquio 48 is the performance of an act of remembrance. Instead of reliving the last moments of the Word's passion, a topos of medieval and Renaissance female mysticism, Maria Maddalena summons the "space" of the Word's absence. Indeed, the entire colloquio takes place in a nonplace. After the mystic's procession to the Word's sepulcher and her gathering with his disciples, Maria Maddalena enters a nonplace, at once the Word's tomb and the Father's bosom, where the two Persons of the Trinity conversed both *before* the Word's incarnation and death and *after* his resurrection. If Maria Maddalena feels the urge to be close to the corpse of her beloved, the Father commemorates the moments in which he had his Son in himself. The vision opens as a procession, but after a few pages it erases any specific localization. As Louis Marin reminds us, parades, corteges, and processions necessarily create an "epiphanic place."[37] "All parades, processions, or corteges can . . . be viewed as a group of proceedings which, while manipulating space, engender space specific to each one according to determined rules and norms" (Marin, "Semiotic Approach," 222–23). However, the more the mystic moves through the "stations" of her remembrances, the more space becomes indistinct. The Word's withdrawal undermines the structure of the procession, since the mystic's procession has lost its goal, the Word himself. More than a reenactment of Christ's itinerary, colloquio 48 enacts its disappearance.

It is apparent that the mystic's utterances have a complex relation to temporality. Her monologue *happens* both in the present (when she is overwhelmed by sheer despair because of her groom's irrevocable absence), in the past (when she speaks from the place where Christ *died*), and in the *pluperfect* (when, speaking in the person of the Father, he/she conjures up the moments of their perfect unity in the Father's bosom). However, her monologue also *foresees* the future, when the Word will come back to her. In fact, the fluctuation of the temporal categories derives from the Word's absence itself. The Word grants and subtracts meaning, structure, and narrative consequentiality. Indeed, never had the mystic held a monologue totally devoid of the Word. In colloquio 48 the Word is either a dead body that the mystic cleans up, or the narration of a past condition. As we shall study in detail, paradoxically the death and resurrection of the Word entails his disappearance. The Word becomes the memory of the Word.

The Word's absence has important consequences also from a diegetic standpoint. If every procession or cortege is "a narrative scenario," the Word's withdrawal from the "stage" of the mystic's performance emancipates the performance from any given "script" (Marin, "Semiotic Approach," 227). In other words, since the main event narrated in colloquio 48 is the Word's nonpresence, the diegesis of his previous presence becomes uncertain. In fact, Maria Maddalena deeply modifies the narration concerning the moments following the Word's deposition from the cross. Becoming the main character of her own "mystery play," in the person of the Virgin she both reprimands and supports the Word's friends. Moreover, she enters the Word's sepulcher and *stays* there commemorating him with his Father. Moreover, when the Father *invades* the mystic's body and speaks through her mouth, the performance's scenario multiplies itself. Maria Maddalena is both herself speaking *in* the Word's tomb and the Word's Father speaking *from* his bosom. The mystic thus comes to embody two different places, along with two distinct identities. On the one hand, she is the widow mourning her dead spouse; on the other, she is the Father commemorating his Son in his own bosom/heart.

Colloquio 48 is based on a radical liminality. Both the mystic as main performer and the "script" of her performance exist as ambiguous areas of performativity. Temporal categories, characters, places, narratives, acquire a fundamental instability. However, it is important to underscore a crucial aspect of the text's liminality. As Turner points out, "liminality may be partly described as a stage of reflection."[38] If we apply Turner's definition to Maria Maddalena's "play," we may say that by blending and trespassing different areas of performativity the mystic questions the core of her performance itself. If colloquio 48 revolves around the dead Savior, the mystic's multiple identifications (she is herself, the Virgin, the Father, etc.), the fluctuant temporality of her performance's diegesis, her unique interpretation of the biblical "script," all these elements achieve the mystic's meditation on the Word. Since the Son has abandoned the stage, the whole process of staging his absence is in fact an attempt to summon the memory of the Word.

Colloquio 48 is structured as follows: First, Maria Maddalena sees the Word's corpse and accompanies it to the tomb. Second, Maria Maddalena is invaded by the Father who holds a long and convoluted sermon about his Son (more than eighty pages in the published edition). Articulating two different voices, the mystic speaks as the Father and as herself. In fact, she limits herself to asking him to explain which kinds of contemplation his Son had in his, the Father's, bosom before becoming incarnate.

In this rapture Maria Maddalena expands and freely interprets a well-known devotional manual on Jesus' passion, *Instrutione et avertimenti per meditare la passione di Cristo nostro Redentore, con alcune meditationi intorno ad esse* (Rome, 1571) by Gaspar Loarte.[39] According to her biographers, this book, an Italian text written by a Spanish

Jesuit, was Maria Maddalena's first reading.[40] Indeed, her confessor gave it to her when she was still a child.[41] In this short book, Loarte follows a medieval and Renaissance tradition of devotional texts that aimed to stir the reader's emotions by asking the reader to visualize the Word's suffering. Loarte's book, in particular, is divided into short chapters, each accompanied by a picture. Although in some cases Loarte, like medieval authors of similar works, limits himself to commenting on a biblical chapter, in a few passages he actually imagines situations that are not present in the biblical text. For instance, Loarte describes in detail the Virgin's despair, when she receives her Son's corpse in her arms (82–83). He invites us to imagine how Christ's mother suffered and how she contemplated his bleeding wounds and amorously kissed them:

> After the deposition, the Savior was placed in the arms of his holy mother. Consider how carefully the holy Virgin received the dead body of her sweet son. When he was taken down from the cross, she gazed at the marks of his open wounds with an infinite despair. She kissed them and her scalding tears flew from her merciful eyes over those bleeding wounds.[42]

Maria Maddalena expands and acts out Loarte's descriptions. As he states in the introduction of his book, Loarte distinguishes among six different kinds of meditations, each of them representing a step up toward a closer relation to the divinity. The six-step process depicts the soul's passage from a participating identification with the Savior's pains to its final joy in his resurrection. The six steps are (3):

1. "generale, historiale, o litterale" (general, historical, and literal)
2. "per via di compassione" (through compassion)
3. "per via di contritione" (through contrition)
4. "per via di imitatione" (through imitation)
5. "per via di allegrezza et di speranza" (through joy and hope)
6. "per via di amore" (through love).

As we shall see, Maria Maddalena's rapture faithfully describes a similar progression from sorrow and contrition to happiness and praise for God.[43] As Loarte points out in his manual, through meditation the soul slowly modifies its image of the suffering Word. Whereas at the beginning the soul primarily visualizes the Savior as a grievous body, later it "purifies" this image, that is, concentrates on a more abstract image. Similarly, whereas in the first part of this vision the mystic depicts the Savior as a corpse, smeared with blood and spit, at the end she will describe him as "perfect goodness" and "pure love."

We may infer that the act of narrating/visualizing the Word's vicis-situdes and death is supposed to lead the subject toward the annihilation of any narrative. The Gospel is nothing but a first step toward its and the Word's erasure. However, Maria Maddalena already starts her process of visualization with the removal of the Word. The Word neither speaks nor acts in this vision. Maria Maddalena has already attained a level in which the narration/visualization of the incarnate Word has eliminated its main character, the Word himself. Loarte's first step of visualization ("general, historical, and literal") has been replaced by the second and third level, compassion and contrition. Both steps characterize the act of mourning and remembering.

As Roland Barthes stresses, the numerous meditation manuals written by Jesuits, all stemming from Ignatius's *Spiritual Exercises*, teach the meditator how to visualize/rewrite his own autobiography. The Word's biography in fact coincides with the believer's. The Word can only be summoned in the subject's mind insofar as the subject "lends" the Word his own memories.[44] The "I" appears in the act of meditation as a "fluid, scattered" subjectivity. "I" is a space filled by the meditator's memories and imaginations, concerning both his own past and the Word's narrated physicality (Barthes, SF, 69). Memory is in fact both "conservation" and "construction," as Merleau-Ponty points out:

> The problem of memory cannot be solved if one hesitates between memory as conservation and memory as construction. It is easy to show that consciousness finds in its "representations" only what it put there. Memory is thus a construction. Another memory is necessary behind the first one, in order to assess the productions of the first one. . . . True memory lies at the intersection of these two forms, at the moment when a remembrance, forgotten and guarded by oblivion, comes back. Indeed, an specific remembrance and oblivion are two modes of our contradictory relation to a past which is present to us through the emptiness it leaves in us.[45]

Life is "set in motion" by our constant production and remembrance of our past. In her visions, Maria Maddalena's imagined/remembered past merges with the Word's. Maria Maddalena's rapture is indeed the dialogue between the two subjects of her performance. Memory, we may say, is a *pas à deux*.

In the act of visualizing the Word's past, the subject's "I" is displaced in the "theater" of his meditation, which essentially concerns the Word's death. This aspect is of crucial relevance if applied to Maria Maddalena's mysticism. I have pointed out that colloquio 48 opens with the Word's occurred withdrawal. Rather than identifying with the Savior, Maria Maddalena identifies with his absence. The mystic's "I" is already missing since the refential "I" (the Word) has disappeared from the stage. If, as Turner states, the performer's liminality is a form of "reflection," we might infer that colloquio 48 is the mystic's reflection on her own mispresence. By realizing and visualizing the Word's withdrawal, Maria Maddalena *sees* her own "I" as a missing reference, a space devoid of any narrativity. This is why in this vision diegesis is such an uncertain, contradictory element, constantly on the verge of disappearing from the performance.

The memorial of the dead Savior is in fact the memorial of the mystic's identity. In other words, the soul's process of individualization corresponds to a meditation on its own dying. Maria Maddalena completes her erasure through the erased Word. If the mystic's sole goal is to "belch forth" the Word, she may attain it only by "belching forth" the narrative of her dying identity. The mystic must accomplish a performance in which she/the Word is absent from it. Her gestures, her words, her movements must "belch forth" her acquired death.[46] This is why colloquio 48 plays such a crucial role in the economy of the entire *I colloqui*. In this vision the mystic succeeds in questioning any possible narrative concerning both Christ and the soul, since the act of contemplation merges the two poles of mystical "reflection."

However, although this vision does not follow a firm diegesis, it does respect the temporal dimension of its biblical referent. As the nuns stress at the very beginning, this vision lasted forty hours, the equivalent of Jesus' stay in the tomb. The writers say that Maria Maddalena entered this vision three hours before Jesus' burial, at nine in the evening. They maintain that, given the length of her forthcoming rapture, God has granted the mystic the ability to come out of her vision whenever she must attend to her physical needs (*i suoi bisogni corporali*). We are told, for instance, that at a certain point Maria Maddalena had a break to eat an egg yolk ("si destò dal ratto, prese un rosso d'uovo e stette un poco," 2:303).

Like colloquio 39, this rapture has a five-part structure: first, an introduction, in which Maria Maddalena clarifies what she is about to experience; second, her actual recounting of her visit to the Word's tomb; third, while his disciples meditate on his death, Maria Maddalena meditates on the time when the Word's soul resided in his Father's bosom. In this long section Maria Maddalena broaches several topics, among them, the different "conformities" (*conformità*), through which the soul relates itself to the Word, the absence of the Word in her soul, and the following assault of the demons. Fourth, Maria Maddalena begins speaking with two different voices, God's and hers. Through her mouth, the divinity delivers a long sermon, interrupted by the mystic's questions and doubts. Fifth and finally, the vision ends with Maria Maddalena's praise of the resurrected Word.

On Friday, May 17, 1585, at 9 p.m., Maria Maddalena entered a rapture (2:285). After a long silence, her first reported words are the following:

> Oh eternal Word, so long? [*silence*] you stayed underground for so long, forty hours, I mean in the sepulcher, and during that time were you in the Father's bosom in Limbo, and underground? And, admiring, I will follow you.

We could say that this introductory passage actually synthesizes the whole colloquio. Maria Maddalena mentions all the central points of her forthcoming vision. First, she tells us that she will follow the Word's corpse underground; for forty hours she will be next to his body. Second, she reminds us that during his stay in the sepulcher the Word rested in his Father's bosom in Limbo; this is actually the topic of the long memorial/sermon delivered by the Father. After having been in the Word's tomb, Maria Maddalena's body is entered by the Father, who will explain to the mystic the kind of relationship he had with his dead Son before his Son embraced the human condition. Finally, the mystic anticipates the concluding section of her vision, in which she will admire and extol the resurrected Word.

After her brief summary, Maria Maddalena introduces the topic of the first section of her vision:

> The period of forty hours will be fulfilled [*silence*] so that I will finish at the dawn of your happy Sunday. Yes [*silence*] one can really call it the day of the Lord. . . . oh yes, you were not in the sepulcher at this time. Oh, then I will enter there too, for sure! [*silence*] during this time the mystery of the Trinity will be fulfilled, because two nights and one day will pass. The day for the eternal Father, the first night for the Word, and the second one for the Holy Spirit [*silence*] two of our nights is one of your days, because you always have light and day [*silence*] and in the meantime I will be able to have you in the Holy Sacrament, because, even though I am with you, I want to have the certainly of you, you know. (2:286)

In this excerpt Maria Maddalena reminds the dead Word that she will visit him in his tomb and will stay by him throughout his three-day death. In the last sentence the mystic says that, although she has the Word close to her, she will attend mass in order to receive communion, because she wants him with certainty ("con certezza").

Indeed, Maria Maddalena had chosen the convent of Santa Maria degli Angeli because the Jesuits allowed the nuns to receive communion daily, whereas in other convents the confessors often did not consider this practice absolutely necessary.[47] Whereas in communion she keeps hold, so to speak, of the incarnate Word through an act of ritualization/remembrance, in her rapture the Word has the presence of a corpse. Once again the mystic shifts temporal levels in her reflection on the Word. *Now* she is both in his tomb and is speaking about her being in his tomb. More importantly, the split temporality of her performance allows her to participate in the mass and to receive the Word as it has become *after* his three-day death. Communion is itself a form of mourning the Word's absence. Although communion *is* the Word's flesh, it also reminds us of the absence of the Word's flesh. "This is my flesh" and "This is my blood" summon the Word's erased flesh and blood. The Word's flesh and blood are present as reminders of absent presences. Similarly, in colloquio 48 Maria Maddalena debates the Word's death as an absence that lingers in her signifiers.

After having introduced the topic of her vision, Maria Maddalena knelt down and looked toward the floor, as if she were contemplating Jesus's corpse: "she knelt down, joined her hands and looked down at the floor. In this way she indicated that she was seeing Jesus taken down from the cross." By this gesture, the writers claim, the mystic starts to identify with the Virgin Mary. At this point, her reenactment of the Word's funeral has already begun. From now on Maria Maddalena will speak both as the distressed Mother of God and as herself. The mystic's gestures, her physical reactions, are fundamental constituents of her performance. According to the nuns, the mystic's gestures clearly imitate some paintings that reproduce the Virgin Mary kneeling over her Son's corpse. The nuns stress this point: "She made some sorrowful and very moving gestures . . . as if she saw Jesus taken down from the cross, as one sees in many Pietàs" (2:287). As Chiara Frugoni points out in her seminal essay "Female Mystics, Visions, and Iconography," "[t]he religious practice of female mystics depended primarily on memorization, and the use of images served a similar mnemonic function" (137).[48]

However, while the mystic's utterances are often obscure to the nuns, her gestures are often even more vague and open to interpretation. For instance, at a certain point the mystic made gestures expressing pity and compassion, similar to those that one might imagine the Virgin Mary to have made when she saw her dead son. Later, the writers see her "look up and down, here and there" and "touch lightly with her hand, *as if* she were cleaning him of clotted blood and spit." As de Certeau stresses, the mystic's body makes her narration "readeable," that is, her physical expressions allow the nuns, the bystanders, to follow the development of her story.[49]

The mystic's body becomes an alternative form of expression, often more powerful and direct than the linguistic one. Her body reenacts, one could say, the narrative about the Word's death. Moreover, in the nuns description of the mystic's gestures the image of a second body arises:

that of the dead Word. Indeed, all her gestures revolve around the corpse of her beloved/son who, according to the nuns' reconstruction, lies in front of her. Christ's body is silent; Maria Maddalena moves her hands toward an invisible being. More than his body in its wholeness, the mystic points to its single parts: his bleeding chest, his feet, his hands, his head. The Word's body is a fragmented image and a silent language. Maria Maddalena is speechless. Both her body and his corpse allude to a lost language. "Anyone could imagine it," the nuns state, "although one who didn't see her could not fully understand everything she did."

Still on her knees Maria Maddalena contemplates Christ's wounded chest and addresses her patron St Mary Magdalen, who was present at the crucifixion:

> Oh love, why do they not fit in your side that is so open and is such a huge cavern? . . . Leave it alone a bit more . . . oh Magdalen, oh Magdalen! [*silence*] you were at those feet, but I am at his mouth, that has narrated so well his Father's eternal will [*silence*] why can't I turn my heart into a sepulcher? (2:288)

Whereas Magdalen lay at the Word's feet, the mystic says, she sits at his mouth, because his mouth has narrated his Father's will. Whereas the Word's flesh is silent, Maria Maddalena mimes both her despair for the absent Word and his "visible" corpse.[50] Once again, the mystic underscores her focus on the Word's mouth, his utterance, his silenced voice. In the act of gazing at his face, Maria Maddalena contemplates her own unfulfilled task.

What in the ritual of the Mass is remembrance, in Maria Maddalena's mystical discourse is the awareness of a perfect oblivion. The priest that performs a Mass speaks the words of the Word, that is, he *announces* the memory of the Word. Maria Maddalena, instead, speaks the memory of the nonpresence of the Word; her words *announce* that the Word has withdrawn from the world. The ritual of the Mass commemorates the resurrection of the Savior in the annihilation of his flesh, whereas Maria Maddalena's monologues equate the Word's flesh with his mouth, his voice. To announce the Word is to give flesh to the Word. A Mass looks at the Word as signifier (the Word is everywhere and is everything, since he has come to embrace and liberate the creation itself), whereas the mystic *wishes that the Word were there*.

The image of the Word's mouth is also present in the next passage of her discourse. Maria Maddalena finally stands up and says:

> Once again, oh eternal Father, I offer you his blood for human kind [*silence*] oh Father, confirm his apostles and his disciples, and let them participate in your vision, because I see them doubt [*silence*] oh my Son, when I had you in my womb, I knew that I would see you in this

way, but oh, oh! [*silence*] oh, I nourished you with all my love, but now I do not contemplate[51] you with less [*silence*] oh, if I could only put my mouth on yours, as you put your mouth on my breast! Oh how willingly I would do so! [*silence*] I gave you my milk, and you want to nourish all of humanity with your blood . . . they will say to me: look at her there, the mother of that crucified one [*silence*] you who are eternal, I see you dead and mortal [*silence*] Oh John, you rested on his chest, but now he rests on yours [*silence*] oh Magdalen, you pay, you pay him the same homage by kissing his feet now, as you did before. (2:289)

In this passage the mystic identifies with the Virgin Mary as mother except in one passage where she speaks as his lover: "if I could only put my mouth on yours, as you put your mouth on my breast." By kissing his mouth, Maria Maddalena would perceive the physicality of his utterance. Her kiss is both a sign of desire, thus of lack, and a wish for perception. Her kiss would make *manifest* that the Word is not here anymore.

In sermon 2 of *On the Song of Songs*, Bernard writes

"Let him kiss me with the kiss of his mouth"; let him whose presence is full of love, from whom exquisite doctrines flow in streams, let him become "a spring inside of me." . . . The mouth which kisses signifies the Word who assumes human nature; the nature assumed receives the kiss; the kiss however, that takes its being both from the giver and the receiver, is a person that is formed by both.[52]

Bernard offers a seminal interpretation of the biblical verse "Let him kiss me with the kiss of his mouth." According to him, the kisser is the Word in the act of assuming his humanity and the mouth kissed is his humanity itself.[53] The Word's flesh (the mouth that kisses and the mouth that is kissed) performs the kiss itself. It is the Word's flesh that kisses itself. In colloquio 48, the mystic wishes she were able to kiss the Word's mouth in order to *touch* the Word's flesh/word. The mystic wants to kiss, and not to be kissed by, a corpse's lips. The mystic will succeed in kissing the Word's lips when she "articulates" his flesh. In other words, whereas in Bernard's sermon the Word kisses the world's physicality by kissing his own lips, in colloquio 48 it is the world, that is, the mystic, that perceives the necessity of kissing the Word's mouth both to summon his withdrawn flesh and its, the world's, being.

If she were allowed to kiss the Word's mouth, Maria Maddalena would perceive that "he and I are like organs of one single intercorporeality" (Merleau-Ponty, *Signs*, 168). To kiss the other means to recognize that his biography is mine, that his death on the cross is mine, and that he needs my kiss to give life to his biography. Conversely, by kissing the other's face and lips I acknowledge that my being lies in the other. When I kiss the other, I keep my eyes closed and erase myself in the other's lips and face.

In colloquio 47 Maria Maddalena had held a long monologue on how the Word kisses and is kissed. "The Word wishes to kiss and to be kissed," she says (2:275). More specifically:

> One gives a kiss with the head, and in particular with the lips and the mouth [*silence*] oh Word, you kiss the face of the soul and you kiss your own face with the lips of your purity and joy; and your lips are reddened by your blood . . . when your lips of purity and joy kiss the face of the soul, they do not leave any sign of pressure, but rather of union, because its spiritual and divine being unifies and transforms the soul into you. (2:275–76)

A kiss, the mystic says, leaves no visible sign. A kiss is a celebration of union and transformation. The act of kissing the face of the soul signifies the Word's silent desire for the soul, and his dedication to it. The Word grants his grace when he *sees* his desire reflected in the face of the soul. Whereas in colloquio 48 it is the soul/Virgin/mystic that would like to reach the Word's face with her lips, in colloquio 47 the Word himself longs for an "osculum unionis," a kiss of union (2:277).

In the above long passage from colloquio 48 a second central aspect must be highlighted. Maria Maddalena hints at themes that she will develop later, such as her encounter with Jesus' disciples, who are confused because of their master's death ("Oh Father, confirm his apostles and his disciples, and let them participate in your vision, because I see them doubt"); the Savior's blood, which will be the crucial topic of the Father's long sermon ("oh eternal Father, I offer you his blood for human kind"); and her conversation with St John, who is the first of Jesus' apostles to talk to Maria Maddalena ("Oh John, you rested on his chest, but now he rests on yours"). In this first part, Maria Maddalena's discourse summarizes the forthcoming stages of her performance.

The mystic then leaves the room of the novices and walks toward the chapel. As the writers underscore, in this vision Maria Maddalena transforms their convent into a biblical landscape, that is, each room, each staircase, even the chapel become a place of Christ's passion. The mystic sees the *sala di novitiato* (room for the novices) as Calvary; then she climbs up the stairs toward the chapel, which becomes the Savior's tomb. In this rapture, space acquires a double meaning: each room of the convent evokes a specific place of Jesus' passion. There is no clear reason why the novices' room is Calvary, or why the choir becomes Jesus' sepulcher. Reality is intrinsically metaphorical; the signs of the Word's passion and death are everywhere. Dinzelbacher calls this kind of rapture "Uebergangsform" (crossing form), by which he means that the mystic has a "double vision," that is, she sees both reality and divine images, the so-called "Fernsicht" (long sight).[54] What is unique in this vision of Maria Maddalena is its public character. In fact, Maria Maddalena does not limit herself to experiencing something, she explains what she sees and/or hears, involving her convent nuns in her performance. The first part of colloquio 48 is an unusual miracle play, in which the main character, the mystic herself, plays all the characters present at the Son's passion and death. Everything reminds the mystic of her bridegroom's death.

As we have seen, Maria Maddalena has moved from the room of the novices to the church, where the actual burial of her Son/Beloved will take place. In this sequence Maria Maddalena bids farewell to the Word, first and foremost seen in his humanity. As I have already mentioned, according to several medieval devotional manuals, among them Loarte's *Instrutione*, the believer, in the act of meditating on Jesus' passion, must move from the Word as mortal creature toward a more spiritual image of him. Kneeling in the choir of the chapel, Maria Maddalena sees the Savior for the last time. Her discourse is a farewell. She invokes his angels, his grave-diggers: "let me have him a bit longer . . . now take him . . . now take him away. . . . Come, you angels, to bury my Son and your Creator" (2:290). She synthesizes this event as follows: "I leave my Son and I take my Word with me [*silence*] I leave him whom I begot and nourished with my milk, and I take with me the essence of the Trinity."

The Savior, as human being, is dead. However, Maria Maddalena takes his word with her, or better yet, she takes on the task to express his being in the world. This is the "essence" of the divinity himself. In this passage, the mystic alludes to the second part of her rapture, where in the person of the Father she will discuss the *past* of the Word. Following the unwritten script of a mystical play, Maria Maddalena mourns her son's death while his angels are digging his grave:

> Why can't I enter with you? [*silence*] but given that I can't enter with you you will enter into me. . . . I was boastful and believed that the virgins would follow me and could boast of having an immortal groom, but now I see you buried. (2:291)

In a crucial sentence ("given that I can't enter with you you will enter into me") the mystic synthesizes the process of "internalization" of the Word's biography. Since the act of meditating on the Word's past is equivalent to the act of reenacting and thus "purging" one's own past, Maria Maddalena progressively appropriates the Word's death. Again, the temporality of this performance lies between the present tense of an absence (the divine corpse, the mystic's mourning, the Father's following memorial) and the past/presence of the appropriation of the Word's narrative. The ambiguity of this vision's temporality stems from the fact that the actants of the performance embody contradictory signifieds. If the second Person of the Trinity is an absence (the dead Christ), his absence is the expected fulfillment of his previous presence (the incarnate Word). His death makes the Word a *forthcoming* presence in the world.

However, the relationship between the Son, the Word, and Christ is even more complex. Indeed, we must remember that the Word is an absence if related to the presence of the (past) Savior in the world (the Christ is still present as a corpse, whereas his word, or the "Word's word," as St Thomas says, is not expressed yet). Yet Christ's current absence (the dead Savior is absent as the incarnate Word) entails the future presence of the Word himself, whose incarnation will occur when the absence of the Christ (his corpse) withdraws from the stage of the performance (Christ's disappearance from the sepulcher and his resurrection).

Maria Maddalena embodies contradictory temporalities as well. As main character of a written text she lives the present tense of the narration. Even though the narrative is composed in the past tense, the character "blessed soul" makes the whole text a "past present." However, as performer of a transcribed performance, Maria Maddalena, the actor whose name is never expressed in the text, is both the mystic who perceives the withdrawal of the incarnate Word from her world, and the "Word's spouse" who cries over his corpse in the past/present occurrence of his death. The performer, however, "forefeels" the forthcoming presence of the Word, that is, his victory over his own death. The mystic, as a Florentine nun who knows the end of the story, interferes in the narrative of the Word's corpse. In Merleau-Ponty's words, memory/unconscious "has a double nature: 'I didn't know it' and 'I have always known it.'"[55] This temporal duplicity is *written* in the flesh of the subject: "This leads to the concept of human body as . . . an idea that is not a final point, since it constantly announces a sequel."[56] The ambiguity of the Savior's identity (Jesus, Son, incarnate Word, forthcoming Word) and that of the performer (nun, mystic, performer of a miracle play, Word's spouse, Word's mother) multiplies the temporality of the text/performance. The future/past of the Word's human experience is both written and expressed in the mystic's gestures.

After having mourned over her son's dead body, the Virgin/mystic rushes to the scriptorium (*lo scrittoio*), which is Mary's house (*la casa di Maria*). It is in the scriptorium that she meets with her Son's disciples. As the writers say, Maria Maddalena goes to the scriptorium door and invites St Peter in:

> Come in, come in Peter, come, come, come here. Come, come in, come in, because, even though you too offended my Word, he is kind, and since he has forgiven you I too forgive you. You know, he has forgiven Magdalen, and will forgive you too. (2:293–94)

Maria Maddalena, the nuns say, seems to accompany St Peter to a seat and, after having reminded him of his future task, the foundation of the Church, she consoles him: "And Peter, strengthen your faith, if you cry now over the past try not to have to cry over the future." Later, she addresses St John, who stands at the door. The mystic merges John the apostle with John the writer of the Gospel: "Oh John! . . . come in, come in, oh John, if my Word recommended me to you, how is it you don't want to stay with me? Come in, come in, come here." In the same way she invites St James, St Joseph, and Nicodemus. In her speech to them the mystic stresses that they doubt themselves and they doubt the Word's forthcoming resurrection: "Preserve the words of the eternal Word, you know that you must be his trumpets." In particular, Maria Maddalena reminds St John that he has a fundamental mission to accomplish, he must recount the Word's incarnation in Mary's womb, his life and his resting in his Father's bosom: "Oh John, you will be so strong, that you will recount what he has done in my womb . . . and you will write that in the beginning he was with his Father."

Maria Maddalena asks Jesus' disciples to meditate on the Word, while she accompanies him through his journey: to the sepulcher, to Limbo, and to his Father's bosom:

> You will meditate on my Word, while in my mind I will accompany him everywhere my Only Begotten goes. If he is in his Father's bosom, I will be in his Father's bosom; if he is in Limbo, I will be in Limbo; if he is in the sepulcher, I will be with him in the sepulcher as well. (2:296)

In this passage Maria Maddalena clarifies the nature of her vision. She actually acts out her visualization of the Word's journey. Although she "sees this in her mind," she engages her daily world (the scriptorium, the kitchen garden, etc.) in her visualization. While she is visualizing her conversation with the disciples, she informs them that she is going to visualize the Word's journey. Her rapture is thus a visualization within a visualization. Reality (the scriptorium) is where the mystic *sees* the Word's friends. Speaking to their images, she says that she will conjure up a second series of images. However, her visualized images *occur* in the here and now of the convent. They inhabit the rooms of the convent. Even the time spent in each visualization is strictly respectful of the referential narrative. In other words, both the world and its temporality dictates the development of Maria Maddalena's mystical performance.

Indeed, by mentioning the three moments of the Word's journey Maria Maddalena anticipates the topic of the final section of the colloquio, which is her long and complex sermon in the person of Father about his relationship with the Word's soul. However, before entering this interaction with the Father, Maria Maddalena introduces this topic by expressing her feelings about the Word's stay in his Father's bosom. In her introduction Maria Maddalena does not follow a strict pattern. She first sees the Word's soul "placed" in his Father's bosom: "Oh, oh, oh! [*silence*] placed" (2:297). This past participle is the actual point word of the entire following section, which describes the positive effects deriving from the union of the Father and the soul both of the "unborn" Word and of the resurrected Savior.

The mystic leans over the scriptorium table, which is next to an open window. She looks out, resting her elbows on the table. Then, Maria Maddalena raises her arms in despair, but she never goes away from the table. Indeed, standing over the table she seems to recite her vision from an invisible text (2:297). The tone of her discourse tends to be highly formal, and she pronounces long passages in Latin.

The first section of this monologue concludes with the expression "placed," which refers to the Word's soul resting in the Father's bosom. After having exalted the perfect union between the Father and the Word ("Vidi animam Verbi collocare Spiritum suum in essentia divinitatis, potentie idee sue, in complacimento animarum nostrarum"), Maria Maddalena goes on to speak of the Word as the "Book of Life" (libro vite), which reports the destiny of every soul:

> Oh, please tell me something about it [*silence*] *libro vite*, yes [*silence*] *et collocavit animas eorum in infernum, et perdent glorie que preparavit eis Verbum* [*silence*] *et superbie eius* [*silence*] *et occidit eos unus ad unum, et collocavit in tenebris e umbre mortis.* (2:299)

In God's "Book of Life," the mystic reads that the Word's soul ascended to his Father's bosom, whereas the evil, stubborn souls fell down into Hell. The expression "Book of Life" has a double meaning: on one hand it is the Bible, the Book of God; on the other, this expression specifically refers to the Word's utterances, transcribed as a written text. The Word's voice, one could infer, has become his "Book of Life."

The expression "libro vite" occurs frequently in *The Book of Revelations*, where it is repeated more than ten times. However, Maria Maddalena freely interprets this expression. In *The Book of Revelations* the "Book of Life" is the text where God has written down the "last things":

> Then I saw a great white throne and the One who was sitting on it. In his presence, earth and sky vanished, leaving no trace. I saw the dead, both great and small, standing in front of his throne, while the book of

life was opened (20:11,12); and anybody whose name was not found written in the Book of Life was thrown into the burning lake. (20:15)

As we shall see in a later passage, the mystic feels that demonic forces have the power to erase this holy Book. The Word's voice, Maria Maddalena will say, must be protected. If he succeeds in erasing the Word's transcribed voice, the devil will also destroy the ultimate sense of the world. To return to the above excerpt, Maria Maddalena states that the Word placed (*collocavit*) the bad souls in Hell among the shadows of the dead. Later, the mystic expands this image when she perceives that bad souls are flying around her. At this point, Maria Maddalena climbs up on the writing-table and opens the window, in order to let the screaming souls fly away:

> [E]t collocavit eos in infernum [silence] who ever saw such speed? . . . go [silence] howl, scream as much as you want [silence] et sublimavit humanitatis nostrae cum confusione eius. (2:300)

Climbing down from the table, Maria Maddalena takes a seat and, after having kept silent for a long while, she says: "Et sublimavit humanitatis nostrae [silence] vidi glorificationis mee and omni creatura in ipsum [silence] surge, quievit e ambulavit." With these words she means that the Word's resurrection brings human kind to perfection. "Surge, quievit e ambulavit" (stand up, he rested and walked) are the first movements of the Word's soul in his Father's bosom.[57] Maria Maddalena mimes these movements, walking up and down the scriptorium five times, both toward the right and the left side of the room, "In a constant movement, without any movement, you go out toward the right and toward the left, and you always return to this place" (2:301). According to the nuns, by this sort of dance the mystic wants to "show how the Word moved in the Father's bosom." In other words, here Maria Maddalena *becomes* the Word who moves in his Father's bosom; her body identifies with his body. This identification is another step toward the appropriation of the Word's biography through meditation. The Word's soul is the mystic's body that walks in a room of a Florentine convent. The mystic performs the Word before his incarnation through the movements of her own body. The Word's soul is gestures, dances, harmonious movements.

Speaking of the perfect "conformity" (*conformità*) between the Father and the Word's soul, the mystic compares the conformities existing between the Word and the Father with those between the Word and the creature. Maria Maddalena distinguishes among five different kinds of conformity existing between human soul and the Word: conformity of ignorance, of nature, of grace, of admiration, and of love (*conformità d'ignorantia, di natura, di grazia, di ammiratione e d'amore*). The first kind of conformity is actually a "nonconformity" (*inconformità*), since it refers to a soul unaware of being ignorant of the Word. The last conformity, that of love, is "sublime" (*una sublimità di conformità*). Maria Maddalena says that "conformity comes from knowledge, and nonconformity comes from a very deep ignorance."[58]

After having recovered from her rapture to take a brief rest and eat an egg yolk, Maria Maddalena concludes her performance of how the Word's soul rested/will rest in his Father's bosom. In this part the mystic dramatizes the resurrected/unborn Word as infinitely distant from her soul. Indeed, on the one hand she recounts the infinite glory of the Word; on the other she sees herself as unworthy of the Word's grace. She repeats a very slow dance around the scriptorium three times and then she says: "Oh, great is our God, great is our God!" At this point, she falls down on the floor, to represent her fall away from the Word's presence, although she can still see his distant glory: "Here I am, on the floor [*silence*] I can't go further down [*silence*] and yes [*silence*] oh, wise folly."

Looking upwards toward the ceiling, Maria Maddalena then sees a series of wonderful cities, all of them glorifying the resurrected Word:

> One hundred twenty-four carry very beautiful vases, full of an extremely delicate perfume, and pour it over the Word's head. These are the wishes of the pure virgins . . . 120 carry a city in their hands . . . in these cities a huge number of people live. Your elect receive your wisdom through your innumerable works . . . the prize of the confessors, yes [*silence*].[59] (2:305)

The Word, the mystic continues, presents himself as a submissive lamb (*docile agnello*) attacked by several fierce beasts. Four groups of young girls (*adolescentule*) protect the Word-Lamb and keep him tied to them by some ropes, which are God's gifts. The Lamb lives in a garden (Jerusalem) that produces wonderful fruits. Maria Maddalena promises to bring as many people as possible to the Word's garden: "Woe is me if I don't come to you and if I don't try to bring you others [*silence*] it is written in the Book of Life, known to you, so that you write it in the book of your heart" (2:307).

Maria Maddalena had already spoken of the "Book of Life" when she had pointed out that devilish souls constantly attempt to cancel the Word's holy Book. However, from a narrative standpoint one would not expect the mystic to visualize the Word's resurrection when she is still speaking from the Savior's tomb. The devils' possible attack could only occur when Jesus becomes the Word's word, that is, when his body disappears and his voice/request echoes in the world.

We could say that Maria Maddalena's description of the union between the Word and the Father has two major facets: on the one hand the mystic contemplates the perfect union between the Son and the Father, on the other she perceives that the Word's "wonderful works" could be jeopardized by negative presences. The devil is a disturbance of one's hearing, a mark that may erase the *text/biography* of the Word. The mystic's discourse oscillates between a well-constructed syntax, when, for instance, she praises the resurrected Word, and a series of fragmented, abrupt utterances, when she either perceives her incapacity to protect the Word from the "beasts," or her exclusion from the Word, who is her "Book of Life":

> There is always someone who tries to erase the writing [*silence*] this is the devil's task, who would like to take away all the good deeds the souls do with their minds; and if he could, he would erase everything that has been written in the Book of Life, so that nobody would be saved. (2:308)

The devil aims to delete the Word's transcribed voice from his Book in order to prevent humankind from reading the world as a *sign* of the Word. By "reading the Word's Book of Life," man can still listen to his holy voice and follow him. Human life, Maria Maddalena says, can be either hell or heaven. Man is in heaven when he listens to the Word's voice and acts according to his teachings; he is in hell when he denies the Word and makes himself deaf to his voice:

> An infinite crowd went up *contra Deum suum*, and they did not want to understand the words that he had placed in their souls . . . my soul will not fail to reveal what she has perceived, and she does not decline to do it [*silence*] more, eternal Word [*silence*] hell and heaven at the same time [*silence*] Moses's bush burned but it was not consumed, whereas I am consuming even though I am not burning [*silence*] oh, Word, no more greatness, no more goodness [*silence*] if I died, once I would taste death without ever dying [*silence*] but living, I die a thousand deaths. (2:309)

The whole passage revolves around the Word's language. Maria Maddalena says that many people heard his words, but they refused to understand them. Maria Maddalena compares herself with Moses's bush, which burned without consuming. However, her soul is consumed by her attempt to utter the Word, that is to say, whereas the biblical bush expresses divine message without being consumed, the mystic's soul is consumed by her striving to utter the Word.[60] The mystic experiences the difficulty of expressing the Word as abandonment by him; her inability to speak his language means that she is distant from him: "Where are you, good Jesus? [*silence*] oh Word, so much pain! [*silence*] oh good Jesus." Her inability to speak (to) the Word means to burn of a fire that consumes without burning. In other words, her saying/fire does not emit light/life. The mystic's fire is the darkness preventing her from gazing at the Word's face. If the bush burned without consuming because it let the Word speak *by means of* its burning branches, the mystic's body *signifies* both the Word's corpse, his absent voice, the mystic's guilt, and her solitude *by means of* a nonpresent fire. The biblical fire did not consume because it *embodied its self*, that is, it expressed itself as a manifestation of the Word. The Word is the sole flesh and blood of the world. The mystic's fire/body, on the contrary, *devastates itself* because it denies itself as fire, as the Word's presence here and now.

Interrupting their transcriptions, the nuns write that at this point the Word is willing to give his heart to Maria Maddalena. However, before receiving this gift, she must understand how, after his *forthcoming* death, his soul *related* to his Father.[61] This will then be the topic of the Father's long memorial, the final part of the colloquio.[62]

God communicates to the soul, the mystic explains, by testing the soul severely: "What happened to Job will happen to me: first he was tested in his belongings, and then in himself . . . first in his body, and then in his soul" (2:311). Approaching an actual encounter with the divinity, Maria Maddalena senses her infinite distance from the divinity himself. Her language turns into a lament. Her pauses become the core of her discourse. The mystic, we could say, speaks to us by means of her silences, which speak of her incapacity to speak the divinity:

> She shook and writhed, as if she were coming apart inside, while saying the following words: "My Jesus, I can't know if you want my body to be destroyed in this way [*silence*] I don't know if I am on earth or in heaven, in Hell or in the abyss [*silence*] oh good Jesus! [*silence*] . . . oh good Jesus! [*silence*] oh my Jesus, it is clear to me, yes [*silence*] *si ascendero in celum tu illic es, si descendero in infernum ades* [*silence*] oh good Jesus! [*silence*] oh good Jesus, you are all love, but you are all pure [*silence*] oh Word, when are you coming? [*silence*] oh good Jesus! [*silence*] my Jesus, you want, yes, yes [*silence*] dear Jesus, good Jesus [*silence*] I understand neither you nor myself. If I am in you, you know it, you come out of yourself [*silence*] I don't know if I am on earth, if I am in heaven, you know."[63] (2:312)

It is apparent that Maria Maddalena's discourse has little in common with the biblical accounts. Following Loarte's *Instrutione*, the mystic's meditation passes from the historical events concerning the Word's bleeding corpse toward a more abstract concept of the Word himself.[64] A crucial aspect in this passage is that the Word's voice *might* be implicitly present in the text. Indeed, in some points Maria Maddalena's utterances have a responsive nature: "Oh good Jesus! [*silence*] oh my Jesus, it is clear to me, yes"; "Oh good Jesus! [*silence*] my Jesus, you want, yes,

yes." The mystic defines herself as "a nothingness" (*un nihilo*); thus, she asks the Word to come down to her: "Word, come, come."[65] To be far away from the Word, the mystic believes, means to be distant from our own source of expression.

The unifying meaning of the above passage is a disturbing sense of lack. It is the mystic's silences, marked in the manuscript as a series of dots, which both hide and hint at the sense of her words. As we have seen, Maria Maddalena has internalized her meditation of the Word's death. The Word's death has become the distintegration of her discourse; his silent corpse is her body striving for expression. The transcribers visualize the mystic's physicality by costructing a "hollow" and discontinuous page, made of dots (silences), exclamations both in Latin and in Italian, repetitions (Oh Jesus, oh, oh). The page has become a map of the mystic's dismembered utterances.

Next, the nuns report a time shift ("It was the tenth hour," 2:313), marking a new phase of their transcription. Maria Maddalena comes out of her rapture in order to go to the night mass. As they reconstruct *a posteriori*, during the celebration the mystic asked the Word to descend upon her when she takes communion. According to the nuns, Maria Maddalena thinks that, as the consecrated host contains his body, his blood, and his soul, so is the believer, who receives the host, made out of blood, body, and soul. In other words, the soul and the Word can only meet on the common ground of their humanity, since the Word is *the* flesh of the world.

In the act of taking communion the mystic's performance acquires a social identity. She *knows* the language of the Catholic ritual; she *knows* that the Word's memory can be summoned by some given gestures and words. Maria Maddalena goes back for a moment to her role as a nun. To take communion means to perform the memory of the Word. The divinity can *at least* be present in the host as a remembrance. The host is a token of the Word's disappeared physicality. Communion is thus a ritualized mourning, whereas the mystic's previous monologue signified the nonsignificance of her gestures and utterances. The mystic joins the world to commemorate the Word, since communion itself is part of the funeral of the Word.

After the mass, the nuns notice that something amazing has occurred to her sister. The mystic's body has been invaded by the Father, who starts to speak through her voice (2:314). Maria Maddalena has now a masculine voice (the Father) and a feminine one (herself). The Father first reminds her of the importance of frequent communion in order to keep close to him. First and foremost, the human soul must be humble and pure if it wants fully to receive him in the host. We have already seen that at the beginning of colloquio 39 Maria Maddalena has broached the topic of the necessity for the soul to attain a perfect purity.

After this brief introduction about the role of Holy Communion in the communication between the soul and himself, the Father delivers a sermon, which will continue for more than eighty pages of the published text.[66] Rather than actually talking, God seems to be reading a memorial, which is occasionally interrupted by the mystic's questions and remarks. This final part of colloquio 48, one could say, no longer belongs to Maria Maddalena; she limits herself to offering her voice to the divinity. Furthermore, at this point her text has reduced to the minimum what Zumthor calls its *index of orality;* her page does not originate from her spoken voice. Even though the mystic has actually uttered this long monologue, her words have an unmistakable written quality.

A crucial question arises at this point: What does God's extremely long sermon/memorial mean? How does it fit into the overall structure of this colloquio? As we have seen, the mystic is in pain because of the Word's distance from her soul. Entering a new phase of her rapture, Maria Maddalena goes to mass and receives the host. It is at this point that God the Father begins to speak through her mouth. The topic of his discourse is the remembrance of his perfect union with his Son's soul. In his sermon God underscores that, after having been tortured and killed, his Son will join him again. As will become clearer later, by letting God describe his forthcoming union with his tortured and martyred Son through her voice, Maria Maddalena comes to participate in their perfect harmony. Maria Maddalena is not only the physical means through which the divinity expresses himself; the mystic is a third element of their love relationship. As we shall see later, at a certain point of the Father's discourse the mystic suddenly begins to interact with the Word, as if the perfect unity described in detail until then was not only between the Father and his Son, but also between the Word and herself. Indeed, at that point the Word will offer her his own heart. As a consequence, in his sermon the Father will address the mystic as "figliuola e sposa Unigenitis mei" (dear daugther and bride of my only Son). We could thus say that the Father *also* symbolizes the mystic's restored unity with the Word. In some passages, Maria Maddalena comes to identify with the Word himself; the perfect union between the Father and the Son is similar to the marriage between Maria Maddalena and the Word, as she has experienced it in colloqio 39.

Both the content and the form of the Father/mystic's discourse has been refashioned during the nuns' final editing. First of all, no pauses, no exclamations, and no interruptions have been reported. Moreover, the length and the perfectly logical form of Maria Maddalena's discourse can hardly correspond to its original oral version. The lengthy sermon she delivers as the Father is clearly an interpolation and not a straightforward transcription of the mystic's words. God's discourse repeats well-known theological concepts; it contains no original interpretations.

Let us examine the overall structure of the Father's sermon. Its major topic is the Father's remembrance of his perfect unity with his dead Son. As we have seen, the mystic had already discussed this theme in the earlier part of her vision. It is Maria Maddalena who, after having announced the major theme of God's sermon, divides it into distinct subsections: "Please, Father, tell me this holy soul's *deeds, words, counsels,* and *contemplation,* when it was in your bosom" (2:317, emphasis mine). In his sermon, the Father will amplify the above four points in long, independent sections. Shifting from a masculine voice to a feminine, humble one, Maria Maddalena will limit herself to interrupting his discourse with simple requests for clarification. For instance: "Padre, non intendo" (Father, I don't understand); "I would like to understand a little what this purity is. You tell me so much about this purity, but I do not understand it." To break God's long monologue, Maria Maddalena also uses brief exclamations, which stress her joy for having grasped God's complex discourse: "O eterno Padre, intendo sì sì" (Oh eternal Father, yes, yes, I understand). As a preacher, in his sermon God/Maria Maddalena makes use of recurrent rhetorical questions, in order to involve the listener (Maria Maddalena herself) in his reasoning:

> What words did he speak? He spoke words of life. . . . Didn't you hear them down there? And yet they were only for you? Didn't you recognize them? No, you did not, for you can know them only through his grace *gratis data.* (2:319)

After having laid out the four major points of God's discourse (the Word's deeds, words, intentions, and contemplations in his Father bosom), the Father takes up each of these themes and, in order to explain them in detail, subdivides them. As far as the first point is concerned, God tells Maria Maddalena that his Son's soul brought about/will bring about deeds of admiration, of might, and of wisdom. His soul transcending to his Father's bosom stirred/will stir the angels' admiration; his might attracted/will attract human souls toward him; his wisdom made/will make man sense his immense ignorance.

Maria Maddalena then asks the divinity to explain the second point of his sermon. God says that in his bosom his Son's soul utters four different kinds of words: nourishing words, attractive words, consoling words, and eternal words, and that all these four kinds could be subsumed under one sole category: words of love. According to the Father, every word the Word's soul utters is a word of love, even though human beings have difficulty in perceiving it. The Word pronounced nourishing words when he agreed to embody our human nature; he pronounced attractive words when he drew his creatures toward his Father: "This is what my Word's soul did in my bosom. He attracted and influenced; he spoke, although he did not speak; without opening his mouth he attracted my glory in order to instill it in you, because he wanted your joy to be perfect" (2:321). The Word speaks, but he does not use language. The Word pronounced consoling words also, when he asked his Father to send his Holy Spirit to each of us. Finally, he spoke eternal words, so that we might acquire eternal life.

Maria Maddalena marks the end of this section with a long exclamation ("Oh, eternal Father, your Word's holy soul gave us so much, when he was in your bosom!"), followed by a new question: Which intentions did the Word's soul have when he was in his Father's bosom? (3:322). God distinguishes among eight different intentions: intention of peace, of union, of freedom, of pity, of might, of justice, of communication, and of love (2:322–32). Intention of love, the Father says, is "to utter love. And what is love? Only by uttering love does the soul feel satisfied" (2:331).

After having examined in detail the above eight intentions of the Word's soul, God focuses on the third central point of his sermon: the Word's types of contemplation (*risguardo*) in his Father's bosom. God enumerates twenty-one different kinds of contemplation: gaze (*miratione*), admiration, love, nothingness, purity, peace, purpose, mercy, freedom, pity, justice, goodness, wisdom, might, communication, truth, union, eternity, clarification, transformation, and glory (2:334).[67] However, before letting the Father explain in detail each kind of contemplation, Maria Maddalena has a brief, but extremely significant, dialogue with the Word. Although the nuns have the impression that, by intervening in God's discourse, the mystic interrupts the flow of his sermon, her unexpected conversation with the Word is consistent with the Father's overall discourse. In fact, the Son's contemplation (*risguardo*) of the Father is similar to Maria Maddalena's contemplation of the Son: "Oh, I am rambling on. For a second I perceive something of you, and then I come back to myself" (2:335).

The first kind of contemplation, that of the gaze (*miratione*), occupies most of God's discourse (2:334–52). It is this part of his sermon that has been certainly interpolated. After a short pause from her rapture (2:352), Maria Maddalena resumes her discourse and in only five pages of the published text (2:352–57) examines the other twenty types of contemplation. However, a crucial change occurs in the second part of the sermon: the mystic herself, and not God, examines the Word's contemplations in the Father's bosom. When Maria Maddalena pronounces her speech with a masculine, divine voice, the nuns feel urged to eliminate any aspect of her spoken discourse, such as repetitions, pauses, and exclamations. When she resumes her discourse with her own voice, the transcribers reintroduce those elements that characterize her oral rhetoric. The transcribers cannot *picture* the Father's discourse as a dissected, fragmented page. The physical fragmentation can only be attributed to the female speaker.

In the first section God examines only one kind of contemplation, that of the gaze. By looking into his Father's bosom, the Son makes two divine streams spring forth: one of milk and one of blood.[68] The first one, God says, is his perfect purity. How can the soul obtain his purity? The Father explains: "one acquires this purity by being nothing, understanding nothing, holding nothing, and desiring nothing, nothing, nothing" (2:345).[69]

As far as the second divine source is concerned, when they receive his blood, each of the Word's two brides, the Church and the soul, generate two more sources: one of milk and one of blood. However, the Church first creates a source of blood and then one of milk, whereas the soul produces first blood and then milk. In both cases, by generating blood and milk both the Church and the soul purify themselves of their sins and open up to God's will. Finally, these two springs produce many good fruits: wisdom, goodness, power, justice, nourishment, and fecundity.

At this point Maria Maddalena introduces the final section of her/the Father's sermon. However, the mystic is no longer speaking as the Father, but as herself. As the contemplation between the Father and the Son equals the contemplation between the Son and the soul, in a similar manner the masculine voice narrating the past/future unity between the Father and the Son finally is equivalent to the soul narrating the future unity between the Son and herself. In this final section the Father is the blessed soul that *will be* the Son.

This is a crucial shift in Maria Maddalena's discourse, in that now she discusses primarily how the Son's death saved all of humanity. Then, after the third kind of contemplation, that of love, Maria Maddalena seemingly abandons this theme and moves on to examine the gifts the Word gave to the soul at the moment of his resurrection.

By shifting the focus of her discourse, the mystic also moves toward the conclusion of her rapture. This vision had begun with a meditation on the Word's corpse in the sepulcher. In the conclusion the mystic goes back to this original theme and connects it to the Father's speech. Indeed, whereas God had commemorated the Word's soul in his past/future unity with the Father, Maria Maddalena focuses on his dead and resurrected body. Both his soul and his body are crucial to the salvation of the soul:

> But, my soul, who loves the Word so much, remember that he is in the sepulcher [*silence*] yes, [his] soul goes to glorify [his] body in the sepulcher, and then in limbo. . . . Oh soul of the Word, yes, come back to glorify his body that is in the sepulcher. (2:353)

In the final pages of this colloquio Maria Maddalena sees the Word's death strictly related to his rebirth in the Virgin's womb.[70] Paradoxically, the incarnate Word's birth/rebirth points to a time *previous* to his stay in the Father's bosom, as if his future incarnation had been *written* in the Word before his generation in/from the Father. The mystic reminds the Virgin: "you called him, *surge gloria mea, surge psalterium meum* (Ps. 102:1–2), your glory, glory of himself, and our glory" (2:361).

The Word is similar to David's ten-string psaltery and he is "played" by his mother's fingers: "Psalterium like David's, made of ten strings" (2:362). The first two strings are his pierced and wounded feet; the third and the fourth are his hands, pierced by nails; the fifth and the sixth strings are his large chest and his heart; the seventh and the eighth are his arms and legs. The final two strings are taken from Jesus' head, tortured by the crown of thorns.

Mary signifies the soul that has learned the language/music of the Word. The Word is the melody of the creation. The "Book of Life" that Satan tries to erase is the memory of the Word's physicality. His wounds speak; his dissected body articulates the music of the world. Mary/the soul has given birth and will give birth to the Word's melody by generating a constant remembrance. Mary mourns the Word by playing his chords. The perfect awareness of the Word's absence, of his occurred death, gives birth to his melody. The music of the Word is a dirge.

Before concluding her vision, Maria Maddalena calls up the other characters that had taken part in the Word's funeral: Magdalen, John, and Peter. Repeating some key terms and expressions used in previous parts of her vision, the mystic synthesizes the theme of her rapture:

> Mary, they will not deceive you! Peter, John, and Magdalen will not do that: they wanted to go anoint him with their ointments. Oh Magdalen, you wanted to anoint him, because you thought that his body was in the sepulcher, but I would have not believed that . . . oh, John, you who rested on his chest! . . . where are the wounds? Where are the beatings, the spit, the offenses, the harm done, and the insults? Is there anything missing in your sacred body? . . . oh Word, you are all divine! There is no pain, no pain any longer. (2:365–69)

The Word's body is missing. The Magdalen wanted to anoint the corpse, but she could not find it. The Word has finally withdrawn from the world. Maria Maddalena *does not see* his wounds, his clogged blood, the spit on his face anymore. The Word has finally become the Word's word, the melody of the world.

The mystic herself has seen her physicality deeply affected by the events of the Word's biography. She has come to identify with the Father, because both of them recall/wish for an amorous union with the Son. Maria Maddalena has trespassed temporal, gender, diegetic categories. She has visited the past of the Son and his future; she has acquired a male identity in order to fathom her/his desire for the Word. Moreover, in order to stage her/his beloved's death, the mystic/Father has invited the mother to commemorate her son by playing his melody.

Colloquio 48 ends with a vision of beauty. The Word's word is the beauty of the world itself. The incarnate Word, which is no more among us, opens the mystic's eyes to the silent melody of the creation.

CHAPTER 4

The Language of Satan

Our Enemy is always with us.
—Origen, *In Lucam Homilia*

God can only be present in the world as absence.
—Simone Weil, *Cahiers III*

As I stressed in my close reading of colloquio 48, the Enemy plays a significant role in Maria Maddalena's mystical performances. Like most of the "living saints" of the first half of the sixteenth century, the Florentine visionary fights against him, yells at him, and cannot help but hear his words. As colloquio 48 clearly shows, demons are disturbances, sound interferences in the ongoing dialogue with the Son. In the vision where she sits next to his corpse in the sepulcher, the devil attacks her as an army, an untamed mob. Let us read this episode one more time:

> [R]aising her head and then lowering it down, she made gestures with her hands and her arms, bending over the window, as if she were sending them down to Hell with her own hands, and saying: "Go [*silence*] howl, scream as much as you want [*silence*] *et sublimavit humanitatis nostre* with their confusion [*silence*] *non cognoscetur amplius*. (2: 299)

The demons scream; they do not possess any sort of idiom.[1] They are beasts, as the medieval iconology often depicts them. In particular, in colloquio 48 the devils attempt to derange the mystic's performance of the Savior's death. They *occur* as a sudden and blurred memory, the Aristotelian *phantasiai* or "after-images" that drift in and out of the mind. Devils are almost-images, almost-feelings, a disquiet arising from nowhere. Devils as afterthoughts. In colloquio 48 Maria Maddalena easily dismisses them, grabbing them as ferocious and noisy animals and throwing them out of the window, down in the courtyard/hell. Like St Anthony tempted in his solitary dwelling, the Italian mystic does not doubt that they are mere images, nothing but *vociferous images*. Her body performs the imaginary act of dumping images in the abyss of absences, hell itself. Hell is indeed the nonplace where the disturbances of the mind annihilate themselves.

However, in colloquio 48 the dismissal of the demonic presences is made less disturbing by the complexity of the mystic's performance. Let us clarify this point. To be assaulted by the devils is both a present occurrence and the reenactment of a remembrance. The Latin sentence "Et collocavit eos in infernum" is in the past tense. The divinity, the mystic says, "placed" the devils in hell. And *now* she herself "places," throws them into hell. The mystic's self-confidence lies in her in-betweenness, in her not-quite-being-there.

Paradoxically, in colloquio 48 the physicality of the devils renders them less threatening. In colloquio 39 Maria Maddalena is tempted by the demons in a quite similar manner. She hears voices. A multitude of "bad angels" swears in her ears:

> [D]uring our conversation we asked her what she had been experiencing when she was shaking so intensively and crying so much that we feared that the Devil himself was hitting her like St Anthony, for she kept saying: "Oh good Jesus," screaming, crying, shaking as if she were being hit.
>
> She told us that no, she was not being hit, but she was rather hearing voices swearing in her ears, so that she was compelled to shake as she did each time that she heard those swears, because those swearers' voices terrified her. (2:16)

In this second passage Maria Maddalena is terrified by voices. She is not assaulted physically; curses echo in her mind. She does not see the Enemy; she hears him. His absence is more haunting than his image. The devil troubles the mystic's attempt to realize her being, which equals the word's Word, as Thomas Aquinas says. The devil exists insofar as he curses the absent Word. The devil's word *may* annihilate the Word.

The devil's word also affects the mystic's body. Whereas his image/body triggers her active response, his word is both a curse and a subtle whispering. As the nuns remark, she shakes as if she were being hit. By entering her mind, the devil comes to endanger the subject's whole identity. The Enemy replaces the subject's thinking with his, the devil's, own thinking. The mind thus becomes divided into two contradictory forms of thinking, a thinking denying one's own thinking. As a consequence, the body as well attacks itself. As the mind questions itself, *the body dissects itself.*

To clarify the relationship between the demonic utterance, the mystic's thinking, the demonic's physicality, and the mystic's physicality, we must analyze *Probation*, a two-volume text containing visions that occurred after *I colloqui*. *Probation* recounts the painful temptations Maria Maddalena faced for five years, from 1585 to 1590. If *I colloqui* focuses on the Word, *Probation* revolves around the Enemy. The devil visits the mystic daily, affecting both her body and her mind with excruciating sufferings. The modalities of the devil's offences are diverse. The devil can *appear* as a beast, as a multitude of roaring creatures, or as himself, although no actual description of his body is given in the text. Unlike the Word, the devil has a body that does not need to be named, for it is *naturally* known to the human being. The Word is a request for being; the devil is a multiplicity of beings.

In the second part of this chapter I will examine how the Church Fathers and the Inquisition interpreted the devil's speaking. In so doing, we will be able to understand better how Maria Maddalena converses with her Foe.

In *Probation* the devil attacked the "blessed soul" for the first time on June 16th, 1585:

> [S]he heard with her ears the horrible screams and howls that the Devil . . . pronounced to offend God. And sometimes these screams occupied her hearing to the point that she had difficulty in under-standing us when we spoke to her. . . . The devils afflicted her body by pushing her down the stairs, making her fall down; and other times, like vipers, they wrapped around her body biting her in the flesh with great cruelty. (*Probation*, 1:33–34)

In this passage the devils' utterance combines the two elements present in colloqui 39 and 48. The devil both screams in the mystic's ears and speaks to her. His speech conveys a message and deafens the mystic's hearing, so that she cannot help but listen to his curses. In another passage (*Probation*, 1:124), the transcribers stress that at times the mystic could not hear them because of the devils' loud swearing. In other words, Maria Maddalena suddenly became deaf to the world's voice.

But why should someone else's cursing affect a believer's faith? Why does the mystic feel that her identity is jeopardized by the demons' offensive words?[2] In fact, the devil articulates a language of negativity that resounds like an echo of the mystic's own utterance. As the guardian angels, according to Origen, repeat our prayers to the divinity without being heard by us, so does the devil encourage the mystic to recognize his words as her own words. In other words, the subject's language and the devil's may overlap, since the signifiers they articulate are the same. To hear the devil's voice *might* mean to hear one's own voice. St Teresa of Avila alludes to a similar experience when, for instance, she writes that "he [Satan] tells us directly, or make us think, that we poor sinners may admire but must not imitate the deeds of the saints."[3]

The devil's word indeed *crosses* the speaker's subjectivity. The Enemy speaks and by speaking *distracts us from our self-awareness*. How should we otherwise interpret the devil's physical offences, his pushing the mystic down the stairs, his biting her stomach, his making her trip down? The Enemy aims to distract her from herself with sudden, disruptive actions. In those moments, when the body falls down, the soul as well *might* fall. The soul, the heart, *might* forget its sole task, the articulation of the Word.

The Enemy's attacks are never physically fatal. In fact, like the Word, the devil needs an interlocutor. He needs to be listened to. On September 17th, 1587, Maria Maddalena became ill. She could not leave her bed; an intense fever gave her painful migraines for more than fifteen days (1:114–15). When she tried to stand up and participate in the morning Mass, the devil made her fall down the stairs. She fell again on November 1st (1:119) and on February 9th (1:134).

Other female mystics experience similar demonic intrusions. Benvenuta Bojanni (Cividale of Friuli, 1255–92) sometimes was taken up in the air by the devil and then thrown on the floor with extreme violence. Once she even wrestled with him on the ground:

> Sometimes it happened that [the devil] took her and rose her up, and then with great violence he hurled her down . . . once . . . she stood up against him, grabbed him and pushed him down under her feet. Then, putting a foot on his neck, she scolded at him with outraged words.[4]

As Maria Maddalena threw the demons out of the window, Benvenuta responded to the devil's physical assaults by fighting back. In *The Life of the blessed Benvenuta Boianne* the devil ends up by begging the strong mystic for mercy. She has humiliated him. Instead of stones, Teresa of Avila uses holy water: "I have learned from the experience of several occasions that there is nothing that the devils fly from more promptly, never to return, than from holy water" (223).

In *Probation* Maria Maddalena has a reaction similar to Benvenuta's and Teresa's. All of a sudden, a devil jumped on her, as if he wished to devour her. She picked up some big stones and threw them at him, screaming: "Leave me alone, you, horrible beast, don't come close to me. In the name of Jesus, I tell you, leave me alone" (1:73). Months later, while she was praying with her sisters in the chapel, the mystic detected a bunch of demons trying to step into the room unnoticed. Since one of them had already entered that sacred place, Maria Maddalena grabbed a crucifix and, using it as a sword, kicked those beasts out of the chapel (1:179).

The relationship between Maria Maddalena and the Enemy, however, only rarely acquires such a distinct theatricality. The devil's *disturbances* are usually less dramatic, but much more distressful, because they tend to refrain from any physicality. Let us resume the narration of Maria Maddalena's sudden and intense fever. When she recovers from her disease, a drastic change occurs in the devil's language. The devil succeeds in making Maria Maddalena think his own words. He starts by instilling doubts about her way of thinking. The mystic has difficulty in drawing the line between his thoughts, his images, and hers:

> [T]he Devil [started] to put doubts and fears in her mind about the holy and austere life she has embraced for God's will. He made her think that that was not God's will, like walking barefoot and wearing only a gown, both in winter and in summer, as she had decided to do a few months before. (1:116–17)

Maria Maddalena went so far as to contemplate the possibility of leaving the convent (1:124). "She had the impression," the nuns report, "that whatever she did, both externally and internally, would deepen her damnation" (1:140). Rather than disrupting her daily life with sudden attacks, the Enemy made the mystic play his own role. The mystic became her own Enemy. As de Certeau says about the notorious possession that took place in the monastery of Loudun, the nuns haunted by the devils stated "I is another."[5] The possessed nuns perceived that they had become the *site* where the Other resided. The battle between the Inquisition and the devil is primarily linguistic. Indeed, the devil refuses to speak as soon as he conquers a creature's identity. In order to defeat him, the judges of the Inquisition must force the possessor to pronounce his name(s).

Maria Maddalena's daily life and her familiar places, which in *I colloqui* had turned into settings of the Word's death—the kitchen garden, the staircases, the dormitory, the scriptorium, the chapel—became *equivocal*. Her life, her sisters write, became "an exile" (1:156)."[6] The language of the devil, his most eloquent utterance, is a sight that doubts its seeing, and thus exiles the subject from herself.[7] The nuns asked Maria Maddalena to explain the nature of the demonic oppression. What did she actually see? Did she see him all the time? Did she always see him with her "corporeal eye"?

> She told us that she does not always see him with her corporeal eye, but she always sees him with the eye of the mind with no respite, as when (similarly) a creature sees something with her corporeal eye, and then that something stays in her mind so clearly that, even if she does not see it concretely, she has the impression that she always sees it. (1:73–74)

The devil has the substance of memory. Remembrances *cross* the subject's mind without any warning. Maria Maddalena knew that, like any memory, the devil had impressed his image in her mind. Not only did he not need to speak, he also did not need to be visible. The devil *is* even before acquiring an image, as any memory lingers in the mind before expressing itself in a picture. Whereas the devil signified his presence through a lack of presence, since the mystic had absorbed his image, the Word's picture resulted intolerable to the mystic's "internal eyes." On January 28th of the same year, Maria Maddalena fainted when she came across a picture of Jesus crucified on the cross: "She cried for a long time and screamed a lot because of the intrinsic light and knowledge that she had of herself; and often she said: 'I would go to hell if there I could undo my offenses'" (*Probation*, 1:133).[8] If in *I colloqui* her pains primarily derived from the devil's cursing in her ear and from his bestial attacks, in *Probation* her anguish came from the vision of the Word.

The Word hurt the mystic by *showing* her her true "nature" through the image of the offenses he received on the cross. In other words, the Word serves the cause of the Enemy by testifying to the devil's power over the soul. However, by showing himself as an image reflecting the Enemy, the Word *shows* the Enemy itself, and thus grants the soul the vision of her hidden Foe. Paradoxically, in *Probation* the Word *signifies* the Enemy; the Word is an *index* of the devil. As I have already pointed out, an *index* is the sign of memory. An *index* says what is not there, like a hole in a wall reminds us of a bullet. Similarly, the picture of the Word's passion is an index of the demons who have crept into the mystic's soul.

In the visions of Caterina Vegri (1413–1463) the image of the Word on the cross serves a totally opposite purpose. In *Sette armi spirituali* (*Seven Spiritual Weapons*) Caterina recounts a vision in which the crucified Christ appeared to her and scolded her because of her deficient obedience to her mother superior. In fact, the Christ on the cross was an impostor.[9] The devil's deceit was a paradox. He said what God was supposed to say. Is not total obedience to one's spiritual guidance (confessor, mother superior, etc.) a necessary practice for every female religious?

One morning, when she entered the church to pray, all of a sudden he [the devil] appeared to her in the form of Christ on the cross. He was crucified with his arms open, suspended above her. And in a friendly and benign manner, as he simply wanted to tell her off, he said: "Thief, you have robbed me. Give me back what you have taken from me." And since she believed that he was Jesus Christ, with reverence and love—because it seemed plausible to her that, given the submission of her mind to him, he would manifest himself with his body—she answered: "My Lord, why do you say that? I have nothing; I am miserable and annihilated to you, and am not submitted to anybody else as I am submitted to you." [And the devil/Christ replies:] "You had promised to offer me your obedience. You gave it to me and then you took it back. This is why I tell you you are a thief." And then she understood that he said that because she had had some thoughts

against the Mother Superior. . . . Thus, she answered: "My Lord, what
can I do? My heart is not free and I can't prevent thoughts from coming up in my mind."[10]

The devil here pronounces the Word's words. What gives him away, so
to speak, is the colloquial virulence of his saying. The mystic thought the
Christ/devil's words over and came to the conclusion that the Impostor's
style was not appropriate to the divinity. However, it is important to
note that the devil used a cornerstone of Catholic doctrine in order to
make the mystic sin. Caterina did not agree with her mother superior's
conduct. The mystic could not help but think this thought. "Thoughts
cross my mind," she said to the Impostor in the attempt to justify herself. As we shall see later, the Church Fathers debated at length about
the scope of the devil's power. Can the Enemy read the creature's mind?
Most of the theologians believe that the devil can instill temptations into
the subject's mind but he cannot know what the subject is actually
thinking. To sin exclusively means to express one's free will. The Church
must defend the axiom that every human being is intellectually and
morally free, and that neither the divinity nor the devil can induce her to
do something if she does not want to. Thus, the Church holds that both
the divinity and the Enemy can speak to the subject but cannot think
their thoughts. In Caterina Vegri's mystical experience, however, this
wiev is undermined. The devil does know that she had disrespectul
thoughts toward her mother superior.

As Maria Maddalena read her sins in the picture of the true Savior,
Caterina read her non-sin in the image of the untrue Savior. Caterina
sincerely believed that the mother superior was in error. Caterina knew
that to disagree with the mother superior could be a sin, but she also
sensed that she had the right to disagree with her spiritual guidance. The
devil thus endeavored to muddle the mystic's self-reflection; he tried to
split her thinking. Again, the Foe is primarily a disturbance, a
sound/image that aims to multiply the voice(s) of one's mind.

However, it is crucial to understand that the devil's multiplicity is
contingent upon the Word's withdrawn presence. Let us remember that
the Word has still to be uttered. The word's Word, as Thomas says, his
manifestation in the world, is a project. The Word is what the Word
could become. The world expects its second creation. The devil uses the
signifier "Word" (his image, his rhetoric, his *mythèmes*, such as his crucifixion, his bleeding side, etc.) and multiplies it. However, the signifier
"Word" signifies nothing, or better yet, signifies a *nothingness*, whereas
"devil" is what the Word's absence has brought about in the creation.
The devil's language is thus the un-uttered language of the Savior.

The "Word" is a "signifier-signified," a nondivision, a word that names itself, a world that contemplates itself in itself like in a mirror. "The Word" embodies the Word and no Enemy can make this embodiment "opaque," uncertain, because the Enemy is deprived of any language since language is exclusively the language of the Word. What the human kind speaks is the memory of the Word, as it has been "rewritten" by the Enemy. However, it is unquestionable that every word we pronounce is a word *directed to* the Word, every word reaches the Word as a failed communication. Our words do not pronounce him. Angela of Foligno refers to this point when she says: "Everything I say is a curse." We may infer that, when the devil cursed in Maria Maddalena's ears, he was echoing Maria Maddalena's own words. As I have pointed out, this is the mystic's most distressing realization, that is, her sudden awareness that the devil's words are able to cross her mind, and that she is pronouncing those very words. The more the subject speaks, the more the devil perceives his language spoken.

As we shall see, the theoreticians of the Inquisition understood that no sacred word can defeat the Enemy. Whereas several medieval Church Fathers theorized that a prayer or a biblical verse had the power of sending the devil away, in the Renaissance some members of the Inquisition questioned the efficacy of any language. Both physical and verbal language are "marred," as Maria Maddalena says, by the Enemy's deceitful duplicity. Every statement is intrinsically double, and thus eludes any single interpretation.

According to Augustine's *The City of God* (book 12), one of Maria Maddalena's basic readings, the Enemy's duplicity derives from the fact that he "has less of being," that is, more than a duplicity, evil is a lack of being:

> Let no one . . . look for an efficient cause of the evil will; for it is not efficient, but deficient, as the will itself is not an effecting of something, but a defect. For defection from that which supremely is, to that which has less of being—this is to begin to have an evil will. Now, to seek to discover the causes of these defections . . . is as if some one sought to see darkness, or hear silence.[11]

To fathom evil's being, Augustine states, is a paradox; it is as if one tried to see darkness or to hear silence. The "Prince of this world," as Augustine says in *Confessions*, speaks a *mute language*, and thus it is its sole interlocutor.[12] When the Son became incarnate, he restored the *possibility* of a dialogue between the world, ruled by the Enemy, and the Trinity. However, as Maria Maddalena's visions show, the only available language between the creature and the Second Person of the Trinity is the Word's death. We might say that in fact the Word became incarnate in order to die.

However, the goal of the "Prince of this world" is to procrastinate the Word's death. Since the death of the Word corresponds to his pronunciation, Satan disturbs the language of the Word's speaker, the world itself. We have seen that in colloquio 48 Maria Maddalena underscores that Satan constantly tries to erase "the Book of Life" (*liber vitae*), the world/text that recounts the incarnation, death, and resurrection of the Word (2:308).

The Church Fathers were aware of the devil's project. Indeed, in their texts they obsessively repeated that the air itself is infected with invisible devils.[13] In *On the Devils' Divination* Augustine states that the devils, being *the* incorporeal inhabitants of the air, travel much faster than any human being. This is why they are able to foretell the future.[14] In the second book of *Moralia* Gregory the Great reiterates the same concept, stressing that the "spirits of the air" are jealous of every wise man that directs his mind toward the "skies," because he reminds the devil of the place he was expelled from.[15] In fact, as Augustine writes, the "vast sea" of the air is at once the devil's reign and his prison. He cannot escape from the air of the world.[16] After having being rejected by the Father, the fallen angel "pervolitat," "vagat," wanders in the air. Like the angels, the demons do not possess a body. Whereas the good angels derive their spiritual physicality from the divinity (the angels feed on God's bread), the fallen angels are envious because they are not allowed to participate in God's banquet.

In sermon 52 Peter Chrysologus offers a striking interpretation of the devil's status as a being residing in the air. His sermon revolves around the episode of the epileptic demoniac in Mark 9 (Cf. Matt. 17:14–21; Luke 9:37–43). Peter Chrysologus underscores that the epileptic's father does not say "attuli filium meum surdum et mutum" (I brought my deaf and mute son) but rather "attuli filium meum habentem spiritum surdum et mutum" (I brought my son who has a deaf and mute spirit).[17] Peter Chrysologus sees a crucial difference between the two statements. The devilish spirit is both deaf and mute, and makes the boy deaf and mute. Do we not know, Peter Chrysologus asks us, that the devil has no body; that the devil does not have a tongue to speak with; that the devil has no bones, no flesh, so that he can cross the air with an extraordinary celerity and can "pierce through" (*transverberet*) our hearts in order to infect our passions and thoughts? (Chrysologus, 345). The devil, the commentator adds, turns the human heart into his own "retreat" (*latebram*).

The devil possesses the boy by preventing him from expressing his status of possessed. Indeed, the Inquisition considered of crucial importance the fact that some possessed souls refrained from speaking or were unable to speak, even under torture. As we have seen, Maria Maddalena experiences something similar. The devil shouted into her ears, so that she would be unable to hear what her sisters tried to tell her. In other words, the devil is able to use language in order to attain his goals, but in fact he does not possess a voice and does not know how to speak. The devil does not have a language.

As Peter Chrysologus stresses, Jesus freed the boy from the deaf and mute spirit by speaking to the spirit himself: "Deaf and mute spirit, I command you: Come out of him." Language *reveals* the devil that does not have a language of his own. As Gregory the Great says, the devil does not possess anything of his own ("Nihil autem maligni spiritus in hoc mundo proprium possidet").[18] Articulating his word, Jesus annihilated the deaf and mute being of the devil. If the world, according to Augustine, is ruled by the Enemy, the world manifests his, the devil's, silence. The world does not perceive its own silence, its incapacity of uttering the Word. If silence rules over the world, chaos and multiplicity blur the world's status of signifier of the divinity. As Augustine states in *On Christian Doctrine*, every "thing" is a verbal expression addressed to the divinity. However, the world is not aware of the fact that *it is constantly speaking to the Word.*

Gregory the Great tackled the problem of the world's deaf and mute language in a crucial passage in *XL Homiliriarum in Evangelia*. In homily 29, Gregory wonders why the early Church pronounced words that had direct, immediate effects in the world, whereas *now* these beneficial effects are not visible any longer. One first reason is that we do not believe in those *signs* anymore: "Nunquidnam, fratres mei, quia ista signa non facitis, minime creditis? Sed haec necessaria in exordio Ecclesiae fuerunt."[19] It is as if, Gregory states, we planted a seed without watering the earth ("si semel radicem fixerint, in rigando cessamus"). Referring to Paul's 1 Corinthians (14:22), Gregory underscores that *signs* are now marred by their speakers. However, Gregory believes that our language does not have visible effects on the world also because *now* our language has become spiritual, whereas *before* it was material. In *De efficacia aque benedicte* (1476) Turrecremata reiterates this point by listing the numerous beneficial effects of holy water. In chapter 5 of his treatise Turrecremata states that, by pronouncing certain words, the priest has the power to turn water into a powerful tool against the "insidias dyaboli" and his illusions.[20] The holy water also brings about a purification of "pestilentie sive aure corrumpentis." In other words, the positive effects of our utterances/signs are still present, albeit not immediately visible. We cannot hear our own *signs* as signifiers anymore, even though they can still generate signifieds: "Sancta quippe Ecclesia quotidie spiritaliter facit quod tunc per apostolos corporaliter faciebat."

It is apparent that Gregory's analysis of our "spiritual" language is unable to solve its basic problem. How can we tell if and when we are uttering a word that believes in itself, that is, a word proceeding from a pure heart? If the devil is *the* master of doubt and silence, how can we know if we are really speaking or not? The Church Fathers must express their unflinching belief in man's free will. In order to sin, a human being *must* know that he/she is sinning. In *Summa Theologica* (Ia. 83:1, 786) Thomas Aquinas writes: "Man is free to make decisions. Otherwise counsels, precepts, prohibitions, rewards and punishment would all be pointless." We might say that, according to Thomas, every language exchange is based on the risks of free will. If, as Gregory the Great reminds us in *Moralia*, the human heart is an "abyss" ("Quid hoc loco abyssum nisi corda hominum vocat? quae et per lapsum fluida et per duplicitatis sunt caliginem tenebrosa"), how can man fathom his own abyss?[21]

If human language springs from one's unknown heart/abyss, a human being cannot detect the (im)purity of his/her speech. This is why the words pronounced by the priests sometimes *work* and sometimes don't. Not only does language express a message directed to the world and to its Prince, it also speaks to the divinity, who can *read* the abyss of the human heart. Language both brings about our sins and formulates our sorrows for those very sins. Psalm 138 says: "The word is not even on my tongue,/God, before you know all about it" (v. 4).

It is clear now why the Word needs to become incarnate in Maria Maddalena's orality. By entering the body/voice of the mystic, the Word would participate in the world and would be able to confront its Prince. When Maria Maddalena performed her visions, she endeavored to make the world speak, and thus to break the silence of its Ruler. In fact, when the devils pushed her down the staircase or bit her belly, they aimed to interrupt, so to speak, the mystic's linguistic apprenticeship.

Maria Maddalena perceived the world's sinful muteness and deafness. Her sisters understood that Maria Maddalena was trying to "belch forth" a different word, a different language. The nuns' manuscripts are the main evidence of their *watching* the mystic in her attempt. Throughout the seven volumes of Maria Maddalena's raptures, the transcribers marked the *signs* of the mystic's performances in order to detect the *site* of her new word.

The devil himself blurs the message communicated by Maria Maddalena's performances. In several passages, the nuns connect the mystic's sudden silence with her being attacked by the Enemy. In other words, the mystic's silence is always read as a *sign* of disturbance. Maria Maddalena must speak. Even her most cryptic gestures can be interpreted and inserted in a narrative structure, but not her pauses. A pause is nothing but the reflection of the world's pause, of its devilish non-speaking or misspeaking. The mystic *must* produce signs.[22] In *La possession de Loudun*, recounting the notorious possession of an entire convent in the seventeenth century, de Certeau highlights the crucial role played by the possessed's body as a "map" illustrating the history of the subject's possession. The words narrating the effects of the possession "describe this surface [the possessed's body] where each sign is a phenomenon; . . . this surface [is] rich with events."[23]

In other words, to interpret one's body means to read it and to read it means to insert the debris of (possible) meanings into a narrative structure. I have stressed that, when the devil visits Maria Maddalena's mind, she starts to doubt her seeing/interpreting. However, the act of doubting is both a curse and a blessing. Let us remember that the Word himself has allowed the devil to enter the mystic's mind in order to purify it. The devil's doubt is a blessing for the subject when she recognizes it as a doubt, when thanks to that doubt the subject comes to question the "less than being" of the world and starts to "narrate" it.

However, in *Probation* Maria Maddalena senses that every narrative is in fact unfounded. Rather than assisting the subject in her act of interpreting the world, every narrative must conceal *some* signs that might blur the world's alleged reading. Moreover, the Florentine mystic comprehends that the main, albeit hidden, character of any narrative is the narrator himself. Although the world is deaf and mute because of the Word's absence, the world needs to believe in the appearance of clear and distinct signs. In *Probation* not only does Maria Maddalena come to perceive the absence of the Word and thus also her sinful nature, she is also invaded by the silence of the Prince of the world.

Her convent sisters attempted to make sense of the mystic's physicality, gestures, exclamations. In other words, the nuns must turn her being into a narrative. Since every manifestation of the world acquires its status of sign by participating in a given narrative, it is imperative to stress the absolutely intentional nature of any narrative. Maria Maddalena's performances could have been read in a totally different manner, that is, as expressions of insanity, of a devilish possession, of a contrived, *insincere* theatricality, and so on. The fact that Maria Maddalena seemed to converse with the Word, that she seemed to follow him through his passion and death, that she seemed to abhor the devil, did not entail that her *readers* would necessarily construct a narrative corresponding to what *seemed to occur*. The construction of a given narrative is exclusively intentional. This is why at the end of each volume containing Maria Maddalena's visions, the transcribers added a list of "testimonies," which did not limit themselves to stating that a given witness was present at the mystic's rapture, they also interpret those events as divine communications. In other words, Maria Maddalena's experiences can be read *only* in a certain manner. For instance, *The Forty Days*, which is the first volume of the mystic's visions, ends with the testimony of seven witnesses, Maria Maddalena's confessor, the mother superior, and five sisters. Sister Maria Pacifica del Tovaglia writes the following declaration:

> I, sister Maria Pacifica del Tovaglia . . . testify that I have seen the aforementioned sister in several raptures and in excesses of love, as it has been written in this book. And I believe that these events were more than human. They proceeded from a heart burning for the true and perfect love of Jesus. (*The Forty Days*, 267)

In fact, most of Maria Maddalena's physical and emotional reactions are strikingly similar to those shown by persons considered possessed by the devil. In *Probation* Maria Maddalena herself is "invaded" by the Enemy. However, the writers of the manuscript held that this intrusion was part of a process of mystical purification. The mystic was "monitored," so to speak, by the Word himself, who allowed the devil to torment the "blessed soul" by showing her the mute and deaf unfoundedness of creation.

However, we must bear in mind that the mystic *was indeed assaulted* by the Enemy. The ambiguity of the mystic's experience should not be overlooked. The theatricality of her struggle with the devil is set on a stage, the world itself (for instance the convent, the dormitory, the scriptorium, the kitchen garden), that neither confirms nor contradicts the nuns' interpretations. The nuns interpreted the seven volumes of their transcriptions as an unusual hagiography (hagiography is necessarily the narration of a dead "blessed soul," whose holiness is recounted *a posteriori*), because they saw the mystic's gestures and monologues as signs at once resulting from and confirming their textuality. From the very beginning Maria Maddalena was the main character of a text. She was made to speak in a clear and distinct manner. As a consequence, we may infer that Maria Maddalena was *saved* by her fictionality.

Salvation or damnation are the two basic poles of the image of the self. A given subject is either destined to heaven or doomed to hell. The Inquisition underscores this crucial element in its obsessive research for clear and distinct signs. The immense production of manuals about how to detect and to punish a witch, are nothing but semiotic texts. Their authors strove to formulate the epistemology of the devil's language. However, as de Certeau stresses, in order to read the devil's signs the interpreter/judge must enter the field of the world/event to be read.[24] A given possession becomes readable only if and when the exorcist is engaged in an act of narration, that is, when he becomes an actant of that event. Only when the judge *gazes at* the possessed body, does that body acquire its status of possessed.

Indeed, in the preface to *Thesaurus exorcismorum* (1608), a popular compilation of late Renaissance treatises on exorcism, Valerio Polidori explains that God allows the devil to assault and possess a soul for a variety of different reasons.[25] First, the divinity may want the soul to realize that the devil does exist, that he is not a legend. A skeptical person might need to be exposed to the devil in order to become more humble. Second, the devil may be God's punishment for the soul's mortal sins. Third, God may withdraw his protection from a soul so that the soul becomes holier and purer. Fourth, by confronting the devil's attack a soul may reveal to the world its holiness. Finally, the devil might be a messenger of God's infinite might. In this case the devil would be a sort of bland sample of God's terrifying omnipotence.

The devil's intervention is thus an event that requires an interpretation. The Enemy may be sent by God either to save the soul or to damn it. The devil does not mean necessarily that the soul abhors God. The devil is a signifier with two contradictory signifieds: God's love and God's condemnation. Thus, the possessed as well must be interpreted. Her body may *mean* either her forthcoming execution or her salvation.

That the detection of a "bad" soul necessitates the judge's participation in the devil's silent saying, is apparent in the notorious *De la démonomanie des sorciers* (1593) by Jean Bodin. Bodin, a jurist, laments the fact that Germans have the erroneous tendency of not executing the persons convicted of witchcraft. Germans are too lenient in believing the witches' expressions of penance.[26] For Bodin, language, in its broadest sense, is not a sign. The language of the world *manifests itself* but its meaning is either hidden or absent. This is why, for instance, prayers have no effect against the devil (Bodin, 24). The possessed can go so far as to confess before taking communion and can even take communion. In fact, Bodin writes, it has been proved that the devil can hide under the possessed's tongue while the possessed receives the body and the blood of Christ (299).

Thus, the judge himself must play a double role. On the one hand, he must show a false compassion for the defendant (Bodin, 322). If the defendant is shy or reluctant, the judge must assure her/him that nobody will be present at her/his deposition (Bodin, 318). In fact, a group of witnesses will be behind a fake wall and will write down everything the victim says. Given "the exceptional situation," the judge should not follow any of the usual procedures (Bodin, 336). In other words, the judge embraces the devil's duplicity in order to unveil his, the devil's, duplicity.

More than evidences (confessions, penance, tears, etc.), *indexes* may be helpful. In fact, for Bodin an *index* always turns out to be an evidence of someone's *present* guilt. The term *index* must be interpreted in the Peircean way, as the sign of memory, of imagination. For her convent sisters, are not Maria Maddalena's long silences indexes of her either conversing with the Word or fighting against the devils? Are not her tears *indexes* of her perceiving the Word's sufferings? Maria Maddalena's performances are *indexes* insofar as they do not point to an "object," but they rather trigger their audience's memory and imagination. However, both silence and tears can be also *indexes* of a devilish possession. In *Malleus maleficarum* (1476) Jacob Sprenger defines silence as "maleficium taciturnitatis."[27] As long as the defendant is alone in a cell, the devil has complete access to her/him (cf. Bodin, 378). Again, the devil speaks (in) silence.[28]

Bodin suggests that the Inquisition place a box next to every confessional, so that people may report anything they consider abnormal or strange (Bodin, 318). In other words, the believers are allowed to accuse whoever stirs their imagination. Since everything in the world is an *index*, everything (for instance, the devil can make the animals speak, Menghi, 212–15) or everyone may be an *index* of the Enemy.

In *Probation* we have seen that the devil is most eloquent when he refrains from speaking and makes the mystic think his thoughts. Maria Maddalena's act of thinking is itself an *index*. We might say that the Inquisition's ruthless cruelty is nothing but a failed attempt to write a grammar of the world. As the Protestant demonologist Lambert Daneau said in *Deux traiez nouveaux très utiles pour ce temps*, it is necessary to torture the body until "truth comes out of her [the possessed's] mouth."[29] Sprenger believes that torture should not be limited to a specific part of the body, for each member may reveal the truth. However, Sprenger stresses that the judge must be careful not to touch the possessed's body. In other words, the body is replete with a language that must be purged and eventually annihilated through fire. By coming into contact with a body contaminated with the Enemy's language, the judge might be infected with the same rhetoric. Each member of the body has something to confess. The body *appears* far too eloquent for the judge, even though he is unable to translate its idiom into his own.

Rather than relying on linguistic expression, the Inquisition pursued the body as the quintessential idiom of the world. Do not the transcribers of *I colloqui* and *Probation* carefully report the mystic's physical expressions, her shaking on the floor, her reddened eyes, her running around the convent? Is not Maria Maddalena's body the site whence the Father comes to articulate his Law? Is not her body the *index* of the devil's presence when she stops speaking?

Every suspect must be totally shaved and examined carefully (Bodin, 358; Menghi, 479). Each part of her/his body may reveal a *sign*, an *icon* of the devil. This is what the torturers look for. They need an *icon*. Satan is believed to mark the possessed with some kind of sign. Interestingly enough, the above demonologists do not specify the nature of this sign. What does this sign depict? However, Bodin stresses the imperative importance of detecting *the* sign. For instance, a man had the devil's sign behind his eyelids. Others may have it under their tongue or under their feet (Bodin, 360). In fact, the devil's *icon* is an *index* itself, that is, the marked body points to a previous occurrence whose nature is not detectable. The sign marked on the body limits itself to *signifying*.

What the Inquisition needed was a body that revealed a narrative event (for instance, the defendant's secret encounters with the devil). The judges wished to bring to the fore a narration of the body and pursued their narrative by inflicting sufferings on the body itself. In a similar manner, female mystics interpreted physical pain as a grace, since through pain their body recalled the Savior's death.

The world's ambiguity lies in its indexicality. The world *is* memory itself, or better yet, it is a mark, possibly a sign, of a past presence. The authors of our parallel texts, that is, the Florentine nuns and the exorcists, *Probation* and Menghi's, Bodin's, and Sprenger's manuals of torture, produce signs out of blurred marks (the possessed's silent body, the mystic's screams, her gestures, etc.). It is however crucial to understand that the act of narrating the other's experiences, such as Maria Maddalena's participation in the Word's funeral or the witches' sexual intercourse with the Enemy, primarily means the legitimization of the author as such.

Are not the above manuals on exorcism both compilations of rituals and anthologies of gruesome short stories? The science of the devil is in fact the narration, the "biography" of the devil. Like the world itself, the devil possesses a powerful but obscure rhetoric that must be exposed to language and then silenced through given behaviors based on "experience," that is, based on previous narrations. Indeed, in their detailed dos and donts (when/if it is necessary to fast, when/if it is good to pray, where one should keep the possessed, if certain herbs are beneficial against the demons, etc.) the authors *always* attempted to manifest the devil's *presence*.[30] The written is itself the means through which the devil is brought to the surface of meaning.

One interesting aspect of the above manuals on demonology may clarify the relationship between seeing/narrating and exposing oneself to the devil. Debating whether the devils are able to perceive man's thoughts or not, Menghi attributes to the devil those skills that the judges would like to master. Repeating a theory present in Augustine's

On the Devils' Divination, Menghi holds that God does not allow the devil to fathom man's thinking. However, given his exceptional expertise, the devil knows how to *read* man's physicality, and thus he can see what man has in mind by examining his gestures, movements, tone of voice, eye expression, and so forth.[31]

The devil interprets and inhabits the world's idiom, its physicality, but he does not possess it. As the Church Fathers stress, the devil is doomed to inhabit the "air" between heaven and earth. In other words, the Enemy knows the language of the world but he is not a "native speaker." He does not belong there. Like the angels, the demons occupy a given physicality only temporarily. The demons invade animals, corpses, trees, because they need a bodily instrument to articulate sounds similar to human language. The devil lives this radical duplicity. He rules over a world that does not belong to him; he performs a language without being capable of speaking.

More than being tempted by the devil, the mystic was allowed to apprehend what I called the indexicality of the world. She came to sense that the world has no meaning, because the world has no memory. The world is an index deprived of memory. However, the mystic's experience of erasure and annihilation (her being abandoned by the Word to a world that means nothing without him) concluded with her receiving the Word as enlightenment, both as an unquenchable and quenched desire for the Word. Whereas the world and its Prince deny any reference, any memory of itself, the Word enacts the memory of desire.

This is the beginning of what the transcribers consider Maria Maddalena's final monologue in *Probation*:

> *Magnus Dominus* [*silence*] it is such a great light [*silence*] it is a seal that the demons can neither take away nor move [*silence*] all the powers of hell cannot take away what you gave me, and who could prevent me from wanting what you want? [*silence*] if everybody saw it, one would take his heart and expose it to that light! [*silence*] it's enough the way it enters the soul [*silence*] this is what transforms and beatifies the soul [*silence*] you cannot ask the creatures about it, nobody can know it. One must accept what you manifest. (*Probation*, 2:262)

Maria Maddalena sees a blinding light. The end of her temptations is in fact marked by blindness. If during her temptations she saw the world as an unstable vision, now she is deprived of that seeing. Not even the devils can take this blindness from her. The act of being marked, "sealed," by the Word, is equivalent to the gift of blindness.[32]

Blindness is the revelation of the Word. The Word reveals himself to the mystic as nonseeing. Maria Maddalena also knows that nobody can explain to her the meaning of that "great" light. Instead of questioning the light, one must "accept what you manifest." What the Word manifests to her after five years of pains and solitude is his being blindness.

If the narrations of the witches' trials inevitably end with the defendants' perceiving their imminent death, Maria Maddalena's "trial" concludes with her realizing that the world is neither an icon nor an index. If an icon shows what it is at present and an index alludes to what it might have been, Maria Maddalena is granted the gift of seeing that the world is nothing but *the deaf and mute sign of what is going to be.* The world is *marked* with the Word's imminent advent.

However, a final element must be clarified. We must keep in mind that both "trials," the witches' and the mystic's, are narratives. Both the demonologists and the Florentine nuns intend their writing both as a reportage and a fiction. By "fiction" I mean a literary genre that is constructed according to the law of meaning. A fiction has a given directionality, that is, it moves toward closure. In Bodin's and Menghi's narrations the end is the execution of a "damned soul." The Inquisition finally detects the *sign* of the devil in the witch's body, and therefore it is entitled to enact the end of the possessed's narrative.

The law of closure is respected in Maria Maddalena's *Probation* as well. After being blinded by the Word, the mystic reencounters the Enemy. *Probation* started with the devil's attack on the mystic's body and mind, and it ends with the mystic's victory over the Enemy. If, at the beginning of the book, Maria Maddalena is silenced by the devil's enlightenment, at the end she turns silence into speech. Having being blessed with the Word's grace, the mystic knows how to read the physicality of the world.

Probation ends with two eloquent chapters. Like every hagiography, the text concludes with the blessed soul healing mortal diseases and humiliating the Enemy.[33] In 1592 a nun called Cherubina became very ill. High fevers tormented her and two open wounds in her side bled incessantly. A priest was asked to confess her because her condition was so critical that her sisters doubted that she would survive. As soon as the priest stepped into the nun's cell, some words crossed Cherubina's mind: "If you want to heal, go to Maria Maddalena's bed" (2:253). Her sisters helped her walk to the mystic's bed. "A marvelous thing" happened. After a few hours of rest in Maria Maddalena's bed, Cherubina felt incredibly better. She stood up and resumed her duties in the convent as if she had never been sick. In other words, Maria Maddalena had already become a holy relic, even her sheets were "soaked" with her santity. *Probation,* we may infer, concludes with the mystic's death as sinful human being. Maria Maddalena could withdraw from her narrative at any time. She could die at any time.

Probation recounts a second final event. In 1601 Maria Maddalena was asked to meet with a young girl who was tormented by numerous evil spirits (*Probation*, 2:254). These demons prevented her from speaking. The young girl, whose nickname is "Wild," reminded the reader of what the mystic experienced at the beginning of the book. However, as soon as she saw Maria Maddalena, the young girl started to chat with her. The mystic also gave the girl her benediction and recited a prayer with her.

Let us remember that the world is neither an icon nor an index, but rather a mark that is not a sign *yet*, because its status of clear and distinct sign will be granted to it at the Word's advent. Maria Maddalena has received the gift of foreseeing/foresensing the Word's presence. Paradoxically, Maria Maddalena has learned that the Word is both still absent from the world and present in his imminent arrival. We may say that *Probation* ends with the mystic's victory over the world's silence. The young girl possessed by the evil spirits went back to the convent a second time. She told Maria Maddalena that, every time she thought of her, the devils left her in peace. The mystic crossed and blessed the girl. All of a sudden, the girl rolled her eyes, shook, and looked as if she were being strangled because her throat gagged incredibly.

Maria Maddalena observed the girl's physical reactions. When the girl resumed control over herself, she told Maria Maddalena that the most cruel spirit just came out of her heart. The devil passed through her throat up to her mouth. That was the devil that used to afflict her heart. Maria Maddalena, the mystic blinded by the imminent Word, had made the Enemy come out of the girl's mouth. As the mystic endeavored to "belch forth" the good Word, the young girl, "Wild," had finally "belched forth" the Prince of our silent, deaf, and mute world.

CONCLUSION

Love Is a Word

Oh, love, love, how is it possible that you have no other name than
love? You are so poor of names, love!
—Maria Maddalena de' Pazzi, *The Forty Days*

You, who are you? You who are not nor ever will be me or mine.
—Luce Irigaray, *I Love to You*

The intermittent experience of the Word, the mystic's striving to give the
Word a face, lips, and a voice, is the kernel of Maria Maddalena's religious discourse. She knows that the Word needs her passion, her dedication, her immolation to his absent face and voice. As we have seen in
chapter 3, the more she longs for him and feels guilty for her inadequate
"performances," the more she realizes that the Word has a "narrative"
face, in the sense that his face can be perceived only within a narrative
frame (the reenactment of his death).

When the Word visits her momentarily, he manifests himself as a
feeling of satisfaction, of being "filled" with grace. However, even if she
feels "full" of the Word, the mystic is still unable to belch forth the
Word's being. Maria Maddalena's sense of content is still a subjective
response to the Word's manifestation, that is, it is a mere abandonment
to his visitation. In *On the Song of Songs* (sermon 74) Bernard of Clairvaux synthesizes this aspect as follows:

> I admit that the Word has also come to me . . . many times. . . . But
> although he has come to me, I have never been conscious of the
> moment of his coming. I perceived his presence, I remembered after-
> wards that he had been with me; sometimes I had a presentiment that
> he would come, but I was never conscious of his coming or his going.
> (4:89–90)

The Word visits the soul unexpectedly. The soul, Bernard stresses, perceives neither his arrival nor his departure. The perception of the Word
is in fact a solipsistic occurrence. The soul senses the presence of a face,
of the Other's loving gaze, which however does not reveal itself. The
soul perceives that the Other is gazing at her with love, that her impossible task of giving him a face, lips, voice is temporarily suspended. In a
similar manner, at the end of colloquio 48 Maria Maddalena briefly per-

ceives the glowing beauty of the resurrected Word. She *perceives* his beauty; *she neither gazes back at his face nor does she belch it forth.*

Indeed, throughout the seven volumes of her visions the mystic never claims that she has granted the Word an idiom. My study on de' Pazzi's mystical language has attempted to show that the uniqueness of her performances lies in her understanding that rather than "speaking love" she can only speak *about* love. Indeed, Maria Maddalena's concept of love is rooted in her awareness of being incapable of giving the Word a voice. "Perfect purity," the quality that, according to the Father (colloquio 48), is necessary to converse with the Trinity, stems from a "perfect" failure. The mystic knows that she may become pure only if she succeeds in embodying her own "baseness," as she says in several monologues.

Love is indeed the core of de' Pazzi's mysticism. To love the Word is equivalent to speaking him. In this final chapter I would like to summarize the major aspects of de' Pazzi's mystical creed by analyzing how she interprets the term "love." Maria Maddalena understands that the human condition is split between the world, ruled by Satan, and the Word's request for being. The Enemy grants the subject silent images/phonemes, a language that articulates "sounds in the air." As we have seen in chapter 4, the Church Fathers underscore that the air itself is full of incorporeal demons who derange our language and deeds. Demons pretend to articulate verbal language by "moving the air" in order to produce sounds familiar to man's ears. Our saying is essentially phonemes, signifiers, sudden and fleeting appearances of memories both in the speaker's and in the interlocutor's mind.[1] The Enemy "moves the air," making us believe that we are actually able to speak an idiom of the Word, which is the idiom of love.

On the contrary, the Word is a constant reminder of the nonbeing of our saying, and thus of the nonbeing of our love. I have stressed that exile is the actual condition of the Florentine mystic, who in *Probation* comes to share the devil's gaze at the world. The devil makes the mystic realize that the world is silent, that the world does not speak love/Word, that the language of the world is nothing but "a movement of the air." Maria Maddalena is left with the memory of the incarnate Word, as it is recounted in the Gospel. The mystic's love is what she retains from her readings; her love is an impulse created by human language. Human love is the act of narrating one's love and springs from the act of reading the Other. Love is both writing and reading one's own love for the Other.

If we analyze how Maria Maddalena broaches the theme of "love" and love, of "the Word" and the Word, we realize that she oscillates between two opposite approaches. On the one hand, following the medieval mystical tradition, she tries to define "love" by drawing up lists of diffent kinds of love. On the other, in some raptures she focuses less on what "love" means than on how she may become able to utter love. These two approaches do not correspond to two different phases of Maria Maddalena's mysticism. We must bear in mind that Maria Maddalena's mysticism does not have a progressive character. The mystic does not *move toward* a more profound understanding of the divinity. Like Bernard of Clairvaux, she is visited by the Word from time to time. Although her task remains unfulfilled, Maria Maddalena varies her attempts to achieve her unachievable goal.

Let us examine the first approach, the more theoretical one. In colloquio 49 Maria Maddalena presents a complete categorization of divine love(s). While she is praying, the Father "calls her to him," because he wants her to learn all his different forms of love. The mystic feels extremely pleased and responds to God's request by repeating the Father's long list of "loves":

> Oh, how numerous are the loves with which you love us! And everything is love [*silence*] separate love, unifying love, recreative love, consuming love, love that always exists and constantly sees its goal; and it is eternal love, glorifying love, beatific love, transforming love, which is a compendium of every love [*silence*] separate love. From what is it separate if it unifies? It is separate from everything that is separate from God; separate from every image and figure; separate from every voice and word; [separate] from every seeing and understanding; separate from every action; separate from myself, eternal, and [it is] even more separate from the essence of my idea [*silence*] the other loves are neither to be tasted nor to be understood, they rather serve it. (2.374–75)

What is striking in the above long list of "loves" is the fact that only "separate" love is actually performed by the soul. All the other forms of love (unifying love, recreative love, consuming love, eternal love, glorifying love, beatific love, transforming love) are received by the soul from the divinity. Moreover, all the other loves "serve" the soul's separate love. The soul loves the Word when it separates itself from itself, if it separates itself from "every image and figure, from every voice and word." By distancing itself from itself, from the world and its phonemes, the soul becomes pure exile. The soul's love for love is exile.

According to Simone Weil, our status as émigrés from ourselves is God's most enduring expression of love: "Through love, he abandons them [the creatures] to affliction and sin."[2] Affliction is the condition proper to exile, and exile is the condition proper to the soul: "The soul," Simone Weil holds, "has to go on loving in the emptiness."[3] Love occurs when the subject perceives her distance from the Word, when she senses the void existing between her longing for the Word and the Word's rejection. We might infer that the soul (and "soul") itself is a synonym for love (and "love"), since both love and the soul result from exile. Neither love nor the soul exist as beings, they rather *occur* thanks to the Word's absence from the world. Indeed, the creature is granted both a soul and love when the Word asks her to summon his being in the world. By so doing, the Word makes the subject realize that she does not have a soul, that she does not have love, that her "I" is a deception of the Enemy. Love is "the soul's looking" at its own impossibility (Weil, *Waiting for God*, 212). Maria Maddalena's long lists of "loves" are indeed attempts to ritualize her existence as "impossibility."

In *Revelations and Knowledge*, Maria Maddalena goes back to this topic in a more detailed manner, dedicating an entire rapture to the various forms of divine loves. Although in this second text she makes use of the same style, that is, she enumerates a series of adjectives that either precede or follow the term "love," in this case she explains each type extensively (*Revelations and Knowledge* 206–12). In this second list of divine "loves" Maria Maddalena modifies the terminology present in her previous rapture. In particular, instead of "separate love" (*amore separato*), she calls the last kind of love "dead love" (*amore morto*), a definition quite common in Western mysticism. Let us read the final passage of this long vision from *Revelations and Knowledge*:

> A passive love, an anxious love, a satiating love, and a dead love. . . . It is lazy, because it contemplates God and sees his supreme goodness . . . but this love, or better yet, the creature, I mean, who has this love, passively considers God's infinitely perfect qualities . . . and lets God do everything . . . anxious love . . . the soul, which has this kind of love, with a constant and passionate desire desires every creature to know God and desires to know God herself, and it desires God to let everyone to know him. . . . The following love is satiating, because it [the soul] enjoys God completely, it takes delight in God. . . . The last love is dead, because it does not desire anything, it does not want anything, it does not long for anything, and it does not look for anything. By abandoning itself to God, the soul with this kind of love desires neither to know him, nor to understand him, nor to enjoy him. . . . All these loves lead to the Word, but one must dwell only in the last one, I mean, in the dead love, which the Word lets his spouse taste a little bit. (210–11)

In this passage the mystic seems to reverse the logic of the previous excerpt from *I colloqui*. Whereas in colloquio 49 she recounts the different ways in which God loves the creatures, now she seems to describe how the soul loves the divinity (passive love, anxious love, satiating love, and dead love). We might see these four loves as four steps toward a closer relation to the divinity. The soul abandons itself to God (passive love); it realizes how distant the other creatures are from God (anxious love); it is filled with a sense of divine satisfaction; and finally, it ceases to feel, think, or perceive anything.

In fact, no actual difference exists between colloquio 49 and the passage from *Revelations and Knowledge*. What does "love" actually mean? Is not "love" the name of love? Is not love a synonym for the Word? The mystic's different "love(s)" are nothing but different names of the Other. Indeed, if we analyze the four loves of *Revelations*, we notice that more than expressing the soul's love for the divinity they are different ways in which the divinity manifests itself in the soul. The Word is a passive, anxious, satiating, and dead love. The soul is never capable of conceiving an "active love" for the Word. It is the Word that allows the soul to call him with *different names corresponding to different manifestations of the word*. "Love," like "Word," is first and foremost a name that needs to be qualified. To qualify the Word means to give "love" a meaning, such as "anxious," "satiating," or "dead."

We might say that "Word" is the proper name of "love." Conversely, "love" is the proper name of "Word." However, this mutual naming is performed by two words that are essentially empty signifiers since they acquire a signified by serving each other as qualifications. In other words, "Word" and "love" mean nothing per se; they obtain the status of signifiers by using each other as signified. To understand better the intrinsic meaninglessness of the words "Word" and "love," let us refer to a crucial text of Renaissance mysticism. In *The Names of Christ* the Spanish scholar and poet Luis de León (1527–91) analyzes the ten most important epithets of the incarnate Word: "Bud," "Face of God," "Way," "Shepherd," "Mountain," "the Everlasting Father," "Arm of God," "King of God," "Prince of Peace," "Husband," "Son of God," "Beloved," and "Jesus." In fact, only the last name seems to be a proper name, whereas the first nine merely express qualities of the Second Person of the Trinity, but not his overall being.

However, before focusing on the second name, "Face of God," which plays a crucial role in Maria Maddalena's mystical discourse, it is imperative to comprehend that even the final name "Jesus" is less a proper name than a facet, a moment, a diegetic occurrence concerning the Father's Only Begotten. Indeed, de León reminds us that the Second Person of the Trinity has a double nature, both human and divine, and thus also two names: "One [the first name] follows the divine nature according to which He is eternally born out of His Father. We call it the Word. Yet He has another name. We call and pronounce this second name, Jesus."[4]

In my reading of colloqui 39 and 48 I have underscored that the names "Jesus" and "Word" play two different roles in Maria Maddalena's reenactment of the Savior's death. For the mystic, "Jesus" is a mere exclamation, an expression of sorrow, of disquiet, whereas "Word" is the actual actant present in her solo play. In Maria Maddalena's mysticism de León's distinction between the Second Person's divine nature (Word) and his historical one (Jesus) are reversed. "Word" is the Father's Only Begotten who became incarnate. In other words, the term "Word" implicitly signify "the humanate Word" or "the incarnate Word." In any case, both in León's and in Maria Maddalena's interpretation the words "Jesus" and "Word" are not proper names—they do not encompass the whole range of possible meanings of the Second Person. For the Florentine mystic, "Jesus" indicates her feeling of being *deprived* of the "Word," and "Word" is a name that needs to become incarnate in the mystic's utterances. Both "Jesus" and "Word" are in fact *empty* words.

In colloquio 48 Maria Maddalena gazes at the Son's corpse and kisses his face and his bleeding wounds. Although at the end of this rapture she perceives the beauty of the resurrected Word, she actually sees and kisses his face only after his death. In this colloquio Maria Maddalena perceives the Word as a mask that does not respond to her gaze and kisses. The love relationship between the Word and the soul paradoxically takes place in this lack of response. The Word, who does not have a proper name, allows the soul to apprehend his "mask," his ashen face and his open wounds, and by so doing he grants the soul the vision of its own face. The Word responds to the soul's gaze by exposing his closed eyelids.[5]

In the above excerpt from *Revelations* Maria Maddalena enumerates a series of different loves that characterize the Word's different approaches to the soul. However, as I will clarify later, the Florentine mystic primarily performs the third kind of love, the so-called "anxious love": "anxious love . . . the soul, which has this kind of love, with a constant and passionate desire desires every creature to know God and desires to know God herself, and it desires God to let everyone to know Him." At that point, the soul identifies with every creature "who neither loves nor knows love," as the mystic says in *The Forty Days* (136).

Luis de León examines the epithet "Face of God" in the first book of *The Names of Christ*. The expression "Face of God" acquire a meaning only if and when the subject turns it into what we might call a "contemplative signifier":

Without seeing him we can with the eyes of our faith contemplate this divine face and these features fashioned by the Holy Spirit, we can see his beautiful face. His grave and sweet posture, his eyes and his mouth, the latter bathed in sweetness, the former with an even more resplendent brightness than that of the sun. . . . Let us rest our eyes upon this perfect beauty and contemplate it. (72–73)

As Maria Maddalena does at the end of colloquio 48, de León primarily focuses on the "beauty" of the Word. However, this act of contemplation does not entail an actual seeing, but rather a series of feelings resulting from a past seeing, that is, a deep sense of pleasure and fulfillment. When de León speaks of the Word's face, eyes, and mouth, he actually refers to the feelings following a nonoccurred sight.[6] In the act of meditating on the expression "Face of God," the "moments of fulfillment" take place when the contemplator erases the words "Face" and "God," and is filled with the perception of the blinding beauty of the divinity. "Love" and love mean past events, remembrances. "Love" can only be uttered in the past tense.

The names "love," "Word," "Face of God," and even "Jesus" start to signify when the subject deletes them. These "names" are both signifiers with infinite signifieds and signifiers with no signifieds. Still, on "Face of God," Luis de León writes: "The more I unfurl the sails, the more space I see to be traversed, and the more I navigate, the more I discover new seas" (77). "Face of God" is an open space, a nonocean, a nonword, if by "word" we intend a set of phonemes evoking a place occupied by meaning. As is well known, in *Divine Names* the Pseudo-Dionysius states that "God is not known, not spoken, not named."[7]

The soul faces the Word's corpse as a challenge to its own significance. If the soul is allowed to gaze at the Other only when the Other keeps his eyes closed, the soul cannot help but wonder about her own eyes, her own gaze. Maria Maddalena's mysticism underscores that the Word grants his gift (his and the soul's face) without gazing at the soul, or better yet, gazing at the soul by means of a nongaze, a nonresponse. This negative gaze, this face that exposes its own death, this mask that excludes the subject, compels the soul to narrate this very absence.

This is a central aspect of Maria Maddalena's mystical discourse. The Other's face, the object of the soul's desire, shows itself as a flat surface, as a nonsignificant being, that is, as a Lacanian *objet a*, that "mute thing" on which the subject projects her own discourse and desire. The closed eyes of the Word urge the mystic to speak, and to attempt to speak the Word's nonexpressive face. Lacan's astute pun "I soul" (*j'âme*) for "I love" (*j'aime*) is a direct response to the mystic's impasse between its desire for the Other and the Other's denied gaze. Lacan asks himself whether we should consider the soul as one of "love's effects" (Lacan, *Feminine Sexuality*, 155):

The soul could only be spoken as whatever enables a being—the speaking being to call him by its name—to bear what is intolerable in its world, which presumes this soul to be alien to that world, that is to say, fantasmatic.

The soul springs from the vision of the Other's closed eyelids. The soul in fact "souls for the soul" (*âme l'âme*). In the act of "souling for" itself, the soul is compelled to speak. The vision of the Word's dead body leads the subject to acknowledge the present absence of her interlocutor and her own, as interlocutor of her interlocutor, absence. "Love" is thus the name pronounced by an absence to an absence.

It is clear now why the above words (Face, Word, Love) are not proper names. A proper name embodies an intrisic directionality (I speak *to*), whereas "Face," "Word," "Love" reside nowhere. Luce Irigaray's *I Love to You* highlights that love as a gaze at the other is "a relation of indirection. . . . The 'to' is the sign of non-immediacy."[8] When Maria Maddalena utters these words ("Oh Word!"; "Oh Love!"), she actually says nothing.

Are the expressions of sorrow, of anxiety directed to someone? Does a body in pain speak in order to communicate, or rather simply to invoke the interruption of his being as suffering? Indeed, "love" is always an invocation, is always an expression of an "anxious love," as Maria Maddalena says, and it should always be written as "Love!" Some of the most involving visions of Maria Maddalena de' Pazzi are dominated by the repeated exclamation "Oh, love!" or simply "love!" Let us read, for instance, a powerful page from *Probation*. As the transcribers report, on May 3rd, 1592, the mystic entered a very painful rapture. Feeling restless and anguished, Maria Maddalena run through the convent and the kitchen garden, and asked her sisters to answer her distressed questions: Do they know Love? Why does no one love love? Does love know that she, Maria Maddalena, is willing to do everything to be with him? While she screamed "love! love!," she started to ring the convent bells to remind her sisters that they must love love. Let us read the last lines of this vision:

> [S]he ran all around the kitchen garden several times, and nearly throughout the entire convent. She said that she was looking for some soul who knew and loved love. And she always either called love or spoke with love. Sometimes, when she met a nun, she grabbed her and holding her tight said to her: "Soul, do you love love? How can you live? Don't you feel as if you were consuming and dying for love?" . . . After having walked through the convent for a while, she grasped the bells . . . and rang them crying out loudly: "Come to love, oh souls, to love love who loves you so much! Souls, come to love!" (*Probation*, 2:189)

Maria Maddalena "grabs a soul" in order to see/face love; she asks a "soul" to utter her love for love/the Word. In this passage the encounter between the subject and her soul is performed as a dramatic confrontation. The mystic "grabs" the image of herself through another nun (a "soul") and questions her/herself about the absence of love.[9] "How can you live?" Maria Maddalena asks her sister, meaning "How can you live without love?" "Don't you feel as if you were consuming and dying for love?" she adds.

As I have pointed out, Maria Maddalena primarily performs an "anxious" love. In her words, "anxious love" takes place when the subject feels the presence of love as a reminder of its absence in the world. "Come to love, souls!" the mystic exclaims, ringing the bell of the convent. It was actually by gazing at her sisters' faces that the mystic recognized that the Word was absent. More than "belching forth" the Word, Maria Maddalena invokes him. To cry out the Word is a performative act that is not directed to the "name" invoked, but rather to those who witness the subject's invocation.

The speaking subject cannot articulate language without having a phantasmatic interlocutor. In the act of talking to oneself the subject faces an interlocutor who is perceived as both absent and present in the sense that, even though he/she is not there, he/she listens to the speaker's words. Words cannot be uttered in a void. The speaker always perceives a presence, or at least the memory of a presence. When the mystic invokes the name of the deceased Savior, she does not direct her saying to the deceased himself. The visionary speaks in order to manifest both the deceased's absence and her distress for the deceased's absence. Maria Maddalena wants the world to "echo" the absence of the Other. We may say that, more than actually invoking the Word/love, Maria Maddalena accuses her own "soul" of not feeling the guilt connected with the Other's absence.

A meaningful element of the mystic's "anxious" love is that in her raptures the traditional discourse about the different kinds and stages of divine love acquires a performative connotation, that is, for Maria Maddalena love is not only a topic to explain, but also and more importantly a truth to show, an inner feeling to perform through both spoken language and her body. As we have seen in chapters 2 and 3, for the Florentine mystic, body and language are connected with each other. When the Word asks her to respond to His request for being, the mystic cannot help but speak and move around the convent. Her voice and her body have the very same task: the expression of the Word. Whereas some of her visions are predominantly discursive, others are dominated by the expressions of her body; words and body are two facets of the same language.

The most "eloquent" vision concerning Maria Maddalena's "anxious" love is in *The Forty Days* (133–80). The nuns tell that during this four-day rapture the mystic was ill and "in an excess of mind." On Monday, June 11, 1584, although she felt restless and anxious, her sisters forced Maria Maddalena to stay in bed and asked her to drink some broth. Maria Maddalena kept repeating "I can't stay here, please let me get out this bed, I can't." She stared at a small crucifix that she kept on the altar in her cell. She posited questions to her sisters and to her confessor, who had been asked to assist the "blessed soul" in her malaise:

> All of a sudden she saw everything God has operated for the creature, who is so base and corrupt that she was forced to scream out loudly, externally, so that she was heard by all those who were present: "Love love, oh God, you love the creature with a pure love, oh God of love, oh God of love."
> And since she saw that the creatures were so ungrateful toward such a great love, she burst out with sorrow, crying and saying:
> "Lord, no more love, no more love, you have too much love for your creatures. No, it's not too much, I mean, for your greatness. But it is too much for the creature, who is so base and corrupt. Lord, why do you give so much love to me?" (*The Forty Days*, 133–34)

What is impressive in this passage is that, like the female speaker of *The Song of Songs*, Maria Maddalena is "sick with love" (2:5c).[10] However, unlike *The Song of Songs*, *The Forty Days* depicts a lover agitated not because of an excess of love, but because God's love reminds her that in fact she does not love love. The Word's love shatters the subject's love by making the lover doubt her own identity as lover. In other words, God's love leads the mystic to perceive the void of her alleged love. More than an actual act of caring, divine love questions the creature's perception of love. Love is, in fact, a reminder of the lack of love. God's love is "too much"; it makes the mystic scream and cry. The Word's love is perceived by the mystic as a persecution: "Why do you give so much love to me?"

Love makes Maria Maddalena sick because love, as the Word, manifests itself as missing. The mystic grabbed the crucifix she had in her cell and stared at it:

> If at least, my Jesus, you were not naked on the cross. Such a dishonor increases their sneer. Yes, love, you wished so. Love love, love drove you crazy, and you went crazy for such an ungrateful creature. Oh, blindness, oh man's malice toward such a great love. No one, no one loves my love. Oh, my love, when will I have you? When will I be united with you perfectly? When will I love you infinitely? . . . My

Jesus, no more love, for I can't take it anymore; and if you want to give it to me, give it to me as much as you want. But give the strength to tolerate it. Oh holy Virgin, how could you be there? You saw him; and he was your son, and he was also God. And you knew that he was doing this because he loves all creatures. (134–35)

The Word, which is love, was "driven crazy" by love. Love deranges both the creature and the divinity who dies for love. Love engenders destruction and death, folly and disease. Love is a negativity, in the sense that it works against the world and its creatures. This is why the mystic can only associate love with death, with the death of love on the cross ("If at least, my Jesus, you were not naked on the cross . . . oh holy Virgin, how could you be there?"). Love is what does not exist in the world, and what makes the creature sense her own nonexistence in the world. Maria Maddalena can only recall the end of love, his dying on the cross for love. Love is always the end of love, since love itself engenders its end: "My Jesus, no more love."

The subject cannot "conjugate love" in the present tense because love is exclusively its past. There would be no love if love were not absent here and now: "Nobody loves my love. Oh, my love, when will I have you?" Love is intrisically nonlove, for it can exist only insofar as the subject longs for it, misses it, and recall his death on the cross. The crucifix is a token of love's death, of his presence in the world as a being-for-death. The subject is unable to love love because of her "baseness." Speaking to the Virgin, Maria Maddalena says: "You saw him; and he was your son, and he was also God. . . . But, I mean, how could you be there without bursting with sorrow? I do not see him and still burst with a great sorrow." Love as sorrow, as remembrance of love's death. Moreover, Maria Maddalena underscores that she loves a love that she has neither seen nor met. Her sorrow springs from an act of remembrance that does not belong to her. She loves someone else's love. Love is not only absence, it is primarily a longing that "makes us sick" without belonging to us.

Maria Maddalena understands that perfect love occurs when the lover loves a memory, that is, a present absence, from which she is excluded. Love does not have an object. Although the incarnate Word has suffered and died for the lover, the lover only converses with the Word/lover/beloved in a void. As I have pointed out at the beginning of this final chapter, the subject is subject to the Other's closed eyelids. What the lover loves is a "mask," the lover loves the beloved when the beloved is not there. As Simone Weil reminds us, more than with the Word the lover *is in contact with* her own vexing memory. The Word loves/loved us by withdrawing from the world. The Word started to love us when he died to the world.

In one of her earlier works, examining the crucial theme of memory in St Augustine, Hannah Arendt stresses that Augustine identifies human knowledge of a "happy life" with self-consciousness. Arendt points out that for Augustine

> [t]he knowledge of the possible existence of the happy life is given in pure consciousness prior to all experience, and it guarantees our recognizing the happy life wherever we should encounter in the future. For Augustine this knowledge of the happy life is not simply an innate idea, but is specifically stored up in memory as the seat of consciousness. Hence, this knowledge points back to the past. When happiness is projected into the absolute future, it is guaranteed by a kind of absolute past.[11]

Arendt refers to a famous passage from book 10 of the *Confessions*, where Augustine asks God how it is possible that the subject has an innate desire for happiness, even though he/she has no experience of it:

> When I seek for you, my God, my quest is for the happy life. I will seek you that "my soul may live" (Isa. 55:3), for my body derives life from my soul, and my soul derives from you. . . . Is not the happy life that which all desire, which indeed no one fails to desire? . . . My question is whether the happy life is in the memory. For we would not love it if we did not know what it is. . . . Even when sad, I remember my times of joy, like a wretched person thinking of the happy life. It is never by bodily sense that I have seen my joy or heard or smelt or tasted or touched it. I experienced it in my mind when I was glad, and the knowledge of it stuck in my memory, so that I could remind myself of it.[12]

Augustine comes to the conclusion that God has instilled the memory of the happy life, that is, of himself, in human consciousness. In fact, a human being remembers what he/she has not experienced. This is why, Augustine infers, everyone spontaneously longs for happiness. According to Augustine, God is the remembrance of a perfect joy: "You [God] conferred this honor on my memory that you should dwell in it" (*Confessions*, 200). Thus, as Arendt points out, "the 'return to oneself' is an act of recollection, it is identical to a return to the Creator. Man loves himself by relating to God as his Maker" (50).

Maria Maddalena de' Pazzi offers a radically different concept of memory and remembrance. Although she shares with Augustine the fundamental idea that to love God means both to remember him and to reenact this very memory in one's own life, she does not believe that God is a memory of a "happy life." As she stresses in many raptures, for her God is the remembrance of his suffering and death for all of humanity. At the beginning was God's suffering for the creation. This is what the creature actually remembers. From the very beginning, from the moment when the Father generated the Son, the divinity descended upon the world as the memory of the Son's forthcoming death. For the Florentine mystic, to love God and to love oneself is equivalent to recalling the Word's death. As she says in many passages from *I colloqui*, Jesus wishes us "to practice pain more than joy," because it is through suffering that the subject "remembers" the Word. Both psychological and physical pain is a sudden insight into the Word's past. Rephrasing Augustine's concept of memory, we might say that for Maria Maddalena God has granted us the memory of his original absence from the world. Whereas for Augustine the divinity, which coincides with a perfectly "happy life," is a sense of a fulfillment similar to Bernard's act of "belching forth the Word," for Maria Maddalena the Word is "history," narration, the tormenting memory of an act of injustice. Injustice, suffering, guilt, affliction, are the actual means through which the soul remembers the Word. In the words of Simone Weil:

> God created through love and for love. God did not create anything except love itself, and the means to love. He created love in all its forms. He created beings capable of love from all possible distances. Because no other could do it, he himself went to the greatest possible distance, the infinite distance. This infinite distance between God and God, this supreme tearing apart, this agony beyond all others, this marvel of love, is the crucifixion. . . . This tearing apart, over which supreme love places the bond of supreme union, echoes perpetually across the universe. . . . This is the Word of God. (Weil, *Waiting For God*, 123–24)

The universe "echoes" the narration of the Word's crucifixion. This is what the creation remembers of its Creator, that is, his dying on the cross. Maria Maddalena acts out her love for love by commemorating his death.

Indeed, in *The Forty Days* the second and third days of Maria Maddalena's vision about divine love clarify her concept of love as remembrance of the Savior's crucifixion. On Tuesday, June 12, the nuns report that the mystic's "disease" intensified. Maria Maddalena "looked crazy"; her screams scared her sisters. She run around her room yelling "love, love!," constantly staring at her small crucifix:

> "Love, love, you laugh, you cry, you scream and keep silent. Love!"
> And turning to those who were present she said:
> "Don't you know it? Oh my Jesus, love, crazy for love, crazy for love, I say it, oh my Jesus. Oh love, you are all lovable, and joyful love! Old and new truth. Love, love, you are recreative, you are consoling, love! Love, love, you are loving and unifying love! Love, you are pain and relief; Love, you are toil and rest, death and life you are, love! Oh

love, what's not in you? What's not in you? Love, love, you are wise
and joyful. High and profound love. Love love, you are admirable,
inexpugnable, unfathomable, incomprehensible, you are love!"
(136–37)[13]

I have stressed that Maria Maddalena has two different approaches
toward divine love. On the one hand, she draws up lists of love; she
attempts to categorize love according to its different stages. On the
other, as this excerpt shows, she gives free rein to her perception of love.
Love is nothing but an exclamation, a performative act that is directed
to nowhere and to no one.

But why does the mystic run around the room? We have seen her accom-
panying love's corpse to his tomb, kneeling down to kiss his bloody face,
wrestling with the devils, throwing them out of the window. But why
running? Maria Maddalena runs, as if she were fleeing from something.
As the third and fourth day of her vision will clarify, love is a persecution, the memory of a crime. Her own flesh is a sign, an icon of *that* past
insult. To perform love is to perform one's own "running away" from
oneself. By running around/away, the mystic performs the oblivion of
the self. Her fever, her "being sick," as the nuns write, is her body's
response to the memory of a transgression against love.[14]
    Love crosses the mystic's body as a reminder of the absence of love.
Indeed, her physicality suffers the "passage" of love as love's suffering
and death. The human body carries the marks of a history that does not
belong to the body itself, but it is inscribed in it. The mystic's running
around the room like an animal in a cage signifies the history of a death.
Paradoxically, this nonperformance, this escaping of the body from
itself, reenacts the history of the Savior's sacrifice. As Daniel Sibony
reminds us, "the root of the religious experience is the paradoxical gesture of *giving back life to God by 'killing him'*; the religious experience
recreates the divinity as the effect of a murder."[15] However, what is central in the mystical experience is the fact that she suffers both as the victim and the murderer torn by an unbearable sense of guilt. Maria Maddalena's body narrates the death of the Word and the memory of that
death. Suffering is the common ground where the divinity and the creature meet.
    Suffering is the central trait of love. "Love," Maria Maddalena says,
"is wounded for love" (138). Love is a wound that love inflicts upon
itself. If the creature can only love love as the memory of love's death,
love itself exists as long as it is "wounded" by its own existence:

Love, love, I see you wounded for love. Please, for love take out that
lance out your open wound that has wounded you for love, so that it

can come and rain down that water that is inside of your grace and of your love. Love, love, rain it over the hearts of your creatures, created for love. (138)

The water gushing out from the Savior's side is love insofar as it cleanses the creature of her dirt/sin. By sprinkling the creature with his "water" the Word's corpse shares his death with the world. Love communicates his death to the creature who is "dying for love," who is "sick for love."

The second day of her "pain for love" ends with the mystic's telling her sisters that "as he finished his external passion soon, my love wants me to finish this vehemence of love that now my body manifests externally. But my love does not want me to cease my interior pain, since he always always wants to be in it; and my love will never leave me" (139). After these words, Maria Maddalena calms down. She remains in bed for the rest of the day. Her external pain has subsided; the internal one still comforts her memory of the love's death.

The third day of the mystic's vision on love (Wednesday, June 13th) revolves around the necessity of uttering the name of love. The mystic entered a rapture as soon as she meditated on "Cor meum et caro mea exultaverunt in Deum vivum, in porticum Salomonis," an interpretation of a verse from psalm 82: "cor meum et caro mea exultavit in Deum vivum/ etenim passer invenit sib1: domum" (3b–4a). Indeed, Maria Maddalena and the psalmist express a similar attitude toward the divinity. Psalm 82 opens with a praise of God's "dwelling-place," where even the sparrow and the swallow find their nest. However, in the second part of the poem the author begs the divinity to grant him the possibility of entering God's dwelling-place: "beati qui habitant in domo tua. . . . Domine Deus virtutum exaudi orationem meam" (5a; 9a). The psalmist thus praises a "place" that he does not know. The psalmist has never visited God's abode.

Maria Maddalena repeats the above verse, first in her mind and then out loudly as a scream, as an invocation to the Word. Both the psalmist and the Florentine mystic formulate an entreaty. Their flesh and their soul long for the Word's loving dwelling. In fact, at the beginning of the vision Maria Maddalena senses that the verse "cor meum et caro mea exultaverunt in te" (*The Forty Days*, 141) is in fact pronounced *by* the Word *to* the creature. The Word asks the creature to let him, the Word, reside in her dwelling-place, that is, her heart. By pronouncing these words in the mystic's mind, the Word indirectly reminds her of pronouncing these words herself. In other words, the Word suggests that the mystic utter that request. The act of residing in God's heart results from a double request, both from the creature and from the divinity himself. When the psalmist and the mystic articulate that invocation to the divinity, they actually lend the Word their voice, so that he may "return" to his own "nest." As Maria Maddalena says, the Word aims "to rest in us."

However, for Maria Maddalena the act of invoking the Word (and that of letting the Word invoke himself through her) is an oral performance. The invocation to the Word is a constant rehearsal. The mystic's voice repeats the biblical verse as if she were trying to achieve a perfect intonation, a perfect articulation of that request. By "perfect articulation" I mean that oral expression that *would break through language and attain the Word*.

After holding a short monologue in her bed, Maria Maddalena told her nurse that she felt as if she were going crazy. She needed to get up. As in the previous two days, she started to run around the room screaming:

> Come, come run with me; help me call love . . . scream loud, loud, louder; you speak so low; he doesn't hear you. . . . Love, love, love. I will never tire of calling you love. Oh, love. *Cor meum et caro mea exultaverunt in te*, my love. (142)

Her sisters did not seem to scream loudly enough; her voice itself did not reach the Word: "Love, love. Oh love, give me a strong voice, so that when I call you I can be heard from the East to the West, and in every part of the world, even in hell, so that everybody will hear and love you, love" (143). By calling the Word, the mystic allows the Word to communicate his message to the world. The world will begin to love love, when the mystic succeeds in uttering the term "love" in/to the world. At that point, the world will perceive "love" as love, as a word that has become incarnate in the mystic's physicality and in her voice.

Maria Maddalena investigates further the meaning of "love" in a crucial, albeit short, passage, where she links "love" to Jesus' last supper and communion:

> Oh, love, you are so strong, and then I see you so weak. So strong that nobody can resist you, but you are also so weak that a creature so base as I am defeats you, overcomes you, just by calling you love. Oh love, love. What you said was right: *Desiderio desideravi*. (144)

In this important excerpt Maria Maddalena clearly explains that the Word does not exist (he is not perceived in the world) unless the mystic's voice makes him participate in the world. Love, the mystic says, is both strong and weak. He is strong as an overwhelming impulse, a force that lies in the soul. However, love is also extremely weak, because the soul "defeats" him by "calling him." How could a human soul possibly "defeat" the Word? The Word's strength resides in the word "love," and this word is a void unless the creature "belches it forth" through her mouth. This is why Maria Maddalena mentions the words the Savior pronounced during his last supper, "desiderio desideravi" (*Luke* 22:15). According to the Florentine mystic, Jesus instituted the sacrament of Holy Communion by expressing his desire for love.

However, the reference to the Mass has also other decisive implications. After pronouncing "desiderio desideravi," Maria Maddalena pauses. Her confessor, who sat next to her, completed her quotation "hoc Pasca manducare vobiscum, ante quam patiar." Maria Maddalena commented on the priest's citation, connecting the institution of communion with the Word's love:

> Oh love, why did you wish to have the last supper? Ah, love, because you wanted to show your love for the creatures. Oh love, love, what a privilege do the priests enjoy when they handle you, love, and administer you to the others. (144)

Priests have the privilege of "handling" (*manipolare*) love as it is manifested as/in bread and wine. Priests reenact the narrative of "love," summoning the symbolic level present in the term "love." However, as Louis Marin points out, the physicality of bread and wine is in fact a symbolic appearance.[16] Bread and wine are linguistic signifiers whose signified is the word "love." "Love" is a signified insofar as it *embodies* love. Love is in fact a word. Maria Maddalena knows that the actual enactment of love can only occur in the articulation of "love." We might thus say that "love" is a signifier, if we read it as a word. But it is also a signified in that love can only be summoned *in* the word "love."

In the Eucharist what is visible (bread and wine) signifies what is at once invisible and "more" real than reality itself. For bread and wine are both signifiers of a past event (the Word's passion and death) and signifieds of that very event, in that they are signified by the Word's death. The term "love" and love, as a result of the utterance of "love," connect reality (bread and wine) with an absence (the Word), which is reality's actual signified. In the act of repeating the words pronounced by Jesus during the Last Supper, bread and wine reveal themselves as absences, in that they are the memory of *that* bread and of *that* wine. In other words, bread and wine are in fact "words" constructing a narration.

Let us go back to Maria Maddalena's vision from *The Forty Days*. In the following section the mystic examines "love" directly, by asking love why he has this name only. The mystic states that Augustine wrote about love more deeply than John, because Augustine "expounded" (*espose*) John's sentence "In principio erat Verbum." In other words, whereas the evangelist limited himself to stating that the Word founded the creation, Augustine analyzed, discussed, *uttered* the Word by means of his commentary on John's statement. Augustine communicated the Word/love to the world:

> Oh, love, love, old and new truth; you are love, love love. Who will I
> say that has written more profoundly about you, either John, who said:
> *In principio erat Verbum*; or Augustine, who expounded those words?
> Love, who will I say that has gone deeper? Augustine, love! Oh, love,
> love, is it possible that you have no other name than love? You are so
> poor of names, love! (145)

It does not suffice to state the Word's supremacy over the creation
(John's Gospel); the Word needs to be "expounded," that is, manifested
to the world (Augustine's writing). Given that the Word has only one
name, "love," Maria Maddalena perceives the difficulty of "finding synonyms" for "Word." Like the "I" of Psalm 82, the mystic is aware of
the fact that the words "love" and "Word" can only be praised,
invoked, longed for. The "Word" is a dwelling-place unknown to the
creature:

> Love, love, you are incomprehensible, you are immense and worthy of
> every praise; but, oh love, no one would ever be able to praise you,
> love, as you deserve. If all human languages, along with the angels and
> all the stars in the sky, the sand of the sea, the plants of the earth, the
> drops of water, the birds of the air, became languages to praise you,
> they would not suffice to praise you, love. (148)

To love love means to praise, to invoke his name. By constantly repeating and exalting the name "love," the subject might succeed in connecting a signifier with its unknown signified. The signified of "love" is a
gift of love; it is love's grace. The discourse of love is a gift of God.
Indeed, when her sisters informed her that they were going to vespers
while she had to stay in bed, Maria Maddalena prayed to God to let the
nuns "give birth to love" each time they spoke a word:

> Let them give birth to love. Every time they speak a word, they will
> give birth to love. Love, love, who tastes you is always satisfied with
> you, love. (152)

The reportage of the third day of the mystic's vision on love ends with
her wishing the other nuns to succeed in pronouncing love during vespers. Maria Maddalena was not allowed to participate. Her "condition"
did not permit it.

The fourth and final day of the mystic's rapture (Thursday, June 14,
1584) opens with her meditation on "In principio erat Verbum et Verbum erat apud Deum, et Deus erat Verbum" (154). We have seen that *I
colloqui* starts with that very citation. The mystic entered a vision by
"considering" these words that crossed her mind all of a sudden. Maria
Maddalena is going to reenact the "history" of the Word. Again, the
mystic's love for love manifested itself in the form of a narration of the
Word's death. However, whereas in colloquio 48 Maria Maddalena

recounted the moments following the Son's death, in *The Forty Days* she performed/narrated the sufferings and humiliations that led to the Word's death. If love's love is a process, in colloquio 48 love had already "loved love," that is, the Word had already completed his act of "tearing apart" himself for love, as Simone Weil suggests, and had withdrawn from the world. In *The Forty Days* Maria Maddalena commemorates the actual occurrence of love's love.

The mystic was still sick in bed. The nurse did not want her to get up. Maria Maddalena told her: "I would like to get out of this bed. Please, let me get up, because I feel my love and I have already, at least it seems to me, run around this room several times, and now I see myself in bed. Let me get up" (*The Forty Days*, 156).

She jumped out of her bed, grabbed her small crucifix, and started to run around as usual, screaming: "Love, love, love" (157). A major narrative shift occurs in the final day of her vision of divine love. The mystic's new narration of the Word's passion and death begins with her addressing the "betrayer":

> Love, love, how little they know you; this one is one of yours and, still, he betrays you, love. Betrayer, betrayer, how little you knew him. You pretend to be a friend of his, and then you betray him, my love. Betrayer. Love, love, oh love. Here he comes, here he is.

The mystic's discourse on love's love starts with the remembrance of love's betrayal. In fact, the narration of divine love *happening* is based on the premise that love occurred when it was betrayed. The mystic's reaction to this sudden awareness is twofold: on the one hand, she insults the "betrayer," that is, the character of the mythic narration. However, her overwhelming sense of despair cannot be explained unless we understand that Maria Maddalena came to identify with the betrayer himself. Her being unable to express the Word coincides with a feeling of having betrayed him. By not articulating the Word, the mystic *executes* him. As the nuns note, Maria Maddalena could not bear the perception of being responsible for the Word's death. She run around the room again, screaming out so loudly that the transcribers were terrified (157).

The nuns treated the mystic as a sick person. Although they never failed to underscore that her disease derived from an "excess of mind," they addressed her as if she were mentally disturbed. The nurse told her: "Sister Maria Maddalena, I want you to go back to bed. You see, Jesus wants it too" (158). Maria Maddalena abode by the nurse's order, but she was unable to lie in bed; she sat on a pillow staring at her small crucifix: "Now now he betrays him, my love." The mystic's identification with the historical betrayer of love becomes evident in what she says immediately after: "Now he leaves him. Oh love, you would have never left me" (159). The meaning of this short sentence is rather complex. The mystic's words might be interpreted as follows. Maria Maddalena visualizes Judas' betrayal. Judas abandons love as the mystic fears that love might abandon her. Both Judas and the Word are personifications of an act of abandonment. However, we might also interpret the mystic's sentence in a different manner. Maria Maddalena might mean "*if* I decided to abandon Jesus as Judas did, Jesus would never let me abandon him, that is, he would never let my soul be deranged by sin." If Judas had shared the Word's affliction, as Simone Weil puts it, he would have not abandoned the Word to death. As a consequence, since the soul exists insofar as it perceives the Other's affliction, Judas ceased to exist in the moment he turned away from the Word. Judas' suicide was the logical conclusion of his act of abandoning himself.

What is also revealing in the mystic's performance is that, whereas in other visions she actively participates in the Word's passion and death, in *The Forty Days* she simply recounts what she is seeing. The death of the Word is experienced by the mystic with a conscious sense of impotence. Indeed, as the nuns report, Maria Maddalena was in bed because she was "sick." The nature of her sickness remains unspecified. Her sisters wanted her to lie in bed; she had to drink the broth they prepared for her.

Still in bed, Maria Maddalena visualized the Word's face. Indeed, what the mystic saw was blood, the Word's face covered with blood: "I see your face full of blood. Oh love, who will come console you? The eternal Father, maybe? Who, love? Oh no, the Father no" (159). The transcribers' narration constructs the experience of the Other's face like the sudden visit of a revenant, the obsessing image of the subject's guilt.[17]

It is evident that Maria Maddalena herself, sick in bed, is the betrayer tormented by the sudden presence of her innocent victim. As the mystic says referring to love's bloody face, "you withdraw; if you did not withdraw you could not suffer" (159). What or who does love withdraw? Love withdraws himself from the world. By so doing, love enacts his suffering and thus attains his full embodiment in the world. Moreover, he allows the world to see his face, only when his face has already been offended and smeared with blood. If this vision begins with the evocation of the Word's traitor, it finally mentions the apathy of the Word's disciples:

> Oh love, they are asleep. You, Peter, Peter, you that seemed so zealous, you can't be on the alert not even for an hour. You don't show that love you seemed to have for Jesus. Oh Peter, you are asleep, yes, you are. And John sleeps. Oh John, and you, you that were the chosen one,

you too, you are asleep. I am not surprised that Peter is sleeping, but that you, you that had tasted the celestial secrets by resting on his chest, now your love fails. I can't believe that. And also that one is asleep. Oh love, everybody is asleep; I am surprised that they are not moved by such a bloody face. There is nothing that makes a face uglier than blood. Oh, oh, it's ominous, it's ominous. (159–60)

In this vision Maria Maddalena speaks to a silenced love. Love shows her his humiliated face, but he does not respond to her. The traitor appears to her "internal eyes," but no interaction occurs between the betrayer and the betrayed. The betrayer is seen by the mystic in the act of leaving. Judas betrays the Word by disappearing from the scene of the mystic's discourse. Moreover, love's disciples, those who in colloquio 48 presented themselves to the mystic and shared her sorrow for the Word's death, are asleep; they do not participate in love's martyrdorm. This entire rapture from *The Forty Days* is dominated by silence. The mystic herself is impotent; she is sick in bed. Her body does not have the energy to flee the Word's death. Love's passion and death happen as if the world were not aware of that. Whereas in other mystical performances Maria Maddalena enacted the struggle between love and the world, between the Word and his Enemy, in this vision the world is already pervaded by the silence following the Word's death. The world, we might say, enacts love's death in a passive manner because it has already been granted the appalling awareness deriving from its execution of love.

Sitting on a pillow in her bed, Maria Maddalena sees love's disciples asleep. She addresses them, or better yet, she mentions their names and scolds them for their apathy. It is apparent that, even if we assumed that her words were pronounced in order to reach a given interlocutor, no actual interaction could occur between the mystic who is "sick" in bed and the apostles who are asleep.

The narration of the Word's death must be enacted, even though no one listens to it. Love, the remembrance of love's sacrifice, is a private practice. The creature recalls the end of love and cannot share this remembrance with any interlocutor. Love is the memory of its end. Love lives in the subject as a sickening past:

Love, love, they are still asleep. And you, Peter, you said *"Relinquimus omnia"*;[18] you said that you had left everything. It doesn't seem that you have left yourselves. And you, John, you had been with him for so long. When two people converse with each other, they usually understand each other's words, but now I see that you do not understand him, because you don't do what to say. (161)

Like the traitor, Jesus himself withdraws from the scene. Maria Maddalena sees him walking away toward the garden where he will pray to the Father. The "scene" is empty. The betrayer and betrayed have met in the act of distancing themselves from each other. The disciples sleep. The Savior goes to pray. The mystic's response is "Love, my love, I burst with sorrow . . . oh, what shall I do now? Nothing, I can't do anything, if love wants to suffer" (162–63).

Then, still in bed, Maria Maddalena saw the Savior addressing a group of soldiers. Three times he says "Ego sum," and three times the soldiers fall down on the ground in a torpor (164). Again, the world does not tolerate love's presence; the soldiers are indeed overwhelmed by the name of love. As soon as the soldiers perceive the name of love, they abandon him by passing out: "Oh love, they leave you" (165).

From this moment on, the vision of love is the silent dramatization of love's death. Maria Maddalena enumerates the different stages of the passion, as a passive spectator of a mystical play. Jesus is chained to the column, where he is whipped and insulted. The mystic does not hear the words pronounced, she rather *sees* them. Her vision turns into a series of silent images, the traditional stations of the cross, where love is depicted in his humble and speechless acceptance of death: "Many things happen. Love, you speak, you become silent, you question, you answer, you act. I don't perceive it" (167). The mystic herself, the nuns report, became silent. She stared at the small crucifix that she held in her hand. According to her sisters, the crucifix was like a mirror reflecting everything that happened during the passion (ibid.).

She resumed her monologue when she saw love being beaten: "Love, why do they beat you so much? What did you do? Is there anything lacking in you? Do you lack wisdom? Goodness? Mercy? Pity? Do you lack love?" (170). What the mystic reiterates for pages and pages is that love is hit and denied. The names of the biblical characters are briefly mentioned as fleeting actants of love's sacrifice. Pilate is the last presence embodying the denial and betrayal of love. Like his disciples, Judas, and the soldiers overwhelmed by the name "love," Pilate makes a silent gesture signifying his abandonment of love: "You washed your hands because you were unworthy to receive the benefice of his passion, nor the gift of his blood. And you did the right thing when you washed your hands, because you wouldn't receive it at all" (174). Like the other traitors, Pilate does not speak. The world, and the mystic as well, seem unwilling to participate in love's destiny. In *The Forty Days* the image of Pilate washing his hands to manifest his final decision becomes an act devoid of any actual impact on the mystic's narrative. The mystic narrates it as something that has already occurred, even though she is recounting it in the present tense, as if it were occurring now, at the moment of her narration. Love's death is a narration whose plot is well-known and "unavoidable." The acts it recounts are memories that have been told innumerable times, and whose horror has become part of the narrator's identity.

In *The Forty Days* love's passion and death cannot be reenacted through a performative act, through gestures, screams, sighs, convulsive movements on the floor. Love's death cannot enter the mystic's physicality. The mystical experience of Maria Maddalena de' Pazzi exclusively focuses on the incarnate Word, on his passion, on his end. However, the Word, love, Jesus, correspond to different narratives of the same *mythème*. Let us remember that in colloquio 48 the name of the Second Person of the Trinity is "the Word," as in most of the mystic's raptures. "Love," on the other hand, is the name evoking the absence of the Word. When the Word becomes mere expression of sorrow, exclamation of disquiet, sudden awareness of the fundamentally absent presence of the Word in the world, it becomes "love." As Lacan has clarified, "love" (*amour*) is always an exclamation ("love!"), a request. To love (*aimer*) is in fact "to soul for" (*âmer*). "I soul for my soul" (*j'âme l'âme*).

The Forty Days thus stages the impossibility of summoning love through language and narration. Although in later raptures the mystic manipulated this *mythème* in very different manners, in *The Forty Days*, the first volume of her visions, Maria Maddalena recounted a silent occurrence. Love died in silence. His spouse, the mystic herself, became "sick." In fact, the mystic's illness stemmed from the fact that she could only observe the taking place of love's death without participating in it. She stared at her small crucifix mumbling scattered words. The characters of the biblical narrations acted in a complete silence as well. Maria Maddalena could not speak to someone who was asleep (the apostles), or withdrew from the "stage" (Judas). The Word himself became silent. He only pronounced "Ego sum," a sentence that makes the soldiers fall asleep.

If, as Simone Weil says, love is present in the world as a remembrance of his affliction, the world can obtain no relief from the act of narrating love's withdrawal from the world. What the vision in *The Forty Days* clarifies is that the act of loving love entails the act of narrating the mute and silent execution of love. The fourth day of Maria Maddalena's vision on love concludes with the following words: "Alas, alas, alas, I can't anymore. No more love. No more, because I can't anymore" (177).

NOTES

INTRODUCTION

1. Some of the translations of *I colloqui* used in this book are from my forthcoming book *Maria Maddalena de' Pazzi: Selected Revelations* (New York: Paulist Press). For my translation I use the sole edition of the mystic's visions: *Tutte le opere di Santa Maria Maddalena de'Pazzi dai manoscritti originali*, ed. Bruno Nardini, Bruno Visentin, Carlo Catena, and Giulio Agresti (Florence: Nardini, 1960–66).

2. I refer to Emmanuel Lévinas's concept of "Otherness" as he formulates it in *Otherwise than Being or Beyond Essence*, trans. Alphonso Lingis (The Hague: Martinus Nijhoff, 1981). In particular, see "Saying and Subjectivity" (chapter 2, 45–56), "Proximity" (chapter 3, 75–93), and "Substitution" (chapter 4, 99–130).

3. Cf. Giovanni Pozzi, *Le parole dell'estasi* (Milan: Adelphi, 1984), 19.

4. I quote from Alison Weber, *Teresa of Avila and the Rhetoric of Femininity* (Princeton, NJ: Princeton University Press, 1990), 117.

5. Louis Marin, *La voix excommuniée* (Paris: Editions galilée, 1981), 46. My translation.

6. Aviad M. Kleinberg, *Prophets in Their Own Countries: Living Saints and the Making of Sainthood in the Later Middle Ages* (Chicago: University of Chicago Press, 1997), 44.

7. As Lacan explains, the *objet petit a* is "the result of a cut (*coupure*) expressed in the anatomical mark (*trait*) of a margin or border—lips, 'the enclosure of the teeth,' the rim of the anus, the tip of the penis, the vagina, the slit formed by the eyelids, even the horn-shaped aperture of the ear" (Lacan, "The Subversion of the Subject and the Dialectic of Desire in the Freudian Unconscious," in *Écrits*, trans. Alan Sheridan [New York: W. W. Norton, 1977], 314–15). As Ellie Ragland explains, "what Lacan called object a is a symbol denoting both an empty *place* in being and body and the 'object' that one chooses to stop it up because this void place produces anxiety" (Ragland, "The Relation between the Voice and the Gaze," in *Reading Seminar XI: Lacan's Four Fundamental Concepts of Psychoanalysis*, ed. Richard Feldstein [Albany: State University of New York Press, 1995], 189). See also Jacques-Alain Miller, "Montré à Premontré," *Analytica* 37 (1984): 28–29; Slavoj Žižek, *The Metastases of Enjoyment* (London: Verso, 1994), 30–33.

8. Lacan, *Écrits*: "It is from the Other that the subject receives even the message that he emits" (305).

9. See Jean-Michel Ribettes, "Le phalsus," in *Folle verité: Vérité et vraisemblance du texte psychotique*, ed. Julia Kristeva (Paris: Seuil, 1979),

116–70. Examining the structure of psychotic discourse from a Lacanian stand-point, Ribettes states that obsessive discourse is "une névrose vraisemblable . . . où la parole est par le sujet éprouvée comme le risque d'une épreuve, une expéri-ence hasardeuse qui examine, interroge et réfléchit intimement le fonctionnement du langage et les conditions mêmes de la langue" (116). Similar to but not iden-tifiable with an obsessive discourse, Maria Maddalena's monologues doubt themselves; they constantly refer to the Word who judges/investigates/under-mines them. As Ribettes reminds us, "la discursivité obsessionelle s'essaie . . . à la récollection des signifiants, à leur comptage exhaustif . . . l'obsessionnel est l'interminable vérificateur indécis, Grand Comptable des signifiants" (136).

10. Cf. Colette Soler, "The Subject and the Other (II)," in *Reading Semi-nar XI*: "in the Other you encounter only signifiers and the void—what Lacan called the interval between signifiers. The interval is a void" (51).

11. As Louis Marin explains, "to speak of orality is to speak of the voice as it occurs in the words that make up speech. Now the voice is 'a thing of the mouth,' [which] constitutes the site where a potentially articulate voice is made to produce or effect words. . . . The mouth is the locus of need, as well as the means by which this need is satisfied. As a result, the mouth is the place where a drive is inscribed." (Louis Marin, *Food for Thought* [Baltimore: Johns Hop-kins University Press, 1989], 35–37).

12. Mark C. Taylor, *Nots* (Chicago: University of Chicago Press, 1993), 11.

13. See Bernard McGinn, *The Foundations of Mysticism* (New York: Crossroad, 1991), 157–82.

14. Claudio Catena, "Ambiente del monastero di S. Maria degli Angeli ai tempi di S. Maria Maddalena de' Pazzi," *Carmelus* 13 (1966): 22 (hereafter cited as AM).

15. Claudio Catena, "Le donne del Carmelo italiano," *Carmelus* 10 (1963): 32 (hereafter cited as DC).

16. Catena explains that originally the Carmelite order admitted four lev-els of religious life, "oblati," "conversi," "confrati," and "familiari" (Catena, DC, 21). Although it is not always easy to define them, these titles corresponded to different duties and vows. Only the male and female *conversi* embraced the strictest Carmelite rule (its three vows) and thus became actual religious. How-ever, women did not have their own monasteries and continued to live by them-selves.

17. Peter-Thomas Rohrbach, O.C.D., *Journey to Carith: The Story of the Carmelite Order* (Garden City, NY: Doubleday, 1966), 127. See also the entry "Carmes" in *Dictionnaire de spiritualité* (Paris: Beauchesne, 1953) 163–64.

18. Catena reminds us that the religious had a "big" scapular that they wore during the day, and a "small" scapular that they wore at night (Catena, DC, 28–29).

19. I have consulted the convent's copy of Capocchi's text. As far as the relationship between death and the body, see pages 47v–48v.

20. For Capocchi's influence on Maria Maddalena, see Claudio Catena, *Santa Maria Maddalena de' Pazzi carmelitana: Orientamenti spirituali e ambi-ente in cui visse* (Rome: Institutum Carmelitanum, 1966), 13–15. Hereafter cited as *Santa Maria Maddalena de' Pazzi carmelitana*.

21. The library of the convent still has Vangelista del Giocondo's memoirs. A sort of hagiographic text was written based on the nun's notes. Vangelista's strict religiosity is apparent in the detached and firm tone of her discourse. For instance, Vangelista addresses her sisters as follows: "You must imagine that you have entered a desert. As you know, in that place nothing is appealing. On the contrary, everything brings about fear and awe, because many animals live there and leaves often fall on the ground and make us fall. . . . Speak very little and not loudly. Avoid any useless word and practice religious modesty in all your deeds." (*Vita della venerabile madre suor Vangelista del Giocondo, monaca di Santa Maria degli Angeli*, quoted in Catena, AM, 82. My translation.)

22. See Bruno Secondin, *Santa Maria Maddalena de' Pazzi: Esperienza e dottrina* (Rome: Institutum Carmelitanum, 1974), 66.

23. On the role of silence in the religious offices, see Gregory Smith, O. Carm., "Liturgic Silence," *Carmelus* 23 (1976): 3–20; Secondin, 72–73.

24. Maria Maddalena suffered from mysterious diseases throughout her life. For an analysis of Maria Maddalena's illnesses, see Claudio Catena, "Le malattie di S. Maria Maddalena de' Pazzi," *Carmelus* 16 (1969): 70–141; Ernest E. Larkin, "The Ecstasies of the Forty Days of Saint Mary Magdalen de' Pazzi," *Carmelus* 1 (1954): 29–71.

25. Gabriella Zarri, "Living Saints: A Typology of Female Sanctity in the Early Sixteenth Century," in *Women and Religion in Medieval and Renaissance Italy*, ed. Daniel Bornstein and Roberto Rusconi (Chicago: University Chicago Press, 1996), 219 (hereafter cited as LS).

26. Bernard McGinn discusses the theological aspects of women's "informal and non-sacramental authority" in "Donne mistiche ed autorità esoterica nel XIV secolo," in *Poteri carismatici e informali: Chiesa e società medioevali* (Palermo: Sellerio, 1992), 153–74.

27. Roberto Rusconi, "Women Religious in Late Medieval Italy: New Sources and Directions," in *Women and Religion in Medieval and Renaissance Italy*, 311.

28. For an analysis of the saint's statements concerning the role of the Church, its relationship with the heretics, and the morality of its ministers, see Ermanno del Sacramento, "La passione di S. Maria Maddalena de' Pazzi per la Chiesa," *Ephemerides Carmelitae* 17 (1966): 405–16. Del Sacramento's study shows that Maria Maddalena limits herself to repeating the rather common criticism on the corruption of some branches of the Church and on the heretics' radical evil.

29. I quote from the first English translation of Puccini's book: *The Life of St. Mary Magdalene of Pazzi, a Carmelite Nunn* (London: Randal Taylor, 1687), 61.

30. For an interesting analysis of the various forms of female mysticism in the Renaissance, see Massimo Petrocchi, *Storia della spiritualità italiana: Il cinquecento e il seicento* (Rome: Edizioni di storia e letteratura, 1978), 7–50.

31. For the concept of "true" versus "false" sanctity in the Renaissance, see Gabriella Zarri, "'Vera' santità, 'simulata' santità: Ipotesi e riscontri," in *Finzione e santità tra medioevo ed età moderna*, ed. Gabriella Zarri (Turin: Rosenberg & Sellier, 1991), 9–39 (hereafter cited as VS).

32. For a detailed analysis of the political and spiritual aspects of the Council, see Adriano Prosperi, "Riforma cattolica, Controriforma, disciplinamento sociale," in *Storia dell'Italia religiosa: II. L'età moderna*, ed. Gabriele de Rosa and Tullio Gregory (Bari: Laterza, 1994), 3–48; Gabriella Zarri, *Le sante vive: Cultura e religiosità femminile nella prima età moderna* (Turin: Einaudi, 1990); William Hudon, *Theatine Spirituality* (New York: Paulist Press, 1996), 7–16; Giuseppe Alberigo, "Dinamiche religiose del Cinquecento italiano tra riforma, riforma cattolica, controriforma," *Cristianesimo nella storia* 6 (1985): 543–60.

33. See Giovanna Paolin, "Confessione e confessori al femminile: Monache e direttori spirituali in ambito veneto tra '600 e '700," in *Finzione e santità tra medioevo ed età moderna*, 366–88; Robert Creytens, "La riforma dei monasteri femminili dopo i decreti tridentini," in *Il Concilio di Trento e la Riforma Tridentina: Proceedings of the Conference held in Trent on September 2–6, 1963* (Rome: Herder, 1965), 1:45–84.

34. For an analysis of Borromeo's text, see Ottavia Niccoli, "Il confessore e l'inquisitore: A proposito di un manoscritto bolognese del Seicento," in *Finzione e santità tra medioevo ed età moderna*, 412–34.

35. Gabriele De Rosa, "I codici di lettura del 'vissuto religioso,'" in *Storia dell'Italia religiosa: II. L'età moderna*, 303–73.

36. Jeffrey Burton Russell, *Witchcraft in the Middle Ages* (Ithaca, NY: Cornell University Press, 1972), 154 (hereafter cited as *Witchcraft*).

37. Jeffrey Burton Russell, *A History of Witchcraft* (London: Thames and Hudson, 1980), 82.

38. Robin Briggs, *Witches and Neighbors* (New York: Viking Penguin, 1996), 202.

39. See Karen-edis Barman, "Cultural Production, Religious Devotion, and Subjectivity in Early Modern Italy: The Case Study of Maria Maddalena de' Pazzi," *Annali d'Italianistica* 13 (1995): 283–306.

40. Fr. Ermanno del S. S. Sacramento, "I manoscritti originali di Santa Maria Maddalena de' Pazzi," *Ephemerides carmeliticae* 7 (1956): 386. My translation.

41. Michel de Certeau, *The Practice of Everyday Life*, trans. Steven F. Rendall (Berkeley: University of California Press, 1984), 156.

1. ORALITY AND TIME IN *I COLLOQUI*

1. Hans Ruef, *Augustin über Semiotik und Sprache* (Bern: Verlag K. J. Wyss Erben, 1981), 82. My translation.

2. Tzvetan Todorov, *Theories of the Symbol*, trans. Catherine Porter (Ithaca, NY: Cornell University Press, 1982), 36.

3. Orlando Todisco underscores that Augustine rejects the Aristotelian vision of language, according to which "words are symbols of affections (pathématon) of the soul, and these are symbols of things" (Orlando Todisco, *Parola e verità: Agostino e la filosofia del linguaggio* [Rome: Anicia, 1993], 29–31).

4. For an analysis of the relationship between time and sign in Augustine's *On Dialectics*, see Cornelius Petrus Mayer, OSA, *Die Zeichen in der Geistigen Entwicklung und in der Theologie des Jungen Augustinus* (Würzburg: Augustinus Verlag, 1969), 239–41.

5. *Serm.* 2, 2.

6. Cf. Giorgio Santi, *Dio e l'uomo: Conoscenza, memoria, linguaggio, ermeneutica in Agostino* (Rome: Città nuova editrice, 1989), 91.

7. St Augustine, *Concerning the Teacher and On the Immortality of the Soul*, trans. George G. Leckie (New York: Appleton Century Crofts, 1938), 13:41–42.

8. Cf. Étienne Gilson, *Introduction a l'étude de Saint Augustin* (Paris: Vrin, 1929), 87–90; Italo Sciuto, *Dire l'indicibile: Comprensione e situazione in S. Agostino* (Verona: Fracisci editore, 1984), 62–66.

9. St Augustine, *On Christian Doctrine*, trans. D. W. Robertson Jr. (Indianapolis: The Bobbs-Merrill Company, 1958), bk. 2, 1:1; bk. 2, 2:3.

10. St Augustine, *On Christian Doctrine*, bk. 1, 22:20–21.

11. Cf. Pozzi, *Parole dell'estasi*, 26: "When he reads her pages, the reader must be aware of the fact that Maria Maddalena never addresses him. . . . The reader is simply overhearing." My translation.

12. Lacan, *Écrits*, 317. Cf. Slavoj Žižek, *Looking Awry: An Introduction to Jacques Lacan through Popular Culture* (Cambridge, Mass: MIT Press, 1991), in particular, "The Real and Its Vicissitudes" (21–47).

13. Cf. Pozzi, *Parole dell'estasi*, 27.

14. In an important chapter of the *Seminar*, "On the Signifier in the Real and the Bellowing-Miracle" (*The Psychosis 1955–1956*, trans. Russell Grigg [New York: Norton, 1993], 130–142), Lacan examines the nature of linguistic interaction. Referring to the words "the peace of the night," which came to his mind all of a sudden, Lacan tries to understand how the deepest meaning of these words can be transmitted and perceived by a listener. Lacan believes that, in order to apprehend fully the sense of these words, we should *not* listen to them, but we should rather let this expression *happen*, as if it were something that came from the outside, such as a echo or murmur: "It's precisely when we are not listening to it, when it's outside our field and suddenly hits us from behind, that it assumes its full value, surprised as we are by this more endophasic, more or less inspired, expression that comes to us like a murmur from without, a manifestation of discourse insofar as it barely belongs to us, which comes as a echo" (138).

15. Pier Aldo Rovatti, *Abitare la distanza* (Milan: Feltrinelli, 1994), 102–3. My translation.

16. In another essay from *The Psychosis*, "I've just been to the butcher's," Lacan states that it is through the Other that the subject comes to perceive himself: "In true speech the Other is that before which you make yourself recognized by it only because it is recognized first. It has to be recognized for you to be able to make yourself recognized" (51).

17. Lacan, *Écrits*, 313.

18. Although *I colloqui* is the result of a complex editorial operation, it is attributed to one person, Maria Maddalena de' Pazzi. A literary text seems to demand a specific attribution, even though, as in the case of *I colloqui*, the book

actually has a number of "authors." Why do we need to name the author? The author's name has at least two major functions. First, "the author's name serves to characterize a certain mode of being of discourse: the fact that the discourse has an author's name shows that this discourse is not ordinary everyday speech . . . on the contrary, it is a speech that must be received in a certain mode and that . . . must receive a certain status" (Michel Foucault, "What Is an Author?" *Foucault Reader*, ed. Paul Rabinow [New York: Pantheon Books, 1984], 107). In other words, in order to acquire its status as text, *I colloqui* needs the name of an author, in this case Maria Maddalena. The saint's name gives this text its identity, its reason for being: "The author's name manifests the appearence of a certain discursive set and indicates the status of this discourse within a society and a culture." Second, the author's name "is . . . the principle of a certain unity of writing—all differences having to be resolved, at least in part" (Foucault, 111).

19. Typically, the mystical literary genre considers God its sole author. In particular, in the case of female mystics many scholars believe that women endeavored to defend themselves against possible attacks from the institutional church by stating that their texts had been dictated by God Himself. Cf. Giovanni Pozzi, "L'alfabeto delle sante," *Scrittrici mistiche italiane*, ed. Giovanni Pozzi and Claudio Leonardi (Genoa: Marietti, 1989), 21–22.

Visions gave women authority, but "each individual woman had to discover for herself how . . . to express her insights within the framework of the teachings of the Church" (E. A. Petroff, *Medieval Women's Visionary Literature* [Oxford: Oxford University Press, 1986], 20). For instance, in Italy only Umiltà of Faenza and Catherine of Siena were widely recognized as authoritative figures within the Catholic church. Bernard McGinn underscores that in some exceptional cases medieval female mystics were granted a theological authority *ex beneficio*, that is, given that the Holy Spirit's grace is unlimited women may be among the elect. Women can teach only when God decides to grant them his knowledge (Bernard McGinn, "Donne mistiche ed autorità esoterica nel XIV secolo," 153–74).

As far as writing is concerned, very frequently female visionaries had to rely on a male scribe, a priest or a monk, who wrote down their discourses (Hildegard of Bingen, Angela of Foligno, Christina of Markyate, Mechthild of Magdeburg, among many others). To lend authority to their mystical experiences, female visionaries needed a male "voice."

Female visionaries not only often needed a male scribe, but they also had to stress that in their texts they had limited themselves to repeating what God himself had communicated to them. For instance, Mechthild of Magdeburg begins *Das fliessende Licht der Gottheit* by underscoring that God is the only the author of her text (Mechthild of Magdeburg, *Das fliessende Licht der Gottheit* [Zurich: Benziger Verlag, 1956], 53).

20. Jonathan Culler stresses that structuralists "postulate the existence of an autonomous level of plot structure underlying actual linguistic manifestation" (Jonathan Culler, *Structuralist Poetics* [Ithaca, NY: Cornell University Press, 1975], 205).

21. In some passages the transcribers notice that the saint's discourses have a sermonic style (colloqui 39 and 41).

22. Maria Maddalena is very respectful of the preachers' role in the convent. In a short but very important passage, the saint clearly states that the divinity speaks to his believers in various manners, sermons among them (1:213).

23. For similar images concerning her convent sisters, see 1:58, 1:67, 1:87–88. Maria Maddalena's discourses usually concern only her convent. However, in occasional passages she also gives us her opinion about the contemporary historical condition. In a vision from *The Forty Days* the saint accuses Queen Elizabeth of England of persecuting the Word: "And that woman, that woman, oh Love, I mean that pestiferous and evil woman, that is persecuting you so; I see her fall and sink like an arrow in the most horrible, gloomy, and deep place. Oh Love, Love.

We understood that she was speaking about Queen Elizabeth of England, the heretic" (150).

24. The saint's remarks about her convent sisters are so frequent that I shall limit myself to one example. In colloquio 4, Maria Maddalena sees some angels putting a group of nuns into the Word's bleeding side. However, the angels reject two of the saint's sisters because these nuns are not "respectable people." Although the angels mention the name of one of them, the nuns do not report it in their transcription (1:87).

25. Paul Ricoeur speaks of "le temps de la narration et le temps raconté." The first kind corresponds to the actual act of narrating a given event, whereas the second is that event in its narrative elements. See Paul Ricoeur, *Temps et récit: 2. La configuration dans le récit de fiction* (Paris: Gallimard, 1984), 149.

26. Saint Augustine's use of his mystical experience in the *Confessions* is in many ways similar to Maria Maddalena's. Augustine tends to mingle atemporal and temporal time. For instance, see the famous book 9 of *Confessions* in which he describes his Ostia rapture.

27. Cf. Jacques Derrida, *De la grammatologie* (Paris: Minuit, 1967), 279–326.

28. Maurice Merleau Ponty, *La prose du monde* (Paris: Gallimard, 1969), 112.

29. See Maurice Merleau-Ponty, *L'oeil et l'esprit* (Paris: Gallimard, 1964), 44–46.

2. THE WORD AND THE LANGUAGE OF THE BIRDS

1. Michael A. Sells, *Mystical Languages of Unsaying* (Chicago: University of Chicago Press, 1994), 1–13.

2. Jacques Lacan, *Feminine Sexuality*, ed. Juliet Mitchell and Jacqueline Rose (New York: W. W. Norton, 1982), 160–61; Lacan *Écrits*, 305. Cf. Žižek, *Looking Awry*, 150–51.

3. Roland Barthes, *Leçon* (Paris: Seuil, 1978), 10.

4. Roland Barthes, *Critique et vérité* (Paris: Seuil, 1966), 27–28.

5. See the seminal analysis by Paul De Man of Nietzsche's conception of rhetoric. De Man underscores that in his notes for a semester course taught at the University of Basel during the winter semester of 1872–73 Nietzsche states

that "the paradigmatic structure of language is rhetorical rather than representational or expressive of a referential, proper meaning." In other words, according to Nietzsche all forms of language are based on tropes (Paul De Man, *Allegories of Reading: Figural Language in Rousseau, Nietzsche, Rilke, and Proust* [New Haven: Yale University Press, 1979], 106).

6. See Roland Barthes, "From Work to Text," in *Image/Music/Text*, trans. Stephen Heath (New York: Farrar, Straus and Giroux, 1988), 155–64. In this seminal essay Barthes stresses that a text is the "field" of the signifier (158). For a discussion of Barthes's interpretation of discoursive practices, see Frances Bartowski, "Roland Barthes' Secret Garden," *Studies in Twentieth Century Literature* 5 (Spring 1981): 133–46.

7. Louis Charbonneau-Lassay, *The Bestiary of Christ*, trans. D. M. Dooly (New York: Arkana, 1992), 425. See also Beryl Rowland, "The Art of Memory and the Bestiary," in *Beasts and Birds in the Middle Ages: The Bestiary and Its Legacy*, ed. Willene B. Clarck and Meredith T. McMunn (Philadelphia: University of Pennsylvania Press, 1989), 12–25.

8. Dante Alighieri, *Purgatorio*, trans. Allen Mandelbaum (New York: Bantam Books, 1982), 17.

9. Gregory the Great, *Homiliarum in Ezechielem*, Patrologia Latina, ed. J.-P. Migné, vol. 76 (Paris: D'Amboise, 1849), bk. 10, 901. Hereafter cited as PL.

10. Honorius, *Elucidarium*, PL, vol. 172, bk. 1, 1113–14.

11. René Guénon, *Fundamental Symbols: The Universal Language of Sacred Science*, trans. Alvin Moore Jr. (Cambridge: Quinta Essentia, 1995), 39. Cf. René Guénon, "Monothéisme et angélologie," in *Mélanges* (Paris: Gallimard, 1976), 26–31.

12. Jacques Lacan, *Seminaire XX* (Paris: Seuil, 1975), 96.

13. Michel de Certeau tackles this problem in *Il parlare angelico*, trans. Daniela De Agostini (Florence: Olschki, 1989), 203.

14. Thomas Aquinas, *Summa Theologica*, in *Basic Writings of Saint Thomas Aquinas*, ed. Anton C. Pegis (New York: Random House, 1945), 494–97.

15. Henry Corbin, *Avicenna and the Visionary Recital*, trans. Willard R. Trask (Princeton, NJ: Princeton University Press, 1988), 55. Corbin refers to Avicenna's Neoplatonic interpretation of the angelic beings: "The idea (common to Islam and Christianity) of the Angel as servant of the supreme God and messenger of his communications to the Prophets is replaced by the Neoplatonic idea of the Angel as "hermeneut of the divine silence"—that is, as annunciation and epiphany of the impenetrable and incommunicable divine transcendence." Examining Avicenna's *The Recital of the Bird* and its influence on Persian mysticism, Corbin synthesizes the so-called "cycle of the bird" as follows: "It is the Imago of the soul perceiving itself as a winged being in the likeness of the Angel, and recognizing its Self in the vision of the celestial being, that gives rise to the 'cycle of the Bird'" (183).

16. Thomas Aquinas, *Summa*, Ia 56, 2:523.

17. Massimo Cacciari, *L'angelo necessario* (Milan: Adelphi, 1994), 132–133. Hereafter cited as AN.

18. Origen, *Comment. in John, Patrologia Greca*, ed. DD. Caroli et Calori Vincentii Delarue, vol. 14 (Paris, 1857), 458–59. Hereafter cited as PG.

19. Desire as "incompletion, an unfulfillment, an aspiration toward the still Unrealized" is a central aspect of Avicenna's angelology (Corbin, 71).

20. Thomas Aquinas, *Summa Contra Gentiles*, in *Opera Omnia* (Stuttgart: Fromann, 1980), bk. 4.14, 121. See Josef Pieper, "Ueber Das Innere Wort," *Sinn und Form* 5 (1995): 706–8.

21. Eusebius Hieronymus, *Commentariorum in Michaeam*, PL, vol. 25, 1206.

22. Origen, *In Lucam Homilia*, PG, vol. 13, 1808: "Fieri enim potest, ut et nunc nobis loquentibus assistat angelus, et tamen quia non meremur, eum videre nequeamus."

23. Peter Dinzelbacher, *Vision und Visionsliteratur im Mittelalter* (Stuttgart: Anton Hiersemann, 1981), 163–64.

24. Brigitta of Sweden, *Life and Selected Revelations*, ed. Marguerite Tjader Harris (New York: Paulist Press, 1990), 102.

25. Kleinberg, *Prophets in Their Own Countries*, 49.

26. Angela of Foligno, *Complete Works*, ed. Paul Lachance (New York: Paulist Press, 1993), 205. For an analysis of this passage from Angela's *Memorial*, see Giovanni Pozzi, *Il libro dell'esperienza* (Milan: Adelphi, 1992), 184–92.

27. As the reader will notice, Maria Maddalena's discourse contains both English (Italian) and Latin; in order to maintain the bilingual nature of the text, I have decided not to translate the Latin passage.

28. See, in particular, John R. Searle, *Speech Acts* (Cambridge: Cambridge University Press, 1969), 54–71. In *La fable mystique* (Paris: Gallimard, 1982, hereafter cited as FM) de Certeau broaches this problem, applying Searle's and Austin's theories to mystical discourse (223–25).

29. John R. Searle, *Intentionality* (Cambridge: Cambridge University Press, 1983), 166.

30. De Certeau hints at this aspect of Searle's philosophy of language in a central part of *La fable mystique*, when he specifically speaks of the "will" (*le vouloir*) expressed by the mystical word (231).

31. Nicholas Wolterstorff, *Divine Discourse: Philosophical Reflections on the Claim That God Speaks* (Oxford: Oxford University Press, 1995), 28.

32. Meister Eckhart, *The Essential Sermons, Commentaries, Treatises, and Defense*, trans. Edmund Colledge, O.S.A. and Bernard McGinn (New York: Paulist Press, 1981), 204 (hereafter cited as ES). Meister Eckhart also suggests: "be silent, and do not chatter about God; for when you do chatter about him, you are telling lies and sinning. But if you want to be without sin and perfect, you should not chatter about God" (207). Joseph Quint discusses this theme in: "Mystik und Sprache," in *Altdeutsche und Altniederländische Mystik* (Wissenschaftliche Buchgesellschaft, 1964), 98–151.

33. Bernard McGinn, "Theological Summary," in Meister Eckhart, *The Essential Sermons, Commentaries, Treatises, and Defense*, 38.

34. Meister Eckhart, *Teacher and Preacher*, ed. Bernard McGinn (New York: Paulist Press, 1986), 259.

35. Bernard of Clairvaux, *On the Song of Songs*, trans. Irene Edmonds, vol. 4 (Kalamazoo, MI: Cistercian Publications, 1980), 7.

36. In colloquio 11 (1:145–46) the Saint speaks of the "idle word" (*parola otiosa*) that prevents God from meeting with us. Our idle word is a "stain" on our soul; God cannot tolerate it. Although this idle word sometimes may seem a minimum flaw to us, it actually makes our communication with the Word impossible.

37. Gilles Deleuze, *Difference and Repetition* (New York: Columbia University Press, 1994), 274. See also Joan Copjec, *Read My Desire* (Cambridge, Mass.: The MIT Press, 1994), 211.

38. George Bataille, *L'expérience intérieure* (Paris: Gallimard, 1990), 56. My translation.

39. In her previous rapture the Word had "plunged" her in his bleeding side twice in order to purify her with his blood. After this purification she would be apt to receive a unique "gift." (47)

40. The sense of this sentence is unclear. The mystic seems to allude to the fact that the disciples had already planned to hold a certain position in God's reign.

41. Pozzi and Leonardi *Scrittrici mistiche italiane*, 196.

42. Cf. Lacan, *Seminaire XX*, 102: "[Q]uelle importance peut-il y avoir dans la doctrine chrétienne à ce que le Christ ait une âme? Cette doctrine ne parle que de l'incarnation de Dieu dans un corps, et suppose bien que la passion soufferte en cette personne ait fait la joussance d'un autre. . . . Le Christ, même, ressuscité, vaut par son corps."

43. This is what de Certeau says about John of the Cross's poetry: "A l'absence du Verbe, s'oppose une assurance: il *doit parler*." (FM, 217)

44. Cf. de Certeau, FM, 195: "il s'agit de paroles 'adressées,' sans qu'on puisse savoir finalement par qui et à qui."

45. This, of course, raises the fundamental question of authority in the text. Although Maria Maddalena is passive toward the divine call, she remains aware of those places in her convent where the divinity visits her. According to Dinzelbacher's different categories of mystical encounters, we could say that Maria Maddalena's raptures are "in-between" visions, what the German scholar calls "Uebergangsformen." By that term he means that the visionary's mind is not totally overwhelmed by the divine communication, but it is still able to distinguish human reality from the supernatural (Dinzelbacher, 37).

46. In Lacanian terms, the *real* is beyond the realm of speech; it can be thought of as the ineffable world of objects and experiences, or as that which is lacking in the symbolic/linguistic order and which may be approached but never grasped.

47. In *De Anima* Aristotle first posits the essential relationship between image, *phantasia*, and word. Although the term *phantasia* has a number of meanings in Aristotle's texts, it is crucial to remember that in *De Anima* "*phantasia* is regarded as a necessary condition of thought ('there is no supposition without it,' 427b15)." However, Aristotle also holds that "*phantasiai* are mere after-images of sense-perception, often false ones" (Dorothea Frede, "The Cognitive Role of *Phantasia*," in *Essays on Aristotle's* De Anima, ed. Martha C. Nussbaum and Amélie Oksenberg Rorty [Oxford: Claredon, 1995], 280). If after-images, summoned by a given utterance, "can become mere appearances

that drift in and out of our consciousness" (Frede, 285), we may infer that the pauses, inserted by the nuns/editors within the mystic's discourse, aim to dispel/annihilate those very after-images created by the edited text. In *I colloqui* graphic pauses (dots in the original manuscripts) thus bring about mental, intellectual "pauses." See also Malcolm Schofield, "Aristotle on the Imagination," in *Essays on Aristotle's* De Anima, 249–77.

48. Derrida's discourse on writing versus orality is implicitly considered at this point. See, for instance, *De la grammatologie*, 207–8.

49. Jack Goody, *The Interface between the Written and the Oral* (Cambridge: Cambridge University Press, 1987), 186.

50. Lauro Flores, "Bilinguism and the Literary Text," *Visible Language* 21 (Winter 1987): 130–52.

51. See Stephen Lubell, "Bilinguism in the Hebrew Text," *Visible Language* 27 (Winter/Spring 1993): 163–204.

52. The literature on Marinetti's visual poetry is incredibly vast. As a starting point, see Michael Webster, "Words-in-Freedom and the Oral Tradition," *Visible Language* 23.1 (1987): 65–87.

53. See Françoise Meltzer, *Salomé and the Dance of Writing* (Chicago: University of Chicago Press, 1987), 129; Mary Lewis Shaw, "Concrete and Abstract Poetry: The World as Text and the Text as World," *Visible Language* 23.1/2 (1987): 29–43.

54. See Estera Milman, "The Text and the Myth of the avant-garde," *Visible Language* 21.3/4 (1987), 335–64.

55. Giorgio Agamben, *Language and Death: The Place of Negativity*, trans. Karen E. Pinkus and Michael Hardt (Minneapolis: University of Minnesota Press, 1991), 47.

56. I find this passage in J. F. M. Hunter, *Understanding Wittgenstein* (Edinburgh: Edinburgh University Press, 1985), 98.

57. Ludwig Wittgenstein. *The Blue and the Brown Books* (New York: Barnes and Noble, 1969), 82.

58. "The term 'imagetext' designates composite, synthetic works (or concepts) that combine image and text" (W. J. T. Mitchell, *Picture Theory* [Chicago: University of Chicago Press, 1994], 89).

59. I study de' Pazzi's different forms of silence in "The Voice and the Silences of Maria Maddalena de' Pazzi," *Annali d'italianistica* 13 (1995): 257–81.

60. Deborah Tannen, "Silence: Anything But," in *Perspectives on Silence*, ed. Deborah Tannen and Muriel Saville-Troike (Norwood, NJ: Ablex, 1984), 97.

61. Deborah Tannen, *Talking Voices* (Cambridge: Cambridge University Press, 1989), 23.

62. See Otto Lorenz, *Das Schweigen in der Dichtung: Hölderlin, Rilke, Celan* (Ruprecht: Vandenhöck 1989), 48. Lorenz holds that silence has a referential function, like a Peircean "index."

63. Meltzer, 23. See also Mitchell's interesting "Ekphrasis and the Other," in *Picture Theory*, 151–81.

64. See Maurice Merleau-Ponty, *Signs*, trans. Richard C. McCleary (Evanston, IL: Northwestern University Press, 1964), 43.

65. Michel de Certeau, *The Writing of History* (New York: Columbia University Press, 1988), 269. Hereafter cited as WH.

66. Kleinberg, *Prophets in Their Own Countries*, 54.

67. Pozzi and Leonardi, *Scrittici mistiche italiane*, 212. The last sentence of the citation is incomplete.

68. In *Fragmentation and Redemption* (New York: Zone Books, 1991), Caroline Walker Bynum studies how the Middle Ages treated the saints' corpses. The saints' bodies were dissected in several parts that were sent to different religious places, such as churches or convents. Those relics were believed to produce miracles because they belonged to the saints' immortal identity (265–97). In *The Resurrection of the Body in Western Christianity, 200–1336* (New York: Columbia University Press, 1995), Bynum recounts St Augustine's discomfort concerning relics: "As a young man in Milan, Augustine had been uninterested in relics, and the councils of 401 held under his influence had tried to limit the practice of moving the dust of the saints. But by 422–23 Augustine had been convinced by accounts of the cures and visions at Uzalis and Carthage; he now ordered Stephen's miracles to be recorded. . . . The dead were materialized by being divided up and distributed; the more the martyr's parts were spread throughout the Mediterranean world, the more he or she came to be seen as housed within the fragment" (105–6).

69. Edith Wyschogrod, *Saints and Postmodernism* (Chicago: University of Chicago Press, 1990), 6.

70. Manfred Frank, *What is Neo-structuralism?*, trans. Sabine Wilke and Richard T. Gray (Minneapolis: University of Minnesota Press, 1989), 43.

71. Manfred Frank, "Die Dichtung als 'Neue Mythologie,'" in *Mythos und Moderne* (Frankfurt am Main, 1983), 17.

72. The strict relationship between physical suffering and love is a *topos* of female mysticism. Pain is first of all the primary way of participating in the Word's passion. However, pain is not exclusively linked to the mystical participation in the Word's passion. Several women mystics encounter "the word of the Word" in the act of suffering from a "natural" disease or from a self-inflicted pain. For instance, Umiliana Cerchi (Florence, 1219–46) experiences the divinity through the intense pains in the stomach that will cause her death. In fact, the more she suffers, the more she feels inspired to sing or to hum her joy (Pozzi and Leonardi, 91). Villana de'Botti (Florence, 1332–61) has an almost masochistic drive toward suffering. She constantly asks God to grant her as many pains as possible. She finally receives a fever similar to a fire that enflames her body (Pozzi and Leonardi *Scrittrici mistiche italiane*, 222).

73. I study de' Pazzi's interpretation of "blood" in "Blood as Language in the Visions of Maria Maddalena de' Pazzi," *Rivista di letterature moderne e comparate* 48 (1995): 219–31.

74. See Giovanni Pozzi, "L'identico del diverso in Santa Maddalena de' Pazzi," *Freiburger Zeitschrift für Philosophie und Theologie* 33 (1986): 517–51.

75. For instance, in a letter to her friend Raimondo from Capua Saint Catherine says that she would like to see him drown "in Christ's extremely sweet blood" (Pozzi and Leonardi, *Scrittrici mistiche italiane*, 228–29).

76. After having asked St Augustine to write that sentence in her heart, the saint addresses St Catherine, who had repeatedly stressed the importance of the Word's blood.

3. THE WEDDING, THE FUNERAL, THE MEMORIAL OF THE WORD

1. Louis Marin, *Sémiotique de la Passion* (Aubier Montaigne: Editions du Cerf, 1971), 386. Hereafter cited as SP.

2. Herbert Blau, "The Surpassing Body," *TDR. The Drama Review* 35.2 (1991): 83.

3. Cf. Jon Erickson "The Spectacle of the Anti-Spectacle: Happenings and the Situationist International," *Discourse* 14.2 (1991): 51.

4. Elaine Scarry reminds us that in the Old Testament God manifests himself by affecting the human body: "God's invisible presence is asserted, made visible, in the perceivable alterations He brings about in the human body: in the necessity of human labor and the pains of childbirth, in a flood that drowns, in a plague that descends on a house, in the brimstone and the fire falling down on a city, in the transformation of a woman in a pillar of salt, in the leprous sores and rows of boils that alter the surface of the skin" (Elaine Scarry, *The Body in Pain, The Making and Unmaking of the World* [New York: Oxford University Press, 1987], 183).

5. In Žižek's words, when "I am driven to despair, thrown into absolute solitude, I can identify with Christ on the Cross. . . . My personal experience of being abandoned by God thus overlaps with the despair of Christ himself at being abandoned by the divine Father. . . . In Lacanian terms, we are dealing with the suspension of the big Other, which guarantees the subject's access to reality: in the experience of the death of God, we stumble upon the fact that 'the big Other does not exist'" (Slavoj Žižek, *The Metastases of Enjoyment* [London: Verso, 1995], 40–42). Žižek refers to Lacan's "Subversion of the Subject and Dialecti of Desire" (*Écrits*, 317). Thus, we may say that Maria Maddalena indirectly performs one more identification, i.e., with the Word himself, abandoned by the Father.

6. Richard Schechner, *Between Theater and Antropology* (Philadelphia: University of Pennsylvania Press, 1985), 295.

7. Jean-Luc Nancy, "Corpus," in *Thinking Bodies*, ed. Juliet Flower MacCannel and Laura Zakarin (Stanford, Calif.: Stanford University Press, 1994), 18.

8. Louis Marin, *La voix excommuniée* (Paris: Éditions Galilée, 1981), 46.

9. Alphonso Lingis, *Foreign Bodies* (London: Routledge, 1994), 23.

10. I find a stunning similitude between the Florentine mystic's sexual ambiguity and "the postmodern dissociation of presence and discourse," as Jill Dolan says about the performances of the male-to-female transsexual Kate Bornstein. "Her [Bornstein's] monologs traded among shifting, constructed identities, layered on a body that has experienced all of these constructions" (Jill Dolan, "In Defense of the Discourse," *TDR. The Drama Review* 33.3 (1989): 66).

11. Hélène Cixous, "Aller à la mer," *Modern Drama* 27.4 (1984): 546.

12. Christopher Smith, "A Sense of the Possible: Miles Davis and the Semiotics of Improvised Performance," *TDR. The Drama Review* 39.3 (1995): 42.

13. As Deleuze states, the body/subject "is not exactly a point but a place, a position, a site . . . a subject will be what comes to the point of view, or rather what remains of the point of view" (Gilles Deleuze, *The Fold: Leibniz and the Baroque*, trans. Tom Conley [Minneapolis: University of Minnesota Press, 1994], 19).

14. I have attempted to connect the biblical passages chosen by the saint to her ritual reading, the breviary. We cannot state that the saint actually cited a certain passage influenced by a recent reading of that very passage. The saint makes use of biblical excerpts according to what she needs to express, more than because of a recent reading. For example, I have come to the conclusion that her choice from the Psalms is absolutely unpredictable. In this colloquio, Psalm 139:12 ("Vir linguosus non dirigetur in terra") was read on Fridays (at vespers), whereas the subsequent one ("Omnes declinaverunt, non est qui faciat bonum, non est usque ad unum") was read on Thursdays (at matins), and the next one ("Et nolunt intelligere ut bene agerent") on Tuesdays (at matins). I have examined the breviary used in the saint's monastery, according to the edition authorized by Pope Pius V: *Breviarum romanum, ex decreto sacrosanti Concilii tridentini restitutum Pii V*, 1577. Bruno Secondin confirms that the convent of Santa Maria degli Angeli had immediately accepted the reformed breviary of Pope Pius V (*Santa Maria Maddalena*, 62).

15. It is crucial to remember that the mystical wedding between God and a soul is not unusual in medieval mystical literature. St Bernard had already theorized the mystical union between the soul and God (see, for example, *On the Song of Songs* 4, 180–87). This theme became central in several hagiographic works. As it is reported in the *Legenda maior* by Raimondo di Capua, St Catherine's marriage to God is the model of all the subsequent mystical weddings. St Catherine Ricci also had the same experience (*Vita di Santa Caterina de' Ricci*, ed. G. M. di Agresti [Florence, 1965], 129–30). Maria Maddalena had read several hagiographic works, primarily the life of St Catherine of Siena. As far as this vision is concerned, we must stress two crucial topoi of a mystical marriage. First, the visionary receives a ring from the Lord. In Maria Maddalena's vision her wedding ring is invisible, whereas in Catherine Ricci it causes the so-called *stigmate anulare* (ring-finger stigmata), a sort of swelling in the visionary's finger. For more on this, see H. Thurston, *Les phénomènes physiques du mysticisme* (Paris, 1963), 161–73.

The central part of colloquio 39 is dedicated to the saint's monologue concerning the meaning and the form of her wedding ring. Another fundamental aspect of a mystical marriage is that the visionary receives Jesus' heart, as if the Lord exchanged his heart with hers. Both Catherine of Siena and Catherine Ricci had the same experience. We find this element also in this vision of Maria Maddalena. For a historical survey of the mystical marriage in Christian tradition, see the entry "mariage spirituel" in *Dictionnaire de Spiritualité* (Paris: Beauchesne, 1953).

16. It is interesting to note that the writers mark the beginning of a new section of her raptures by a point sentence, that is, a sentence that summarizes

the content of the following visionary discourse. As we shall notice in several other passages, in her point sentences Maria Maddalena freely interprets the sacred text, often combining two verses together. In my analysis of this chapter I loosely refer to some basic concepts of sociolinguistics. In particular, I use Stephen Tyler, *The Said and the Unsaid* (New York: Academic Press, 1978).

17. I could not find any direct reference in the Bible. The metaphor expressed by the sentence "comedi iniquitatem" is not present in the Bible. However, Scripture contains several metaphors related to the act of eating. For instance, Hosea 4:8 presents the following image: "Peccata populi mei *comedent*: et ad *iniquitatem* eorum sublevabunt animas eorum" ("They shall eat the sins of my people, and shall lift up their souls to their iniquity"). I use *The Holy Bible* (Chicago: Good Counsel Publishing Company, 1963).

Maria Maddalena probably also refers to the well-known description of the Last Supper (Matt. 26:26).

18. Cf. Psalm 39:5: "Non respexit in vanitates et insanias falsas" ("[who] turns not to idolatry or to those who stray after falsehood"); Psalm 106:26: "Ascendunt usque ad coelos, et descendunt usque ad abyssos" ("They mounted up to heaven; they sank to the depths; their hearts melted away in their plight"). In particular, the expression "profundum abyssi" is not rare in the Bible (cf. Eccl. 1:2, 23:28, 24:8).

19. As far as the relationship between Italian and Latin is concerned, we must remember that these two languages correspond to two different linguistic frames. Whereas Latin is the language of the religious ceremonies and of the sacred texts, Italian is the language used in everyday conversations. It seems to me that the saint makes use of Latin not only when she quotes from the Bible or from her breviary, but first and foremost, when her discourse becomes highly ritualized. Again, only by listening to her actual voice could we perceive a shift in her discourse. For example, in the above passage the nuns inserted their explanation between the first and the second part. They marked a pause between the two sections. A very interesting case is also when the two languages, Latin and Italian, merge in the same utterance. This interaction between the two languages is due to two different emotional fields. First, she begins by using Latin, but later she breaks the formal tone of her Latin speech and introduces Italian. Second, she starts to speak in Italian, but later it seems that she finds this language inadequate to communicate the gravity of her statements. In both cases, the shift from one language to the other represents a frame shift.

From a grammatical standpoint, the nuns do not report correct Latin. We do not actually know whether the improprieties of the Latin were introduced by the transcribers themselves or whether the saint herself expressed them in her discourse. For instance, in this very passages we find "dolores inferni circunde*dit* me"; "comed*it* me dolores inferni"; "cadunt in iniquita*te*" but "cadunt in profundum abyssi"; "non habitab*it* in dom*um* tu*am* qui blasfem*ant* nomin*is* tu*i*." Claudio Catena reminds us that the nuns were encouraged to meditate together in Italian on the Latin passages read during the Mass. A sort of bilingualism thus dominated the everyday life in the convent of Santa Maria degli Angeli. During their meditation, also called "refectio spiritualis" (spiritual meal), the nuns freely intermingled Latin and Italian, first of all where the two languages either sounded or actually were similar (Catena, *Santa Maria Maddalena de' Pazzi carmelitana*, 35). In my translation I turn every Italian word into English. The most common case is "e" ("et" in Latin) translated as "and."

20. See Reinahrt Herzog, "Non in sua voce," in *Das Gespräch*, ed. Karlheinz Strierle und Painer Warning (Munich: Fink, 1984), 214–50; F. E. Consolino, "Interlocutore divino e lettori terreni: La funzione-destinatario nelle Confessioni di Agostino," *Materiali e discussioni* 6 (1982): 119–46; L. F. Pizzolato, *Le "Confessioni" di Sant'Agostino* (Milan: Vita e pensiero, 1968).

21. Claire Kahane, *Passions of the Voice: Hysteria, Narrative, and the Figure of the Speaking Woman, 1850–1915* (Baltimore: Johns Hopkins University Press, 1995), 17–18. Kahane speaks of the relationship between Freud and Dora, his patient in "Fragment of a Case of Hysteria."

22. Jean E. Jackson, "'After a While No One Believes You': Real and Unreal Pain," in *Pain as Human Experience: An Anthological Perspective*, ed. Mary-Jo Delvecchio Good (Berkeley: University of California Press, 1992), 138–68.

23. The judges of the Inquisition were aware of the ambiguity of the body's language. Although they claimed that tears would be a sign of repentance, they also knew that tears can be *false*, and thus signs of stubbornness. See chapter 4.

24. Ps. 52:4.

25. Ps. 35:4. The mystic modifies the actual verse: "et noluit intelligere un bene ageret."

26. Dianne Hunter, "Hysteria, Psychoanalysis, and Feminism: The Case of Anna O," in *The (M)other Tongue: Essays in Feminist Psychoanalytic Interpretation*, ed. Shirley Nelson Garner (Ithaca, NY: Cornell University Press, 1995), 102. Hunter discusses a fascinating case of the history of psychoanalysis. Bertha Pappenheim, known as "Anna O." in *Studies of Hysteria* published by Freud and Breuer in 1895, suffered from a sudden attack of aphasia. "When she regained her ability to talk, Bertha Pappenheim was unable to understand or speak her native tongue, although she proved surprisingly fluent in foreign languages" (Hunter, 92). She progressively lost her capacity of formulating complete sentences, ending up by making up words and using only verbs in the infinitive. "Hysteria expresses in the language of the body what psychoanalysis says in words" (Hunter, 114).

27. Meister Eckhart believes that we blaspheme God whenever we try to define him. This is a typical aspect of the so-called apophatic approach to God. For instance, in his sermon 83 Eckhart writes: "[B]e silent, and do not chatter about God; for when you do chatter about him, you are telling lies and sinning. But if you want to be without sin and perfect, you should not chatter about God." (Meister Eckhart, ES, 207)

28. I refer to Heinrich Lausberg, *Elementi di retorica* (Bologna: Il Mulino, 1969).

29. She modifies the famous verse "Cantate Domino canticum novum: cantate Domino omnis terra" from Psalm 95:1.

30. From Psalm 46:2. The complete verse is "Omnes gentes plaudite manibus: jubilate Deo in voce exultationis."

31. In a rapture reported in the second volume of *Probation*, for example, Maria Maddalena tells the Lord that she would like her participation in the Word's funeral to be a secret between him and herself.

32. Louis Marin, "Voix et énonciation mystique," in *La voix au XVIIe siècle*, ed. Patrick Dandrey (Paris, 1990), 172.

33. According to Bernard McGinn, Maria Maddalena could have chosen St Catherine and St Augustine as witnesses at her wedding also because of some possible paintings in her convent that reproduced these two saints together. Mystical literature is indeed highly influenced by iconographic elements. On this, see Millard Meiss, *Painting in Florence and Siena after the Black Death* (New York: Harper & Row, 1951), 105–31; Chiara Frugoni, "Female Mystics, Visions, and Iconography," in *Women and Religion in Medieval and Renaissance Italy*, 130–64.

However, we must remember that St Catherine and St Augustine have a specific symbolic meaning. Maria Maddalena had read several hagiographies of St Catherine. For Maria Maddalena, Catherine was the most influencial Italian mystic.

34. In *Probation* (1:174) Maria Maddalena says that she had been attracted to the Word through St Augustine's words, because his words are strictly united to the Word's. In the same book, the saint also states that St Augustine wants to write down the name of every nun of the convent (1:89).

35. The image of the mirror is present in other of her visions. For instance, in *The Forty Days* Maria Maddalena says that the Word's wounds are mirrors in which the soul can see itself (124). In the same book, she sees the Virgin Mary's eyes as two mirrors in which the believers can see themselves (260–61). In *Probation* (1:234), Maria Maddalena states that God gives three divine mirrors to the intellect. The first is God's purity, the second is his communication, the third is the charity of every blessed soul.

36. In *The Forty Days* Maria Maddalena gives us a different interpretation of this biblical verse. She sees the Father belch forth the Word. In this case, the "belched" Word is all His creatures (180). Cf. Meister Eckhart: "The Father speaks the Son out of all his power, and he speaks in him all things." (Meister Eckhart, ES, 205)

37. Louis Marin, "A Semiotic Approach to Parade," in *Time Out of Time: Essays on the Festival*, ed. Alessandro Falassi (Albuquerque: University of New Mexico Press, 1987), 220–28.

38. Victor Turner, *The Forest of Symbols. Aspects of Ndembu Ritual* (Ithaca, NY: Cornell University Press, 1967), 105.

39. Gaspar Loarte was born in Medina del Campo in 1498. He became a disciple of Juan de Avila in 1537 and later taught theology in Baeza. After joining the Jesuits, he moved to Rome in 1554 and there became friends with Saint Ignatius of Loyola. He wrote several devotional texts in Italian. His readers were first and foremost "the simple souls," that is, whoever needed direct and uncomplicated instructions on how to live a perfect Catholic life. His most important works are: *Esercitio della vita christiana, dove si tratta dei principali essercitii ne' quali il christiano con molto frutto spirituale possa spender la vita sua* (Rome, 1557); *Instruttione et avisi per meditare la passione di Christo, nos-*

tro Redentore, con alcune meditationi di essa (Rome, 1570); *Istruttione et aver-timenti per meditar i misterii del Rosario della Santissima Vergine Madre* (Rome, 1573); *Avisi di sacerdoti et confessori* (Parma, 1579). On Loarte and the first Jesuit authors, see Jean-François Gilmont, *Les écrits spirituels des premiers jésuites* (Rome: Institutum Historicum S.I., 1961), 260–68.

40. In *The Forty Days*, the saint's confessor suggests that she reread Loarte, in order to solve some personal problems (73).

41. Secondin, *Santa Maria Maddalena*, 100–101.

42. I quote from the copy in the library of the convent.

43. The mystic's sisters are aware of that fact that her visions tend to reproduce this structure. Indeed, in colloquio 47 the nuns point out that in her raptures the saint tends to follow the same pattern: first, she feels sorrow and fear; then, she slowly moves toward joy and happiness. According to the nuns, this invariable structure is a clear sign of the divine origin of her visions: "almost always at the beginning of her raptures she feels awe, fear, and suffering, but slowly she becomes happier and surer, that she ends her raptures in joy and happiness. This clearly means that these raptures come from God."

44. Roland Barthes, *Sade. Fourier. Loyola* (Paris: Seuil, 1971), 68. Here-after cited as SF.

45. Maurice Merleau-Ponty, *Résumés de cours (Collège de France, 1952–1960)* (Paris: Gallimard, 1968), 71–72. My translation.

46. Jacques Derrida, *The Gift of Death*, trans. David Wills (Chicago: University of Chicago Press, 1995), 15. Commenting on Plato's *Phaedo*, Derrida states that "the psyche as life, as breath of life, as *pneuma*, only appears out of [the soul's] concerned anticipation of dying."

47. Catena, *Santa Maria Maddalena de' Pazzi carmelitana*, 25–26.

48. Frugoni also underscores that "female mystics were often uneducated—or at least their biographers sought to emphasize the similarities between their models and the public to which they were presented. They were generally capable of reciting the Lord's Prayer and the Creed. . . . When they happened to possess great learning, this was presented as an ineffable divine gift; and if learning was openly desired and pursued, the miraculous gift of the vision was lost" (136).

49. Michel de Certeau, *La possession de Loudun* (Paris: Gallimard, 1990), 69: "Le corps visible devient, dans la pratique, la lisibilité même de l'histoire." De Certeau examines a notoriuos case of possession, which occurred in a small village, Loudun, at the beginning of the seventeenth century. He explains how the exorcists attempted to understand the nature of this demoniac possession by interpreting the gestures of the possessed. Although I do not see any theological similarity between those possessed nuns and Maria Maddalena de' Pazzi, I consider it important that in both cases physical expression plays a linguistic role.

50. Cf. Nadia Seremetakis, *The Last Word* (Chicago: University of Chicago Press, 1991). In her fascinating study of death rituals in some rural areas in Greece, Seremetakis explains that for female mourners "*discoursed pain* and *discourse in pain* constitute truth. . . . The female body as gesture and as speech . . . becomes the preeminent threshold for the disturbing passage of . . . truth into the social order" (120–21). In other words, the distressed voice of the

mourner and her gestures "embody" the inner sense of death.

51. Maria Maddalena uses the complex term "risguardare," which is almost a synonym for "contemplare" (to contemplate). For an analysis of this crucial term, see my introduction to my forthcoming translation of de' Pazzi's texts (*Maria Maddalena de' Pazzi: Selected Revelations* [New York: Paulist Press]).

52. Bernard of Clairvaux, *On the Song of Songs* 1, trans. Kilian Walsh (Spencer, MA: Cistercian Publications, 1971), 9–10.

53. As Ann Matter reminds us, Bernard holds that "the kiss of union, the 'kiss of the mouth,' is not attained immediately, . . . but rather through a series of ascending spiritual kisses: Bernard describes moving from the 'kiss of the feet' to the 'kiss of the hand,' before attaining the 'kiss of the mouth'" (Ann Matter, *The Voice of My Beloved: The Song of Songs in Western Medieval Christianity* [Philadelphia: University of Pennsylvania Press, 1990], 126). Maria Maddalena clearly refers to the "kiss of the feet" when she mentions Mary Magdalen. The mystic says that, unlike Mary Magdalen, she will not limit herself to kissing the Word's feet.

54. Dinzelbacher, 37. Dinzelbacher mentions the case of Elisabeth of Schönau, who once in a church saw a celestial stair descending from the ceiling toward the altar and two adolescents coming down from this stair.

55. Merleau-Ponty, *Résumés de cours (Collège de France, 1952–1960)*, 179.

56. Ibid. 179–80.

57. I maintain the odd syntax of the original.

58. Cf. Matt. 11:27: "All things have been delivered to me by my Father; and no one knows the Son except the Father; nor does anyone know the Father except the Son, and him to whom the Son chooses to reveal him."

59. This passage derives from Rev. 21, a description of the messianic Jerusalem: "I saw the holy city, and the new Jerusalem, coming down from God out of heaven. . . . One of the seven angels that had the seven bowls full of the seven plagues came to speak to me and said, 'Come here and I will show you the bride that the Lamb has married.'"

60. Exodus 3:3–4: "And the angel of the Lord appeared to him in a flame of fire out of the midst of a bush; and he looked, and lo, the bush was burning, yet it was not consumed. . . . When the Lord saw that he turned aside to see, God called to him out of the bush, 'Moses, Moses!'"

61. "Oh, my Jesus, you will have to preserve it, when you give it to me [*silence*] but before I receive it, I have to understand something about your holy soul, what it did in your Father's bosom during this time."

62. Other mystics describe the gift of receiving the Word's heart. For instance, in *Letter 22* Hadewijch speaks of those who "burn with interior desire without ceasing, because everything is inclined toward them: The mouth is open; the arms are outstretched; and the rich Heart is ready. . . . The rich wonders overflowing out of his Heart cause them to experience desires above reason. . . . And the truth of his rich open Heart says to their spirit that he shall be totally theirs" (Hadewijch, *The Complete Works*, trans. Mother Columba Hart, O.S.B. [New York: Paulist Press, 1980], 98).

63. The whole passage contains echoes of the so-called *Pietà* of the Virgin Mary, the sorrowful discourse delivered by the Word's Mother at his death. Several *pietà* were composed during the Middle Ages. We could say that Maria Maddalena mourns the Word's distance from her soul as his Mother mourned her Son's death. Let us remember, for example, Jacopone da Todi's famous poem "Donna de Paradiso."

64. In this above passage Maria Maddalena intermingles brief references to the events in the biblical account ("Omnes vos qui transitis per viam, attendite e videte si est dolor sicut dolor meus"; "Si ascendero in celum tu illic es, si descendero in infernum ades") with her own expressions of grief.

65. The language of the whole passage fails to construct a unified meaning. We can identify four primary components: (1) the saint's exclamations, which seem to arise from an unexpressed state of despair, marked by silence; (2) the saint's brief attempts at describing her inner feelings; (3) biblical quotations, interpreted according to her despair; (4) short questions directed to the Word himself (*Quando verrai?*/ When will you come?).

66. As Bruno Secondin points out (*Santa Maria Maddalena*, 240–46), the preachers' sermons highly influenced the nuns' religious education. As she explicitly says in *Renovation of the Church* (167), Maria Maddalena had read the so-called *Institutiones*, an anthology of North European mystics, among them Meister Eckhart and Tauler. Tauler, in particular, had artfully blended the two main forms of sermon prevailing in the fourteenth century: the homily and the thematic sermon. From a structural standpoint, and this corresponds to the last section of colloquio 48, in the thematic sermon the preacher made use of two basic rhetorical devices: dilation and amplification. After having announced the theme of his sermon, the preacher divided it into several sections (divisions), and then he amplified them in specific subchapters (distinctions). A "clausio," a sort of summary of both divisions and distinctions, led to a brief closing prayer. Although he did not adhere strictly to this structure, Tauler, and God's voice in this colloquio as well, loosely refers to it. I refer to: Josef Schmidt, "Introduction" to Johannes Tauler, *Sermons*, trans. Maria Shrady (New York: Paulist Press, 1985), 1–34. On Tauler's presence in Italy, see A. M. Walz, "Tauler im italienischen Sprachraum," in *Johannes Tauler, ein Deutscher Mystiker, Gedenkschrift zum 600. Todestag* (Essen, 1961), 371–95. See also George A. Kennedy, *Classical Rhetoric and Its Christian and Secular Tradition from Ancient to Modern Times* (Chapel Hill: University of North Carolina Press, 1980), 190–92; James Murphy, *Rhetoric in the Middle Ages* (Berkeley: University of California Press, 1974), 269–355.

67. It is impossible to find a direct source for the Father's list of mutual contemplations between the Father and the Son. Some late medieval handbooks use a similar style when they describe the relationship between the soul which has been freed from sin and God. For example, Nicolas Kempf, *Tractatus de Mystica Theologia*, ed. Jeanne Barbet and Francis Ruello (Salzburg: Analecta Cartusiana, 1973), 353: "[A]cquiritur vera humilitas, perfecta paciencia et sui ipsius quoniam nichil sit recognicio . . . illis eciam perficiuntur Spiritus sancti dona, primo sapiencie et intellectus in superioribus porcionibus voluntatis et racionis; in racione perficiuntur consilii et fortitudinis, et inferiore porcione sci-

encie et pietatis et timoris Domini." See also the final chapter of *Die siben strassen zu got* by Rudolf of Biberach (Florence: Spicilegium Bonaventurianum, 1969), 165–85.

68. Maria Maddalena uses this image of the two sources in many visions. However, in *The Forty Days* the two sources spring fron the Virgin Mary's breast and not from the Word's chest (108).

69. It is important to remember that in the very first colloquio the saint stresses the theme of the soul's purity as a necessary element in her receiving the Word.

70. The mystic underscores the interrelationship between the Word's birth and his death in *Probation*, 1:149.

4. THE LANGUAGE OF SATAN

1. Some Renaissance treatises on demonology analyze the "nonlanguage" of the devil. In particular, see Laurentius Anania, *De natura daemonum* (Venice, 1581), 77–83; Sylvester Prierio, *De strigimagarum Daemonumque Mirandis* (Rome, 1575), 76–84. For a brief introduction to Prierio's important text, see Henry Charles Lea, *Material toward a History of Witchcraft*, vol. 1 (Philadelphia: University of Pennsylvania Press, 1939), 358–65.

2. Radically different are the words that the devil yells at Margherita da Cortona (Lavinio, 1247–97). In *Legenda de vita et miraculis beatae Margaritae de Cortona* we read: "he assaulted her, yelling at her that her entire life was nothing but a deception and that her internal sweetnesses did not come from Jesus" ("[I]n eam repente irruit, et cum impetu dixit eidem, quod tota ejus vita nihil erat aliud quam deceptio, et quod illae non erant suavitates internae ab ipso Jesu," Pozzi and Leonardi, *Scrittrici mistiche italiane*, 125). The devil and the mystic are two distinct interlocutors. The mystic does not express any doubt about her faith. It is the devil that, out of envy, attacks the woman with his direct, and thus less insidious, language.

3. St Teresa of Avila, *The Life of Saint Teresa of Avila by Herself*, trans. J. M. Cohen (London: Penguin Books, 1957), 89.

4. Pozzi and Leonardi, *Scrittrici mistiche italiane*, 189.

5. De Certeau, *La possession de Loudun*, 102. My translation.

6. As Czeslaw Milosz writes: "Despair [is] inseparable from the first stage of exile. . . . Exile is morally suspect because it breaks one's solidarity with a group, i.e., it sets apart an individual from the rest of his collegues" (Czeslaw Milosz, "Notes on Exile," in *Altogheter Elsewhere: Writers on Exile*, ed. Marc Robinson [New York: Harcourt Brace & Company, 1994], 37–38).

7. See Frances Bartkowski, *Travelers, Immigrants, Inmates* (Minneapolis: University of Minnesota Press, 1995). Particularly interesting is what Bartkowski says about the close relationship between wonder and shame: "Travel writing, immigrant autobiographies, and also concentration camp memoirs . . . provide a textual unfolding of the relation between wonder and shame. Each of these narrative forms shows writers differentially placed along this axis. How they are positioned is dependent on their relation to power and language

as they move from place to place" (89). Maria Maddalena shares these two basic feelings when she suddenly senses that she "does not belong there" anymore. She both sees her daily places as a new environment and suffers from the displacement that this feeling entails.

In an essay on the relationship between immigrants and the foreign language of their new country, Julia Kristeva speaks of the "mourning of the mother-tongue." Kristeva examines how the loss of the mother-tongue sometimes brings about physical and emotional ailments (Julia Kristeva, "En deuil d'une langue?," in *Deuils: Vivre, c'est perdre*, ed. Nicole Czechowski and Claude Danziger [Paris: Editions Autrement, 1992], 27–36).

8. Maria Maddalena has a similar insight of her "baseness" in *The Forty Days*. On July 22, 1584, the Father had marked her heart with his seal. The same day the mystic has a "marvelous sight" of her nothingness and of her constant offences to the divinity (248–50).

9. The devil tempts Maria Maddalena in a similar way. He appears to her in the form of two nuns, one dressed in white and the other in grey, and tells her that she shouldn't have joined the convent (*Probation*, 1:115).

10. Pozzi and Leonardi, *Scrittrici mistiche italiane*, 266–67.

11. St Augustine, *The City of God*, trans. Marcus Dods, D.D. (New York: The Modern Library, 1950), 387. For a good introduction to book 12, see Italo Sciuto, "Interiorità e male nel *De civitate Dei*," in *Interiorità e intenzionalità nel "De civitate Dei" di Sant'Agostino*, ed. Remo Piccolomini (Rome: Institutum Patristicum "Augustinianum," 1991), 87–116.

According to Lactantius, whose doctrine was severely criticized by the Church and was certainly unknown to Maria Maddalena de' Pazzi, the intrinsic duplicity of evil results from the duplicity of the creation itself. In the second book of *Divinarum Institutionum* Lactantius states that God "produced" two "rivers" or spirits, that is, two Words. Whereas at the beginning God's nature inhabits both rivers, it withdraws from the second one after a short period of time. (Lactantius, *Opera Omnia*, PL, vol. 6, 293–97). As a consequence, this second Word/river "was infected with the poison of envy" (294). Moreover, according to Lactantius God "gave the devil absolute power over the world." Only later God sent his angels to support the human kind in its battle against the devil (330). For that matter, the idea that the devil's fall was due to both pride and envy is repeated by Ireneaus in the fourth book of *Adversus Haereticos* (chapter 78) and by Augustine in the first book of *De Genesi ad litteram*, PL, vol. 34, 436.

12. St Augustine, *Confessions*, c. 21.

13. For instance, Cassian writes that "[t]anta vero spirituum densitate constipatus est aer iste, qui inter coelum terramque diffunditur, in quo non quieti nec otiosi pervolitant" (Joannis Cassiani, *De principatibus seu potestatibus* [PL vol. 49], 740).

14. St Augustine, *Contra academicos*, PL 32, 1:20, 916: "talia cum in memoriam nostram incurrerint, non mirum est, si sentiri possunt ab hujus aeris animalibus quibusdam vilissimis, quos daemones vocant"; cf. St Augustine, *De Genesi ad litteram*, PL 34, c. 14, 436.

15. Gregory the Great, *Moralia*, PL 75, 590: "Scimus quod immundi spiritus, qui e coelo aethereo lapsi sunt, in hoc coeli terraeque medio vagantur: qui

tanto magis corda hominum ascendere ad coelestia invident, quanto se a coelestibus per elationis suae immunditiam projectos vident." For an introduction to Gregory's theology, see Bernard McGinn, *The Growth of Mysticism* (New York: Crossroad, 1994), 34–79.

16. St Augustine, *Enarratio in Psalmum CIII*, PL 37, sermo 4, 1382: "Ipse cadens peccato suo de sublimi habitatione coelorum, et ex angelo factus diabolus, accepit quemdam locum suum in hoc mari magno et spatioso. Regnum ejus quod putas, carcer ejus est."

17. Peter Chrysologus, *Opera Omnia*, PL 52, 345.

18. Gregory the Great, *XL Homiliarum in Evangelia*, PL 76, 1233.

19. Ibid., 1215.

20. Turrecremata, *Tractatus de efficacia aque benedicte* (Concilii Basiliensis compilatus, 1476).

21. Gregory the Great *Moralia*, 76. For that matter, it is interesting to see how in *On Free Choice of the Will* Augustine interprets a crucial verse from Psalm 18:13–14: "Ab occultis meis munda me, Domine, et ab alienis parce servo tuo." Augustine stresses that there are two kinds of sins. Man either sins because he wants to or because he is seduced by some negative influences (another human being or the devil). However, Augustine does not consider that the first part of the psalm concerns those impurities that are hidden to the subject himself. (Augustine, *On the Free Choice of the Will*, trans. Anna S. Benjamin and L. H. Hackstaff [Indianapolis: Bobbs-Merrill, 1964], 1285.)

22. An interesting similitude can be seen between the nuns' attitude toward Maria Maddalena's raptures and Freud's and Charcot's attempts to pin down the *signs/symptoms* of their patients suffering from hysteria. Charcot goes so far as to take photos of his patients. As de Marneffe underscores, "hysteria, the Sphinx of disorders, presented a challenge to the creation of a uniform clinical picture" (Daphne de Marneffe, "Looking and Listening: The Construction of Clinical Knowledge in Charcot and Freud," *Signs*, Autumn 1991, 79).

Charcot needs clear signs from his patients. However, like Maria Maddalena's performances, Charcot's hysterics often send mixed messages, confused communications, that he tries to rationalize by means of photographs. "A major feature of Charcot's view of hysterics was an emphasis on hysterical dissimulation and the hysteric's goal of making the doctor a fool" (de Marneffe, 100).

Also, the nineteenth-century Italian criminologist Cesare Lombroso used photos in his scientific research. Lombroso attempted to detect those physical traits that every "female offender" might share. The female body "was made an object of a variety of specialized reading practices: scientific measurements and evaluations that struggled to overcome the female body's epistemological resistance and contain its dangerousness" (David G. Horn, "This Norm Which Is Not One: Reading the Female Body in Lombroso's Anthropology," in *Deviant Bodies*, ed. Jennifer Terry and Jacqueline Urla [Bloomington: Indiana University Press, 1995], 109).

23. Michel de Certeau, *La possession de Loudun*, 69. My translation.

24. Ibid., 76.

25. Valerio Polidoro Patavini, *Thesaurus exorcismorum* (Coloniae: Lazari Zetzneri, 1608), 7–8.

26. Jean Bodin, *De la démonomanie des sorciers* (Paris: Arnould Couiux, 1593), 335. For a recent study of Bodin's texts, see Sophie Houdard, *Les sciences du diable* (Paris: Cerf, 1992), 57–103.

27. Jacob Sprenger, *Malleus maleficarum*, trans. Montague Summers (London: The Pushkin Press, 1951), 229.

28. Tears as well may be *indexes* of the devil's possession. In *Compendio dell'arte essorcistica* (1605), Girolamo Menghi reminds us that the devil can put fake tears in the victim's eyes, as deceitful signs of her/his insincere penance. Even when she is tortured, the possessed is supported by the devil with counterfeit expressions of suffering. In fact, when a human being becomes possessed, she is unable to cry.

29. Lambert Daneau, *Deux traiez nouveaux tres utiles pour ce temps* (Paris: Jacques Baumet, 1579), 114.

30. For more on this, see Alfonso M. di Nola, *Il diavolo: Le forme, la storia, le vicende di Satana* (Rome: Newton Compton, 1987), 292–98.

31. According to Menghi, "not only the devil but also other human beings may understand our thoughts. However, the devil apprehends them in a much deeper way. . . . He can apprehend them also through the expressions of one's face and of one's heart, since it beats according to its different situations. We have a clear example in the physicians, who are able sometimes to detect our diseases by the wrist's pulse. . . . [T]his is why the malign spirits can perceive our thoughts and feelings" (83). My translation.

32. See Jacques Derrida, *Memoirs of the Blind*, trans. Pascale-Anne Brault and Michael Naas (Chicago: University of Chicago Press, 1993), 32–39.

33. For a fundamental analysis of the role of ending in any form of coherent narration, see Frank Kermode, *The Sense of an Ending: Studies in the Theory of Fiction* (New York: Oxford University Press, 1967).

CONCLUSION

1. In the fascinating, albeit underestimated, *Beiträge zu einer Kritik der Sprache* (Hildesheimer 1969) Fritz Mauthner highlights the central role played by memory in any form of language articulation (185–90). According to Mauthner, every linguistic sign is in fact a "memory sign" (*Gedächtniszeichen*), in that every sign embodies the speaker's remembrances connected with his or her expression of that sign (when he/she became familiar with that word; when someone used it in his/her presence on a particularly significant occasion; when that word was inserted in a discourse directed to the speaker; etc.).

2. Simone Weil, *On Science, Necessity, and the Love of God*, trans. Richard Rees (London: Oxford University Press, 1968), 153.

3. Simone Weil, *Waiting For God*, trans. Emma Craufurd (New York: Harper Colophon Books, 1973), 121.

4. Luis de León, *The Names of Christ*, trans. Manuel Duran and William Kluback (New York: Paulist Press, 1984), 343. For an introduction to León's work, see Aubrey Bell, *Luis de León* (Oxford: Oxford University Press, 1925); Manuel Durán, *Luis de León* (New York: Twayne, 1971).

5. Vincent Brümmer highlights that "since love is a reciprocal relation, God is also dependent on the freedom and responsability of human persons in order to enter into a loving relation with them. Of course, this autonomy is *bestowed* on us by God as our creator. We do not owe our autonomy as persons to ourselves" (Vincent Brümmer, *The Model of Love: A Study in Philosophical Theology* [Cambridge: Cambridge University Press, 1993], 162–63).

6. Cf. Georg Simmel, *On Women, Sexuality, and Love* (New Haven, CT: Yale University Press, 1984), 133: "The moments of fulfillment lie in its [love's] pauses."

7. Pseudo-Dionysius Areopagita, *The Divine Names and Mystical Theology*, trans. John D. Jones (Milwaukee: Marquette University Press, 1980), 179.

8. Irigaray, *I Love to You*, 109. Cf. Weil, *Waiting for God*, 135.

9. For an interesting discussion of the image of the self as reflection of/in the other, see Umberto Curi, *Endiadi: Figure della duplicità* (Milan: Feltrinelli, 1995), 60–78.

10. For an introductory commentary on this crucial passage from *The Song of Songs*, see Othmar Keel, *The Song of Songs: A Continental Commentary*, trans. Frederick J. Gaiser (Minneapolis: Fortress Press, 1994), 84–88.

11. Hannah Arendt, *Love and Saint Augustine* (Chicago: University of Chicago Press, 1996), 47.

12. St. Augustine, *Confessions*, trans. Henry Chadwick (Oxford: Oxford University Press, 1991), 196–97.

13. For the importance of the crucifix as an inspirational picture, see Frugoni, "Female Mystics," 138–39.

14. Cf. Daniel Sibony, *Le corps et sa danse* (Paris: Seuil, 1995), 269–70: "The mystic dances a strange disease. Her dance signifies her body's change into God, [her] human change into God, but primarily their mutual . . . tearing apart. And . . . her disease is a 'disfigurement' of her body—she makes her body unsteady; she dissects it, molds it, manipulates it . . . the body is the place of a 'folly' that attempts to expel itself " My translation.

15. Daniel Sibony, *Perversions: Dialogues sur des folies "actuelles"* (Paris: Grasset, 1987), 245. My translation.

16. Louis Marin, *La critique du discours: Sur la "Logique de Port-Royal" et les "Pensées" de Pascal* (Paris: Minuit, 1975), 96.

17. Late-nineteenth-century literature is replete with such descriptions. The Other, tortured and killed, comes back to the person who has offended him and shows him/her his face smudged with blood: "To face the [Other's] gaze is . . . always to experience a certain "horror" or "mortification" (Kaja Silverman, *The Threshold of the Visible World* [New York: Routledge, 1996], 150).

18. Matt. 19:27.

SELECT BIBLIOGRAPHY

RELIGIOUS SOURCES

Agresti, G. M., ed. *Vita di Santa Caterina de' Ricci*. Florence, 1965.

Anania, Laurentius. *De natura daemonum*. Venice, 1581.

Angela of Foligno. *Complete Works*. Edited by Paul Lachance. New York: Paulist Press, 1993.

Augustine. *De Genesi ad Litteram*. Patrologia Latina (PL), ed. J.-P. Migné, vol. 34. Paris: D'Amboise, 1849.

———. *Enarratio in Ps. CIII*. PL, vol. 37.

———. *Concerning the Teacher and On the Immortality of the Soul*. Translated by George G. Leckie. New York: D. Appleton-Century Company, 1938.

———. *The City of God*. Translated by Marcus Dods, D.D. New York: The Modern Library, 1950.

———. *On Christian Doctrine*. Translated by D. W. Robertson Jr. Indianapolis: The Bobbs-Merrill Company, 1958.

———. *On the Free Choice of the Will*. Translated by Anna S. Benjamin and L. H. Hackstaff. Indianapolis: The Bobbs-Merrill Company, 1964.

———. *Confessions*. Translated by Henry Chadwick. Oxford: Oxford University Press, 1991.

Bernard of Clairvaux. *On the Song of Songs*. Translated by Kilian Walsh. Vol. 1. Spencer, MA: Cistercian Publications, 1971.

———. *On the Song of Songs*. Translated by Irene Edmonds, vol. 4. Kalamazoo, MI: Cistercian Publications, 1980.

The Holy Bible. Chicago: Good Counsel Publishing Company, 1963.

Bodin, Jean. *De la démonomanie des sorciers*. Paris: Arnould Couiux, 1593.

Breviarum romanum, ex decreto sacrosanti Concilii tridentini restitutum Pii V. Rome, 1577.

Brigitta of Sweden. *Life and Selected Revelations*. Edited by Marguerite Tjader Harris. New York: Paulist Press, 1990.

Cassiani, Joannis. *De principatibus seu potestatibus*. PL, vol. 49.

Daneau, Lambert. *Deux traiez nouveaux très utiles pour ce temps*. Paris: Jacques Baumet, 1579.

Pseudo-Dionysius Areopagita. *The Divine Names and Mystical Theology*. Translated by John D. Jones. Milwaukee: Marquette University Press, 1980.

Hadewijch. *The Complete Works*. Translated by Mother Columba Hart, O.S.B. New York: Paulist Press, 1980.

Eusebius Hieronymus. *Commentariorum in Michaeam*. PL, vol. 25.

Gregory the Great. *Moralia*. PL, vol. 75.

————. *Homiliarum in Ezechielem*. PL, vol. 76.

————. *XL Homiliarum in Evangelia*. PL, vol. 76.

Honorius. *Elucidarium*, PL, vol. 172.

Kempf, Nicolas. *Tractatus de Mystica Theologia*. Edited by Jeanne Barbet and Francis Ruello. Salzburg, Austria: Analecta Cartusiana, 1973.

The Koran. Translated by E. H. Palmer. Delhi: Motilal Banarsidass, 1965.

Lactantius, *Opera Omnia*, PL, vol. 6.

León, Luis de. *The Names of Christ*. Translated by Manuel Duran and William Kluback. New York: Paulist Press, 1984.

Loarte, Gaspar. *Instrutione et Avertimenti*. Rome, 1571.

Mechthild of Magdeburg. *Das fliessende Licht der Gottheit*. Zurich: Benziger Verlag, 1956.

Meister Eckhart. *The Essential Sermons, Commentaries, Treatises, and Defense*. Translated and edited by Edmund Colledge, O.S.A., and Bernard McGinn. New York: Paulist Press, 1981.

————. *Teacher and Preacher*. Edited by Bernard McGinn. New York: Paulist Press, 1986.

Menghi, Girolamo. *Compendio dell'arte essorcistica*. Venice: Pietro Bertano, 1605.

Origen. *In Lucam Homilia*. Patrologiae Graeca (PG), ed. DD. Caroli et Calori Vincentii Delarue, vol. 13. Paris: D'Amboise, 1857.

————. *Comment. in Joan*. PG, vol. 14.

Pazzi, Maria Maddalena de'. *Tutte le opere di Santa Maria Maddalena de'Pazzi dai manoscritti originali*. Edited by Bruno Nardini, Bruno Visentin, Carlo Catena, and Giulio Agresti. 7 vols. Florence: Nardini, 1960–66.

Peter Chrysologus. *Opera Omnia*. PL, vol. 52.

Polidoro Patavini, Valerio. *Thesaurus exorcismorum*. Coloniae: Lazari Zetzneri, 1608.

Prierio, Sylvester. *De strigimagarum Daemonumque Mirandis*. Rome, 1575.

Rudolf of Biberach. *Die siben strassen zu got*. Florence: Spicilegium Bonaventurianum, 1969.

Sprenger, Jacob. *Malleus maleficarum*. Translated by Montague Summers. London: The Pushkin Press, 1951.

Tauler, Johannes. *Sermons*. Translated by Maria Shrady. New York: Paulist Press, 1985.

Teresa of Avila. *The Life of Saint Teresa of Avila by Herself*. Translated by J. M. Cohen. London: Penguin Books, 1957.

Thomas Aquinas, *Summa Theologica*. In *Basic Writings of Saint Thomas Aquinas*, edited by Anton C. Pegis. New York: Random House, 1945.

————. *Summa Contra Gentiles*. In *Opera Omnia*. Stuttgart: Fromann, 1980.

Turrecremata. *Tractatus de efficacia aque benedicte*. Concilii Basiliensis compilatus, 1476.

Weil, Simone. *Cahiers III*. Paris: Plon, 1956.

————. *On Science, Necessity, and the Love of God*. Translated by Richard Rees. London: Oxford University Press, 1968.

————. *Waiting For God*. Translated by Emma Craufurd. New York: Harper Colophon Books, 1973.

Other Primary Texts

Dante Alighieri, *Purgatorio*. Translated by Allen Mandelbaum. New York: Bantam Books, 1982.

PHILOSOPHICAL SOURCES

Agamben, Giorgio. *Language and Death: The Place of Negativity*. Translated by Karen E. Pinkus and Michael Hardt. Minneapolis: University of Minnesota Press, 1991.

Arendt, Hannah. *Love and Saint Augustine*. Chicago: University of Chicago Press, 1996.

Barthes, Roland. *Critique et vérité*. Paris: Seuil, 1966.

――. *Sade. Fourier. Loyola*. Paris: Seuil, 1971.

――. *Leçon*. Paris: Seuil, 1978.

――. "From Work to Text." In *Image/Music/Text*. Translated by Stephen Heath. New York: Farrar, Straus and Giroux, 1988.

Bataille, George. *L'expérience intérieure*. Paris: Gallimard, 1990.

Brümmer, Vincent. *The Model of Love: A Study in Philosophical Theology*. Cambridge: Cambridge University Press, 1993.

Cacciari, Massimo. *L'angelo necessario*. Milan: Adelphi, 1994.

Certeau, Michel de. *La fable mystique*. Paris: Gallimard, 1982.

――. *The Practice of Everyday Life*. Translated by Steven F. Rendall. Berkeley: University of California Press, 1984.

――. *The Writing of History*. New York: Columbia University Press, 1988.

――. *Il parlare angelico*. Translated by Daniela De Agostini. Florence: Olschki, 1989.

――. *La possession de Loudun*. Paris: Gallimard, 1990.

Curi, Umberto. *Endiadi: Figure della duplicità*. Milan: Feltrinelli, 1995.

Deleuze, Gilles. *The Fold: Leibniz and the Baroque*. Translated by Tom Conley. Minneapolis: University of Minnesota Press, 1994.

――. *Difference and Repetition*. New York: Columbia University Press, 1994.

Derrida, Jacques. *De la grammatologie*. Paris: Minuit, 1967.

――. *Memoirs of the Blind*. Translated by Pascale-Anne Brault and Michael Naas. Chicago: University of Chicago Press, 1993.

――. *The Gift of Death*. Translated by David Wills. Chicago: University of Chicago Press, 1995.

Irigaray, Luce. *I Love to You*. Translated by Alison Martin. New York: Routledge, 1996.

Keel, Othmar. *The Song of Songs: A Continental Commentary*. Translated by Frederick J. Gaiser. Minneapolis: Fortress Press, 1994.

Lacan, Jacques. *Seminaire XX*. Paris: Seuil, 1975.

――. *Écrits*. Translated by Alan Sheridan. New York: W. W. Norton, 1977.

――. *Feminine Sexuality*. Edited by Juliet Mitchell and Jacqueline Rose. New York: W.W. Norton, 1982.

――. *The Psychosis 1955–1956*. Translated by Russell Grigg. New York: Norton, 1993.

Lévinas, Emmanuel. *Otherwise than Being or Beyond Essence*. Translated by Alphonso Lingis. The Hague: Martinus Nijhoff, 1981.

Merleau-Ponty, Maurice. *L'oeil et l'esprit*. Paris: Gallimard, 1964.

———. *Signs*. Translated by Richard C. McCleary. Evanston, IL: Northwestern University Press, 1964.

———. *Résumés de cours (Collège de France, 1952–1960)*. Paris: Gallimard, 1968.

———. *La prose du monde*. Paris: Gallimard, 1969.

Ricoeur, Paul. *Temps et récit: 2. La configuration dans le récit de fiction*. Paris: Gallimard, 1984.

Rovatti, Pier Aldo. *Abitare la distanza*. Milan: Feltrinelli, 1994.

Searle, John R. *Speech Acts*. Cambridge: Cambridge University Press, 1969.

———. *Intentionality*. Cambridge: Cambridge University Press, 1983.

Sibony, Daniel. *Perversions: Dialogues sur des folies "actuelles."* Paris: Grasset, 1987.

———. *Le corps et sa danse*. Paris: Seuil, 1995.

Simmel, Georg. *On Women, Sexuality, and Love*. New Haven, CT: Yale University Press, 1984.

Wittgenstein, Ludwig. *The Blue and the Brown Books*. New York: Barnes and Noble, 1969.

Wolterstorff, Nicholas. *Divine Discourse: Philosophical Reflections on the Claim That God Speaks*. Oxford: Oxford University Press, 1995.

SECONDARY SOURCES

Alberigo, Giuseppe. "Dinamiche religiose del Cinquecento italiano tra riforma, riforma cattolica, controriforma." *Cristianesimo nella storia* 6 (1985): 543–60.

Barman, Karen-edis. "Cultural Production, Religious Devotion, and Subjectivity in Early Modern Italy: The Case Study of Maria Maddalena de' Pazzi." *Annali d'Italianistica* 13 (1995): 283–306.

Bartkowski, Frances. *Travelers, Immigrants, Inmates*. Minneapolis: University of Minnesota Press, 1995.

Blau, Herbert. "The Surpassing Body." *TDR. The Drama Review* 35.2 (1991): 74–98.

Briggs, Robin. *Witches and Neighbors*. New York: Viking Penguin, 1996.

Burton Russell, Jeffrey. *Witchcraft in the Middle Ages*. Ithaca, NY: Cornell University Press, 1972.

———. *A History of Witchcraft*. London: Thames and Hudson, 1980.

Catena, Claudio. "Le donne del Carmelo italiano." *Carmelus* 10 (1963): 9–55.

———. "Ambiente del monastero di S. Maria degli Angeli ai tempi di S. Maria Maddalena de' Pazzi." *Carmelus* 13 (1966): 21–96.

———. *Santa Maria Maddalena de' Pazzi carmelitana: Orientamenti spirituali e ambiente in cui visse*. Rome: Institutum Carmelitanum, 1966.

———. "Le malattie di S. Maria Maddalena de' Pazzi." *Carmelus* 16 (1969): 70–141.

Cixous, Hélène. "Aller à la mer." *Modern Drama* 27.4 (1984): 546–48.

Consolino, F. E. "Interlocutore divino e lettori terreni: La funzione-destinatario nelle Confessioni di Agostino." *Materiali e discussioni* 6 (1982): 119–46.

Corbin, Henry. *Avicenna and the Visionary Recital.* Translated by Willard R. Trask. Princeton, NJ: Princeton University Press, 1988.

Creytens, Robert. "La riforma dei monasteri femminili dopo i decreti tridentini." In *Il Concilio di Trento e la Riforma Tridentina: Proceedings of the Conference held in Trent on September 2–6, 1963.* Rome: Herder, 1965.

Culler, Jonathan. *Structuralist Poetics.* Ithaca, NY: Cornell University Press, 1975.

Dinzelbacher, Peter. *Vision und Visionsliteratur im Mittelalter.* Stuttgart: Anton Hiersemann, 1981.

Dolan, Jill. "In Defense of the Discourse." *TDR. The Drama Review* 33.3 (1989): 58–71.

Erickson, Jon. "The Spectacle of the Anti-Spectacle: Happenings and the Situationist International." *Discourse* 14.2 (1991): 36–58.

Foucault, Michel. "What Is an Author?" In *Foucault Reader*, edited by Paul Rabinow. New York: Pantheon Books, 1984.

Flores, Lauro. "Bilinguism and the Literary Text." *Visible Language* 21 (Winter 1987): 130–52.

Frank, Manfred. "Die Dichtung als 'Neue Mythologie.'" In *Mythos und Moderne.* Frankfurt am Main: Suhrkamp, 1983.

———. *What Is Neo-structuralism?* Translated by Sabine Wilke and Richard T. Gray. Minneapolis: University of Minnesota Press, 1989.

Frede, Dorothea. "The Cognitive Role of *Phantasia.*" In *Essays On Aristotle's "De Anima,"* edited by Martha C. Nussbaum and Amélie Oksenberg Rorty. Oxford: Claredon, 1995.

Frugoni, Chiara. "Female Mystics, Visions, and Iconography." In *Women and Religion in Medieval and Renaissance Italy*, edited by Daniel Bornstein and Roberto Rusconi. Chicago: University of Chicago Press, 1996.

Gilmont, Jean-François. *Les écrits spirituels des premiers jésuites.* Rome: Institutum Historicum S.I., 1961.

Goody, Jack. *The Interface between the Written and the Oral.* Cambridge: Cambridge University Press, 1987.

Guénon, René. *Fundamental Symbols: The Universal Language of Sacred Science.* Translated by Alvin Moore Jr. Cambridge: Quinta Essentia, 1995.

Herzog, Reinahrt. "Non in sua voce." In *Das Gespräch*, edited by Karlheinz Strierle and Painer Warning. Munich: Fink, 1984.

Horn, David G. "This Norm Which Is Not One: Reading the Female Body in Lombroso's Anthropology." In *Deviant Bodies*, edited by Jennifer Terry and Jacqueline Urla. Bloomington: Indiana University Press, 1995.

Hudon, William. *Theatine Spirituality.* New York: Paulist Press, 1996.

Hunter, Dianne. "Hysteria, Psychoanalysis, and Feminism: The Case of Anna O." In *The (M)other Tongue: Essays in Feminist Psychoanalytic Interpretation*, edited by Shirley Nelson Garner. Ithaca, NY: Cornell University Press, 1995.

Hunter, J. F. M. *Understanding Wittgenstein.* Edinburgh: Edinburgh University Press, 1985.

Kahane, Claire. *Passions of the Voice: Hysteria, Narrative, and the Figure of the Speaking Woman, 1850–1915.* Baltimore: Johns Hopkins University Press, 1995.

Kennedy, George A. *Classical Rhetoric and Its Christian and Secular Tradition from Ancient to Modern Times.* Chapel Hill: University of North Carolina Press, 1980.

Kleinberg, Aviad M. *Prophets in Their Own Countries: Living Saints and the Making of Sainthood in the Later Middle Ages.* Chicago: University of Chicago Press, 1997.

Kristeva, Julia. "En deuil d'une langue?" In *Deuils: Vivre, c'est perdre,* edited by Nicole Czechowski and Claude Danziger. Paris: Editions Autrement, 1992.

Jackson, Jean E. "'After a While No One Believes You': Real and Unreal Pain." In *Pain as Human Experience: An Anthological Perspective,* edited by Mary-Jo Delvecchio Good. Berkeley: University of California Press, 1992.

Larkin, Ernest E. "The Ecstasies of the Forty Days of Saint Mary Magdalen de' Pazzi." *Carmelus* 1 (1954): 29–71.

Lea, Henry Charles. *Material toward a History of Witchcraft,* vol. 1. Philadelphia: University of Pennsylvania Press, 1939.

Lingis, Alphonso. *Foreign Bodies.* London: Routledge, 1994.

Lorenz, Otto. *Das Schweigen in der Dichtung: Hölderlin, Rilke, Celan.* Ruprecht, Germany: Vandenhöck, 1989.

Lubell, Stephen. "Bilinguism in the Hebrew Text." *Visible Language* 27 (Winter/Spring 1993): 163–204.

Man, Paul de. *Allegories of Reading: Figural Language in Rousseau, Nietzsche, Rilke, and Proust.* New Haven, CT: Yale University Press, 1979.

Marin, Louis. *Sémiotique de la Passion.* Aubier Montaigne, France: Editions du Cerf, 1971.

———. *La critique du discours: Sur la "Logique de Port-Royal" et les "Pensées" de Pascal.* Paris: Minuit, 1975.

———. *La voix excommuniée.* Paris: Editions galilée, 1981.

———. "A Semiotic Approach to Parade." In *Time Out of Time: Essays on the Festival,* edited by Alessandro Falassi. Albuquerque: University of New Mexico Press, 1987.

———. *Food for Thought.* Baltimore: Johns Hopkins University Press, 1989.

———. "Voix et énonciation mystique." In *La voix au XVIIo siècle,* edited by Patrick Dandrey. Paris: Aux Amateurs De Livres, 1990.

Marneffe, Daphne de. "Looking and Listening: The Construction of Clinical Knowledge in Charcot and Freud." *Signs,* Autumn 1991, 78–91.

Matter, Ann. *The Voice of My Beloved: The Song of Songs in Western Medieval Christianity.* Philadelphia: University of Pennsylvania Press, 1990.

Mauthner, Fritz. *Beiträge zu einer Kritik der Sprache.* Stuttgart: J. G. Cotta, 1912–21.

Mayer, Cornelius Petrus, O.S.A. *Die Zeichen in der Geistigen Entwicklung und in der Theologie des Jungen Augustinus.* Wurzburg, Germany: Augustinus Verlag, 1969.

McGinn, Bernard. *The Foundations of Mysticism.* New York: Crossroad, 1991.

———. "Donne mistiche ed autorità esoterica nel XIV secolo." In *Poteri carismatici e informali: Chiesa e società medioevali*. Palermo, Italy: Sellerio, 1992.

Meiss, Millard. *Painting in Florence and Siena after the Black Death*. New York: Harper & Row, 1951.

Meltzer, Françoise. *Salomé and the Dance of Writing*. Chicago: University of Chicago Press, 1987.

Miller, Jacques-Alain. "Montré à Premontré." *Analytica* 37 (1984): 28–29.

Milosz, Czeslaw. "Notes on Exile." In *Altogheter Elsewhere: Writers on Exile*, edited by Marc Robinson. New York: Harcourt Brace & Company, 1994.

Mitchell, W. J. T. *Picture Theory*. Chicago: University of Chicago Press, 1994.

Nancy, Jean Luc. "Corpus." In *Thinking Bodies*, edited by Juliet Flower MacCannel and Laura Zakarin. Stanford, CA: Stanford University Press, 1994.

Niccoli, Ottavia. "Il confessore e l'inquisitore: A proposito di un manoscritto bolognese del Seicento." In *Finzione e santità tra medioevo ed età moderna*, edited by Gabriella Zarri. Turin: Rosenberg & Sellier, 1991.

Paolin, Giovanna. "Confessione e confessori al femminile: Monache e direttori spirituali in ambito veneto tra '600 e '700." In *Finzione e santità tra medioevo ed età moderna*.

Petrocchi, Massimo. *Storia della spiritualità italiana: Il cinquecento e il seicento*. Rome: Edizioni di storia e letteratura, 1978.

Pieper, Josef. "Ueber das Innere Wort." In *Sinn und Form* 5 (1995): 706–708.

Pizzolato, L. F. *Le "Confessioni" di Sant' Agostino*. Milan: Vita e pensiero, 1968.

Pozzi, Giovanni. *Le parole dell' estasi*. Milan: Adelphi, 1984.

———. *Il libro dell' esperienza*. Milan: Adelphi, 1992.

Pozzi, Giovanni and Claudio Leonardi, eds. *Scrittrici mistiche italiane*. Genoa: Marietti, 1989.

Petroff, E. A. *Medieval Women's Visionary Literature*. Oxford: Oxford University Press, 1986.

Prosperi, Adriano. "Riforma cattolica, Controriforma, disciplinamento sociale." In *Storia dell'Italia religiosa. II. L'età moderna*, edited by Gabriele de Rosa and Tullio Gregory. Bari, Italy: Laterza, 1994.

Puccini, Vincenzo. *The Life of St. Mary Magdalene of Pazzi, a Carmelite Nunn*. London: Randal Taylor, 1687.

Ragland, Ellie. "The Relation between the Voice and the Gaze." In *Reading Seminar XI: Lacan's Four Fundamental Concepts of Psychoanalysis*, edited by Richard Feldstein. Albany: State University of New York Press, 1995.

Ribettes, Jean-Michel. "Le phalsus." In *Folle verité: Vérité et vraisemblance du texte psychotique*, edited by Julia Kristeva. Paris: Seuil, 1979.

Rohrbach, Peter-Thomas, O.C.D. *Journey to Carith: The Story of the Carmelite Order*. Garden City, NY: Doubleday, 1966.

Rosa, Gabriele de. "I codici di lettura del 'vissuto religioso.'" In *Storia dell'Italia religiosa. II. L'età moderna*.

Ruef, Hans. *Augustin über Semiotik und Sprache*. Bern: Verlag K. J. Wyss Erben, 1981.

Rusconi, Roberto. "Women Religious in Late Medieval Italy: New Sources and Directions." In *Women and Religion in Medieval and Renaissance Italy*.

Sacramento, Ermanno del. "I manoscritti originali di Santa Maria Maddalena de' Pazzi." *Ephemerides carmeliticae* 7 (1956): 323–400.

——. "La passione di S. Maria Maddalena de' Pazzi per la Chiesa." *Ephemerides Carmelitae* 17 (1966): 405–16.

Santi, Giorgio. *Dio e l'uomo: Conoscenza, memoria, linguaggio, ermeneutica in Agostino.* Rome: Città nuova editrice, 1989.

Scarry, Elaine. *The Body in Pain: The Making and Unmaking of the World.* New York: Oxford University Press, 1987.

Schechner, Richard. *Between Theater and Antropology.* Philadelphia: University of Pennsylvania Press, 1985.

Secondin, Bruno. *Santa Maria Maddalena de' Pazzi: Esperienza e dottrina.* Rome: Institutum Carmelitanum, 1974.

Sells, Michael A. *Mystical Languages of Unsaying.* Chicago: University of Chicago Press, 1994.

Seremetakis, Nadia. *The Last Word.* Chicago: University of Chicago Press, 1991.

Silverman, Kaja. *The Threshold of the Visible World.* New York: Routledge, 1996.

Smith, Christopher. "A Sense of the Possible: Miles Davis and the Semiotics of Improvised Performance." *TDR. The Drama Review* 39.3 (1995): 41–55.

Smith, Gregory O. Carm. "Liturgic Silence." *Carmelus* 23 (1976): 3–20.

Soler, Colette. "The Subject and the Other (II)." In *Reading Seminar XI: Lacan's Four Fundamental Concepts of Psychoanalysis.*

Tannen, Deborah. "Silence: Anything But." In *Perspectives on Silence,* edited by Deborah Tannen and Muriel Saville-Troike. Norwood, NJ: Ablex, 1984.

——. *Talking Voices.* Cambridge: Cambridge University Press, 1989.

Taylor, Marc C. *Nots.* Chicago: University of Chicago Press, 1993.

Todisco, Orlando. *Parola e verità: Agostino e la filosofia del linguaggio.* Rome: Anicia, 1993.

Todorov, Tzvetan. *Theories of the Symbol.* Translated by Catherine Porter. Ithaca, NY: Cornell University Press, 1982.

Turner, Victor. *The Forest of Symbols: Aspects of Ndembu Ritual.* Ithaca, NY: Cornell University Press, 1967.

Walker Bynum, Caroline. *Fragmentation and Redemption.* New York: Zone Books, 1991.

——. *The Resurrection of the Body in Western Christianity, 200–1336.* New York: Columbia University Press, 1995.

Weber, Alison. *Teresa of Avila and the Rhetoric of Femininity.* Princeton, NJ: Princeton University Press, 1990.

Wyschogrod, Edith. *Saints and Postmodernism.* Chicago: University of Chicago Press, 1990.

Zarri, Gabriella. *Le sante vive: Cultura e religiosità femminile nella prima età moderna.* Turin: Einaudi, 1990.

——. "'Vera' santità, 'simulata' santità: Ipotesi e riscontri." In *Finzione e santità tra medioevo ed età moderna.*

——. "Living Saints: A Typology of Female Sanctity in the Early Sixteenth Century." In *Women and Religion in Medieval and Renaissance Italy.*

Žižek, Slavoj. *Looking Awry: An Introduction to Jacques Lacan through Popular Culture.* Cambridge, MA: The MIT Press, 1991.

——. *The Metastases of Enjoyment.* London: Verso, 1994.

INDEX